The Concise Encyclopaedia of
SCOTTISH FOOTBALL

The Concise Encyclopaedia of
SCOTTISH FOOTBALL

Phil H Jones and David Potter

Pitch Publishing Ltd
A2 Yeoman Gate
Yeoman Way
Durrington
BN13 3QZ

Email: info@pitchpublishing.co.uk
Web: www.pitchpublishing.co.uk

The publisher makes no representation, express or implied, with regard to the accuracy of the information contained
in this book and cannot accept any legal responsibility for any errors or omissions that may be made.

A CIP catalogue record for this book is available from the British Library.

13-digit ISBN: 9781909626294

Cover design by Olner Design.
Typeset by Iolaire Typesetting, Newtonmore
Printed in Great Britain. Manufacturing managed by Jellyfish Print Solutions Ltd.

DEDICATED TO

All the Scotland players who won the 'Victory Shield' in 2013
by beating England and Northern Ireland, and drawing with Wales

The Victory Shield is an annual tournament for under-16 teams representing Scotland, England, Wales and Northern Ireland. It takes place over a period of several weeks during the first half of each season, with each country playing a single match against the three others. Home advantage alternates each year, which means that in a given season Scotland will be playing either two home matches and one away from home, or one home match and two away. The results are compiled into a league table, and the country (or countries) with the most points becomes the holder (or joint-holder) of the Victory Shield.

INTRODUCTION

The Encyclopaedia of Scottish Football contains hundreds of entries, and is a very comprehensive reference book that is packed with in-depth information about the history of football in Scotland. The first edition, which was produced in 2008, was followed by an expanded second edition in 2011, and over the years a number of readers contacted the editors to discuss aspects of Scottish football that were of interest to them. After listening to what they had to say, it became apparent that there is a need for a concise edition which focuses on the key topics that Scottish football fans want to refer to on a regular basis. This updated edition has been produced to meet that need, and it provides the information from the full encyclopaedia that relates to the following essential topics:

Club Football in Scotland
- Scottish league football
- Scottish Cup
- Scottish League Cup
- Scottish League Challenge Cup

Club Football in Europe
- The European Cup
- The Champions League
- The European Cup-Winners' Cup
- The Inter-Cities Fairs Cup
- The UEFA Cup
- The Europa League

International Football

- International football arranged according to all the countries that Scotland has ever played
- A list of all the men who have played for Scotland, including the number of appearances and goals scored by each one
- Scotland managers

International Tournaments

- European Championship campaigns
- World Cup campaigns

As well as in-depth coverage of these topics, each entry is introduced with a collection of facts that are little nuggets of information for followers of the Scottish game to enjoy.

Glasgow Corporation Transport.

International Football Match,

HAMPDEN PARK.

In addition to the regular service on the routes converging on Hampden Park, arrangements have been made to augment the undernoted services:—

Mount Florida	and Paisley Road Toll.
,, ,,	and Monkland Street.
,, ,,	and Seamore Street.
Clarkston or Battlefield	and Kelvingrove.

This will mean that 237 cars per hour, providing 15,000 seats, will be running between the City and Hampden Park, from 12.30 p.m.

The following Bus Services are convenient for Hampden Park:—

Knightswood & King's Park.		2
Possilpark & ,, ,,		7
Carntyne & ,, ,,		10
So. Carntyne & ,, ,,		13
Balornock & Aikenhead.		4a
Muirend & Lennox Av. or Knightswood.		5 & 5a

Seventy-four buses per hour, providing 3,780 seats, will be converging on Hampden Park from 12.30 p.m.

46 Bath Street,
23rd March, 1931.

The programme for the 1931 match between Scotland and England provided information about tram and bus services to Hampden Park

Hampden Park in the inter-war years

ACKNOWLEDGEMENTS

This edition contains some new pictures as well as many that appeared in the previous editions, and thanks are due to Jim Howie and Tom Cairns, who have provided new material.

These websites have been invaluable sources of information:
- www.scottishleague.net
- www.scottish-football-historical-archive.com
- www.rsssf.com

Well-thumbed books include:
- *The Breedon Book of Football Records* by Gordon Smailes
- *The First 100 Years: The Official Centenary History of the SFL* by Bob Crampsey
- *Sky Sports Football Yearbooks*
- *Up for the Cup: British Football Clubs in Europe since 1955* by John Ladd
- *The Roar of the Crowd* by David Ross

Thanks are also due to: John Adamson, Tom Campbell, Brian McColl (Scottish Football Historical Archive), David Ross (scottishleague.net), Robbie McPhail, Ian Simpson, Brian Wright, Jim Crawford, Russell Shepherd, Gordon Gilchrist and the authors' wives Rosemary and Margaret.

CONTENTS

CLUB FOOTBALL IN SCOTLAND

SCOTTISH FOOTBALL LEAGUE (1890–2013)
SCOTTISH PREMIER LEAGUE (1998–2013)
SCOTTISH PROFESSIONAL FOOTBALL LEAGUE (Formed 2013)

1890–1891	Division One (10)	
1891–1892	Division One (12)	
1892–1893	Division One (10)	
1893–1900	Division One (10)	Division Two (10)
1900–1901	Division One (11)	Division Two (10)
1901–1902	Division One (10)	Division Two (12)
1902–1903	Division One (12)	Division Two (12)
1903–1905	Division One (14)	Division Two (12)
1905–1906	Division One (16)	Division Two (12)
1906–1912	Division One (18)	Division Two (12)
1912–1913	Division One (18)	Division Two (14)
1913–1914	Division One (20)	Division Two (12)
1914–1915	Division One (20)	Division Two (14)
1915–1917	Division One (20)	
1917–1919	Division One (18)	
1919–1921	Division One (22)	

1921–1922	Division One (22)	Division Two (20)	
1922–1923	Division One (20)	Division Two (20)	
1923–1926	Division One (20)	Division Two (20)	Division Three (16)
1926–1932	Division One (20)	Division Two (20)	
1932–1939	Division One (20)	Division Two (18)	
1939–1940*	Division A (20)	Division B (18)	
1945–1946#	Division A (16)	Division B (14)	
1946–1947	Division A (16)	Division B (14)	Division C (10)
1947–1949	Division A (16)	Division B (16)	Division C (12)
1949–1950	Division A (16)	Division B (16)	Division C NorthEast-16	Division C SouthWest-18
1950–1952	Division A (16)	Division B (16)	Division C NorthEast-16	Division C SouthWest-16
1952–1953	Division A (16)	Division B (16)	Division C NorthEast-15	Division C SouthWest-14
1953–1954	Division A (16)	Division B (16)	Division C NorthEast-13	Division C SouthWest-14
1954–1955	Division A (16)	Division B (16)	Division C NorthEast-13	Division C SouthWest-13
1955–1956	Division A (18)	Division B (19)	
1956–1974	Division One (18)	Division Two (19)	
1974–1975	Division One (18)	Division Two (20)	
1975–1986	Premier Division (10)	First Division (14)	Second Division (14)
1986–1988	Premier Division (12)	First Division (12)	Second Division (14)
1988–1991	Premier Division (10)	First Division (14)	Second Division (14)
1991–1994	Premier Division (12)	First Division (12)	Second Division (14)
1994–1998	Premier Division (10)	First Division (10)	Second Division (10)	Third Division (10)
1998–2000	SPL (10)	First Division (10)	Second Division (10)	Third Division (10)
2000–2013	SPL (12)	First Division (10)	Second Division (10)	Third Division (10)
2013–	Premiership (12)	Championship (10)	League One (10)	League Two (10)

The figure in brackets gives the number of clubs in each division at a given time
* Abandoned season; # Unofficial season

Rangers won the League Championship in 1924/25, as well as the Glasgow Cup and the Glasgow Merchants Charity Cup

- 1890/91: The first season of the Scottish Football League began with eleven clubs in a single division (Abercorn, Cambuslang, Celtic, Cowlairs, Dumbarton, Hearts, Rangers, Renton, St Mirren, Third Lanark and Vale of Leven), but Renton were expelled after just five matches for contravening the amateur code. Dumbarton and Rangers were declared joint champions after finishing the season on equal points and then drawing 2–2 in a play-off (goal-average had not yet been introduced).

- 1893/94: Division Two was created after three seasons with just one division, and the number of clubs increased to twenty. There were ten clubs in each division, and new clubs Dundee and St Bernard's went straight into Division One.

- 1921/22: This was the first season with automatic promotion and relegation; before then the clubs in Division One simply elected any new members. There had been no Division Two since 1914/15, but it was re-introduced in 1921 and Alloa Athletic became the first club to be automatically promoted.

- 1922/23: 'Goal-average' was introduced to separate teams with an equal number of points (the number of goals scored divided by the number of goals conceded). It was first called upon to settle a championship in 1929/30, when Leith Athletic and East Fife were level on points at the top of Division Two, but Leith had a better goal-average.

- 1923/24: The Scottish League created a Division Three of sixteen clubs, which only lasted for three seasons. Its members experienced such severe financial problems that in 1925/26 only one club (Helensburgh) was able to complete its fixtures. Brechin City and Montrose (three seasons), Queen of the South (two seasons), East Stirlingshire and Forfar Athletic (one season) all belonged to this short-lived third division.

Bill Struth was manager of Rangers between 1920 and 1954, during which time his teams won eighteen Scottish League Championships

- 1946/47: In its first official post-war season, the Scottish League comprised three divisions, known as 'A', 'B' and 'C'. Six clubs from the pre-war Division Two were placed in Division C, as well as Stirling Albion, who replaced King's Park; the numbers were made up with the reserve teams of other clubs. Only first teams could win promotion to Division B and Stirling (the first champions) were promoted with Leith Athletic. Division C lasted until 1955, although in 1949 it was merged with the Scottish Reserve League and split into two regional sections for its final six seasons.

- 1971/72: 'Goal difference' replaced 'goal average' as the system for separating teams with an equal number of points (the number of goals scored minus the number of goals conceded); it was believed that the previous system encouraged defensive football by putting an emphasis on conceding as few goals as possible. That very first season it was used to decide the championship of Division Two when Dumbarton edged ahead of Arbroath.

- 1975/76: A major re-structure arranged the clubs into three levels instead of two – the Premier, First and Second Divisions. Two clubs were promoted and relegated in each case. Whilst the clubs in the Premier Division played each other four times, the other clubs only played each other twice and their fixtures ended in late February. To compensate, a

Willie Bauld won League Championship medals with Hearts in both 1957/58 and 1959/60

Alan Gilzean heads a goal for Dundee against Third Lanark at Cathkin Park in 1963. His team had won the League Championship in 1961/62

'Spring Cup' was introduced for the First and Second Divisions, but it only lasted one season and from 1976/77 these clubs played each other three times.

- 1991/92: The Premier Division was enlarged from ten teams to twelve; a change which spared St Mirren from relegation. Falkirk and Airdrieonians were promoted to increase the numbers and the top two divisions undertook an exacting fixture-list of forty-four matches until 1994, when the Third Division was created. (The top two divisions had also played forty-four league games in 1986/87 and 1987/88).

- 1994/95: The Scottish Football League adopted a system of three points for a win instead of two, and also created a fourth tier for the first time in its history. There were now ten clubs in each of the Premier, First, Second and Third Divisions – a total of forty clubs instead of the previous season's thirty-eight. The two new clubs were Ross County and Caledonian Thistle (as the Inverness club was then known).

- 1994/95, 1995/96 and 1996/97: For three seasons the second-bottom club in the Premier Division and the runners-up in the First Division (second tier) took part in a play-off for a place in the following season's Premier Division. The three winners were Aberdeen (stayed in Premier Division), Dundee United (promoted) and Hibernian (stayed in Premier Division).

Willie Waddell, manager of Kilmarnock, leads the celebrations after his team has won the League by beating Hearts 2–0 at Tynecastle in 1965

- 1998/99: This was the first season of the Scottish Premier League after ten clubs broke away from the Scottish Football League (Aberdeen, Celtic, Dundee, Dundee United, Dunfermline, Hearts, Kilmarnock, Motherwell, Rangers and St Johnstone). The first champions were Rangers, with Celtic second and St Johnstone third.

- 2000/01: The Scottish Premier League was enlarged from ten teams to twelve and the 'split' was introduced. After the clubs have played each other three times (thirty-three matches), their points are carried over into a second phase. Those who finish in the top six play each other once more (five matches) to compete for the championship and European qualification, whilst the teams who finish in the bottom six play each other once more to compete for survival in the top flight. A team in the lower section cannot finish the season higher than seventh in the league.

- Two more clubs (Elgin City and Peterhead) were admitted to the Scottish Football League in 2000/01, taking the total to forty-two. This meant that there were still ten clubs in each of the First, Second and Third Divisions, despite the enlargement of the Scottish Premier League.

- 2005/06: Play-offs were introduced between (i) the second-bottom club in the First Division and the second, third and fourth clubs in the Second Division (ii) the second-bottom club in the Second Division and the second, third and fourth clubs in the Third Division. The first winners were Partick Thistle (promoted to First Division) and Alloa Athletic (stayed in Second Division).

- 2013/14: This was the first season of the Scottish Professional Football League, following the merger of the Scottish Premier League and the Scottish Football League into a single body. The new league maintained the previous structure of four divisions, but they were renamed 'Scottish Premiership', 'Scottish Championship', 'Scottish League One' and 'Scottish League Two'. Other changes included the introduction of play-offs to decide promotion and relegation between the first and second tiers, and new arrangements for the distribution of money amongst the clubs.

The Scottish Football League was formed in Glasgow on 30 April 1890 and only five of the eleven founder members remain in senior football. Cambuslang disappeared in 1892, Cowlairs in 1895, Abercorn in 1915, Renton in 1922, Vale of Leven in 1926 and Third Lanark in 1967.

In 1998, after decades of wrangling about the distribution of income, ten teams broke away from the SFL to form their own organisation, which they called the Scottish Premier League. This left the SFL to run three divisions, from which the top club in the First Division earned promotion to the SPL, provided its ground accommodation met SPL requirements (in 2003 the Scottish Premier League blocked promotion for Falkirk because their ground, Brockville, was deemed to be unsuitable).

On 27 June 2013 the Scottish Premier League and Scottish Football League agreed to merge into a single body known as the Scottish Professional Football League – a decision that enacted one of the recommendations by Henry McLeish in his Review of Scottish Football. Neil Doncaster, who had been chief executive of the Scottish Premier League, became the new league's first chief executive. All forty-two clubs became full members, with no associate membership. The SPFL also organises the Scottish League Cup, as well as the Scottish League Challenge Cup for clubs that are not in the top division.

The champions of the various divisions of the league over the years are listed over:

	Division One	Division Two
1890/91	Dumbarton & Rangers (Shared)	
1891/92	Dumbarton	
1892/93	Celtic	
1893/94	Celtic	Hibernian
1894/95	Hearts	Hibernian
1895/96	Celtic	Abercorn
1896/97	Hearts	Partick Thistle
1897/98	Celtic	Kilmarnock
1898/99	Rangers	Kilmarnock
1899/00	Rangers	Partick Thistle
1900/01	Rangers	St Bernard's
1901/02	Rangers	Port Glasgow
1902/03	Hibernian	Airdrieonians
1903/04	Third Lanark	Hamilton Academical
1904/05	Celtic	Clyde
1905/06	Celtic	Leith Athletic
1906/07	Celtic	St Bernard's
1907/08	Celtic	Raith Rovers
1908/09	Celtic	Abercorn
1909/10	Celtic	Leith Athletic
1910/11	Rangers	Dumbarton
1911/12	Rangers	Ayr United
1912/13	Rangers	Ayr United
1913/14	Celtic	Cowdenbeath
1914/15	Celtic	Cowdenbeath
1915/16	Celtic	No competition
1916/17	Celtic	No competition
1917/18	Rangers	No competition
1918/19	Celtic	No competition
1919/20	Rangers	No competition
1920/21	Rangers	No competition
1921/22	Celtic	Alloa Athletic
1922/23	Rangers	Queen's Park
1923/24	Rangers	St Johnstone
1924/25	Rangers	Dundee United
1925/26	Celtic	Dunfermline Athletic
1926/27	Rangers	Bo'ness
1927/28	Rangers	Ayr United
1928/29	Rangers	Dundee United

1929/30	Rangers	Leith Athletic
1930/31	Rangers	Third Lanark
1931/32	Motherwell	East Stirlingshire
1932/33	Rangers	Hibernian
1933/34	Rangers	Albion Rovers
1934/35	Rangers	Third Lanark
1935/36	Celtic	Falkirk
1936/37	Rangers	Ayr United
1937/38	Celtic	Raith Rovers
1938/39	Rangers	Cowdenbeath
	Suspended because of the Second World War	
1946/47	Rangers	Dundee
1947/48	Hibernian	East Fife
1948/49	Rangers	Raith Rovers
1949/50	Rangers	Morton
1950/51	Hibernian	Queen of the South
1951/52	Hibernian	Clyde
1952/53	Rangers	Stirling Albion
1953/54	Celtic	Motherwell
1954/55	Aberdeen	Airdrieonians
1955/56	Rangers	Queen's Park
1956/57	Rangers	Clyde
1957/58	Hearts	Stirling Albion
1958/59	Rangers	Ayr United
1959/60	Hearts	St Johnstone
1960/61	Rangers	Stirling Albion
1961/62	Dundee	Clyde
1962/63	Rangers	St Johnstone
1963/64	Rangers	Morton
1964/65	Kilmarnock	Stirling Albion
1965/66	Celtic	Ayr United
1966/67	Celtic	Morton
1967/68	Celtic	St Mirren
1968/69	Celtic	Motherwell
1969/70	Celtic	Falkirk
1970/71	Celtic	Partick Thistle
1971/72	Celtic	Dumbarton
1972/73	Celtic	Clyde
1973/74	Celtic	Airdrieonians
1974/75	Rangers	Falkirk

	Premier Division	First Division	Second Division
1975/76	Rangers	Partick Thistle	Clydebank
1976/77	Celtic	St Mirren	Stirling Albion
1977/78	Rangers	Morton	Clyde
1978/79	Celtic	Dundee	Berwick Rangers
1979/80	Aberdeen	Hearts	Falkirk
1980/81	Celtic	Hibernian	Queen's Park
1981/82	Celtic	Motherwell	Clyde
1982/83	Dundee United	St Johnstone	Brechin City
1983/84	Aberdeen	Morton	Forfar Athletic
1984/85	Aberdeen	Motherwell	Montrose
1985/86	Celtic	Hamilton Ac.	Dunfermline Ath.
1986/87	Rangers	Morton	Meadowbank This.
1987/88	Celtic	Hamilton Ac.	Ayr United
1988/89	Rangers	Dunfermline Ath.	Albion Rovers
1989/90	Rangers	St Johnstone	Brechin City
1990/91	Rangers	Falkirk	Stirling Albion
1991/92	Rangers	Dundee	Dumbarton
1992/93	Rangers	Raith Rovers	Clyde
1993/94	Rangers	Falkirk	Stranraer

Dundee United with the Premier League trophy in 1982/83

Forfar Athletic – winners of the Second Division championship in 1983/84

	Premier Div.	First Div.	Second Div.	Third Div.
1994/95	Rangers	Raith Rovers	Morton	Forfar Athletic
1995/96	Rangers	Dunfermline A.	Stirling Albion	Livingston
1996/97	Rangers	St Johnstone	Ayr United	Inverness CT
1997/98	Celtic	Dundee	Stranraer	Alloa Athletic

Henrik Larsson of Celtic scored fifty-three goals in 2000/01, including thirty-five
league goals. Celtic won the SPL with ninety-seven points from thirty-eight
games

	SPL	First Div.	Second Div.	Third Div.
1998/99	Rangers	Hibernian	Livingston	Ross County
1999/00	Rangers	St Mirren	Clyde	Queen's Park
2000/01	Celtic	Livingston	Partick Thistle	Hamilton Ac.
2001/02	Celtic	Partick Thistle	Queen of the S.	Brechin City
2002/03	Rangers	Falkirk	Raith Rovers	Morton
2003/04	Celtic	Inverness CT	Airdrie Utd.	Stranraer
2004/05	Rangers	Falkirk	Brechin City	Gretna
2005/06	Celtic	St Mirren	Gretna	Cowdenbeath
2006/07	Celtic	Gretna	Morton	Berwick Rangers
2007/08	Celtic	Hamilton Ac.	Ross County	East Fife
2008/09	Rangers	St Johnstone	Raith Rovers	Dumbarton
2009/10	Rangers	Inverness CT	Stirling Albion	Livingston
2010/11	Rangers	Dunfermline A.	Livingston	Arbroath
2011/12	Celtic	Ross County	Cowdenbeath	Alloa Athletic
2012/13	Celtic	Partick Thistle	Queen of the S.	Rangers
	Premiership	**Championship**	**League One**	**League Two**
2013/14	Celtic	Dundee	Rangers	Peterhead

SCOTTISH CUP

- First Scottish Cup final: Queen's Park beat Clydesdale 2–0 at the first Hampden Park on 21 March 1874 (Scorers: W. McKinnon and Leckie). They had been two of the eight founding members when the SFA was formed in 1873, along with Vale of Leven, Dumbreck, Third Lanark, Eastern, Granville and Kilmarnock.

- 1883/84: Queen's Park were awarded the cup after Vale of Leven failed to turn up, following a dispute about the date. The match was due to be played at the first Cathkin Park on 23 February 1884.

- 1892/93: Queen's Park won the cup even though the club was not a member of the Scottish Football League, which had been formed in 1890. They beat Celtic 2–1 at the first Ibrox on 11 March 1893.

- 1895/96: The final was played outwith Glasgow for the only time. Hearts beat Hibernian 3–1 at Logie Green, the Edinburgh home of St Bernard's FC, on 14 March 1896.

- 1908/09: The cup was withheld after a riot on 17 April 1909; spectators had expected extra time following the second of two drawn matches between Celtic and Rangers.

- 1937/38: East Fife of Division Two became the only club to win the cup whilst in a division of the league that was not the top one. They beat Kilmarnock 4–2 at Hampden Park on 27 April 1938 in a replayed match.

- 1954/55: The 1–1 draw between Clyde and Celtic on 23 April 1955 was the first Scottish domestic club fixture to be televised live; the replay on 27 April, which Clyde won 1–0, was not broadcast on television.

- 1974/75: Celtic played in a Scottish Cup final for a seventh consecutive year when they beat Airdrieonians 3–1 at Hampden Park on 3 May 1975.

- 1980/81: This was the last occasion on which the final was replayed. Rangers and Dundee United drew 0–0 at Hampden Park on 9 May 1981 and played again at the same venue three days later, when Rangers won 4–1.

- 1989/90: The Scottish Cup final was decided on penalties for the first time when Aberdeen beat Celtic 9–8 following a 0–0 draw at Hampden Park on 12 May 1990 (there had also been penalty shoot-outs in previous rounds for ties that were still level after a replay).

- 2007/08: The winners of junior football's four main competitions were admitted into the Scottish Cup for the first time. The first clubs to qualify in this way were Culter (North Region Premier League), Linlithgow Rose (East Region Superleague and Scottish Junior Cup) and Pollok (West Region Superleague Premier Division).

First competed for in 1873/74, the actual cup is the oldest trophy competed for in football history for, although the English FA Cup is two years older, there have been three actual trophies, whereas the Scottish Cup has remained the same since 1874. The success of the tournament lies in the fact that it retains the same format, and has a straight draw. Three teams, Queen's Park, Dumbarton and Kilmarnock have entered every single competition.

The first games were on 18 October 1873 and the results were:

Alexandra Athletic	3	Callander	0
Renton	2	Kilmarnock	0
Western	0	Blythswood	1
Third Lanark walkover versus Southern			

Queen's Park, who received a bye, went on to win the first trophy, beating Clydesdale 2–0 in the final.

The record winners' medal holder is Charlie Campbell of Queen's Park with eight, although in one cup final, that of 1884, no game took place, as Vale of Leven didn't turn up! Bobby Lennox of Celtic also has eight winners' medals, but he started in only five finals, came on once as a substitute and on another two occasions was an unused substitute. Three men have seven winners' medals – Jimmy McMenemy (six with Celtic and one with Partick Thistle), Bob McPhail (six with Rangers and one with Airdrie) and Billy McNeill (all seven with Celtic). In 2007 Steven Pressley completed a remarkable treble of Scottish Cup medals with three separate clubs – Rangers in 1993, Hearts in 2006 and Celtic in 2007.

The Scottish Cup final is regarded as one of the showpieces of the season. It was televised live in 1955 and 1957 (in both cases the first game, but not the replay) and from 1977 onwards. The final has had a variety of venues, but only once has it been played outwith Glasgow, and that was in 1896 when Logie Green in Edinburgh, the home of St Bernard's, housed the all-Edinburgh final between Hibernian and Hearts.

The cup final results since 1874 are as follows:

1874	21 March	Queen's Park	2	0	Clydesdale	1st Hampden Park
		W. McKinnon Leckie				
Queen's Park: Dickson, Taylor, Neill, Thomson, Campbell, Weir, Leckie, W. McKinnon, Lawrie, McNeil, A. McKinnon						
Clydesdale: Gardner, Wotherspoon, McArley, Henry, Raeburn, Anderson, Gibb, Wilson, Lang, McPherson, Kennedy						
Referee: J. McIntyre						2,500

1875	10 April	Queen's Park	3	0	Renton	1st Hampden Park
		A. McKinnon Highet W. McKinnon				
Queen's Park: Neil, Taylor, Philips, Campbell, Dickson, McNeil, Highet, W. McKinnon, A. McKinnon, Lawrie, Weir						
Renton: Turnbull, A. Kennedy, McKay, Scallion, McGregor, Melville, McRae, M. Kennedy, J. Brown, Glen, L. Brown						
Referee: A. Campbell, Glasgow						7,000

1876	11 March	Queen's Park	1	1	Third Lanark	Hamilton Crescent
		Highet			Drinnan	
Queen's Park: Dickson, Taylor, Neil, Campbell, Philips, Lawrie, McGill, Highet, W. McKinnon, A. McKinnon, McNeil						
Third Lanark: Wallace, Hunter, Watson, White, Davidson, Crichton, Drinnan, Scoular, Walker, Millar, McDonald						
Referee: A. McBride, Vale of Leven						10,000

1876	18 March	Queen's Park	2	0	Third Lanark	Hamilton Crescent
		Highet (2)				
Queen's Park: Hillcote and Smith replaced Lawrie and A. McKinnon						
Third Lanark: As per first game						
Referee: A. McBride, Vale of Leven						6,000

1877	17 March	Vale of Leven	1	1	Rangers	Hamilton Crescent
		Paton			McDougall o.g.	
Vale of Leven: Wood, McIntyre, Michie, Jamieson, McLintock, Ferguson, Paton, McGregor, McDougall, Baird, Lindsay							
Rangers: Watt, Vallance, Gillespie, Ricketts, W. McNeill, M. McNeill, Watson, Dunlop, Campbell, Marshall, Hill							
Referee: J. Kerr, Hamilton							12,000

1877	7 April	Vale of Leven	1	1	Rangers	Hamilton Crescent
		McDougall			Dunlop	a.e.t.
Vale of Leven: As per first game						
Rangers: As per first game						
Referee: J. Kerr, Hamilton							15,000

1877	13 April	Vale of Leven	3	2	Rangers	1st Hampden Park
		Watson o.g. Baird Paton			Campbell W. McNeill	
Vale of Leven: As per first and second games						
Rangers: As per first and second games						
Referee: J. Kerr, Hamilton							8,000

1878	30 March	Vale of Leven	1	0	Third Lanark	1st Hampden Park
		McDougall				
Vale of Leven: Parlane, McLintock, McIntyre, McPherson, Jamieson, Ferguson, McFarlane, McGregor, James Baird, McDougall, John Baird							
Third Lanark: Wallace, Somers, J. Hunter, Kennedy, McKenzie, Miller, A. Hunter, Lang, Peden, McCririck, Kay							
Referee: R. Gardner, Clydesdale							5,000

1879	19 April	Vale of Leven	1	1	Rangers	1st Hampden Park
		Ferguson			Struthers	
Vale of Leven: Parlane, McLintock, A. McIntyre, J. McIntyre, McPherson, McFarlane, Ferguson, James Baird, McGregor, John Baird, McDougall							
Rangers: Gillespie, A. Vallance, T. Vallance, Drinnan, McIntyre, Hill, Dunlop, Steel, Struthers, Campbell, McNeil							
Referee: J. Wallace, Beith							6,000
Vale of Leven awarded the cup after Rangers failed to appear for the replay on 26 April							

1880	21 February	Queen's Park	3	0	Thornliebank	1st Cathkin Park
		Highet (2) Ker				
Queen's Park: Graham, Somers, Neil, Campbell, Davidson, Richmond, Weir, Highet, Ker, Kay, McNeil							
Thornliebank: Cadden, Jamieson, Marshall, Henderson, McFetridge, A. Brannan, Clark, Wham, Anderson, Hutton, T. Brannan							
Referee: D. Hamilton, Ayr							7,000

1881	9 April	Queen's Park	3	1	Dumbarton	Kinning Park
		Smith (2) Ker			Meikleham	

Queen's Park: McCallum, Watson, Holm, Campbell, Davidson, Anderson, Fraser, Ker, Smith, Allan, Kay

Dumbarton: Kennedy, Hutcheson, Paton, Miller, Anderson, Meikleham, Brown, Lindsay, McAulay, McKinnon, Kennedy

Referee: D. Hamilton, Ayr	10,000

This game followed a protested 2–1 win for Queen's Park on 26 March at Kinning Park. Dumbarton claimed that crowd encroachment prevented the referee or the umpire seeing if the ball had crossed the line before Queen's Park scored. The SFA upheld the appeal.

1882	18 March	Queen's Park	2	2	Dumbarton	1st Cathkin Park
		Harrower (2)			Brown Meikleham	

Queen's Park: McCallum, Watson, A. Holm, Davidson, J. Holm, Fraser, Anderson, Ker, Harrower, Richmond, Kay

Dumbarton: Kennedy, Hutcheson, Paton, P. Miller, Watt, Brown, Meikleham, McAulay, Lindsay, Kennedy, J. Miller

Referee: J. Wallace, Beith	12,000

1882	1 April	Queen's Park	4	1	Dumbarton	1st Cathkin Park
		Richmond Ker Harrower Kay			J. Miller	

Queen's Park: Campbell for J. Holm

Dumbarton: Watt for McKinnon

Referee: J. Wallace, Beith	15,000

1883	31 March	Dumbarton	2	2	Vale of Leven	1st Hampden Park
		Paton McArthur			Johnstone McCrae	

Dumbarton: McAuley, Hutcheson, Paton, P. Miller, Lang, Keir, R. Brown I, R. Brown II, J. Miller, Lindsay, McArthur

Vale of Leven: McLintock, McIntyre, Forbes, McLeish, McPherson, Gillies, McCrae, Johnston, Friel, Kennedy, McFarlane

Referee: T. Lawrie, Queen's Park	15,000

1883	7 April	Dumbarton	2	1	Vale of Leven	1st Hampden Park
		Anderson R. Brown I			Friel	

Dumbarton: Anderson for Lang

Vale of Leven: as per first game

Referee: T. Lawrie, Queen's Park	8,000

1884	23 February					1st Cathkin Park
Queen's Park beat Vale of Leven after Vale of Leven failed to turn up, following a dispute about the date. Queen's Park's team would have been: McCallum, Arnott, Holm, Campbell, Gow, Christie, Allan, Smith, Harrower, Anderson, Watt						

1885	21 February	Renton	0	0	Vale of Leven	2nd Hampden Park
Renton: Lindsay, Hannah, A. McCall, Kelso, McKechnie, Barbour, Kelly, McIntyre, J. McCall, Thomson, Grant						
Vale of Leven: James Wilson, A. McIntyre, Forbes, Abraham, John Wilson, Galloway, D. McIntyre, Ferguson, Johnstone, Gillies, Kennedy						
Referee: J. E. McKillop, Cartvale						2,500

1885	28 February	Renton	3	1	Vale of Leven	2nd Hampden Park
		J. McCall McIntyre Unknown			Gillies	
Renton: As per first game						
Vale of Leven: McPherson for John Wilson						
Referee: J. E. McKillop, Cartvale						3,500

1886	13 February	Queen's Park	3	1	Renton	1st Cathkin Park
		Hamilton Christie Somerville			Kelso	
Queen's Park: Gillespie, Arnot, Watson, Campbell, Gow, Christie, Somerville, Hamilton, Allan, Harrower, Lambie						
Renton: Lindsay, Hannah, A. McCall, Kelso, McKechnie, Thomson, Grant, Barbour, J. McCall, McIntyre, Kelly						
Referee: J. E. McKillop, Cartvale						7,000

1887	12 February	Hibernian	2	1	Dumbarton	2nd Hampden Park
		Smith Groves			Aitken	
Hibernian: Tobin, Lundy, Fagan, McGhee, McGinn, McLaren, Lafferty, Groves, Montgomery, Clark, Smith						
Dumbarton: McAulay, Hutcheson, Fergus, Miller, McMillan, Kerr, Brown, Robertson, Madden, Aitken, Jamieson						
Referee: R. Brown, Queen's Park						10,000

1888	4 February	Renton	6	1	Cambuslang	2nd Hampden Park
		McCall (2) D. Campbell J. Campbell McCallum McNee			H. Gourlay	
Renton: Lindsay, Hannah, A. McCall, Kelso, Kelly, McKechnie, McCallum, J. Campbell, D. Campbell, J. McCall, McNee						
Cambuslang: Dunn, Smith, Semple, McKay, J. Gourlay, Jackson, James Buchanan, John Buchanan, Plenderleith, H. Gourlay, J. Gourlay						
Referee: A. McA. Kennedy, Dumbarton						10,000

1889: This Third Lanark side won the Scottish Cup at the Second Hampden Park. When the Third Hampden Park was opened fourteen years later, the club would take over the site of this ground and build 'New Cathkin Park' on it

1889	9 February	Third Lanark	2	1	Celtic	2nd Hampden Park
		Oswald (minor) Marshall			McCallum	

Third Lanark: Downie, Thomson, Rae, Lochead, Auld, McFarlane, Marshall, Oswald (minor), Oswald (major), Hannah, Johnstone

Celtic: John Kelly, Gallacher, McKeown, W. Maley, James Kelly, McLaren, McCallum, Dunbar, Groves, Coleman, T. Maley

Referee: C. Campbell, Queen's Park	16,000

Followed a game played on 2nd February at 2nd Hampden Park that was declared a friendly, because of shocking ground conditions. Third Lanark won 3–0.

1890	15 February	Queen's Park	1	1	Vale of Leven	1st Ibrox
		Hamilton			McLachlan	

Queen's Park: Gillespie, Arnot, Smellie, McAra, Stewart, Robertson, Berry, Gulliland, Hamilton, Sellar, Allan

Vale of Leven: Wilson, Murray, Whitelaw, Sharp, McNicol, Osborne, McLachlan, Rankin, Paton, Bruce, McMillan

Referee: C. Campbell, Queen's Park	10,000

1890	22 February	Queen's Park	2	1	Vale of Leven	1st Ibrox
		Hamilton Stewart			Bruce	

Queen's Park: As per first game	
Vale of Leven: As per first game	
Referee: C. Campbell, Queen's Park	14,000

1891	7 February	Hearts	1	0	Dumbarton	2nd Hampden Park
		Russell				

Hearts: Fairbairn, Adams, Goodfellow, Begbie, McPherson, Hill, Taylor, Mason, Russell, Scott, Baird	
Dumbarton: McLeod, Watson, Miller, McMillan, Boyle, Keir, Taylor, Galbraith, Mair, McNaught, Bell	
Referee: T. R. Park, Cambuslang	14,000

1892	9 April	Celtic	5	1	Queen's Park	1st Ibrox
		Campbell (2) McMahon (2) Sillars o.g.			Waddell	

Celtic: Cullen, Reynolds, Doyle, Gallacher, Kelly, Maley, Campbell, Dowds, McCallum, McMahon, Brady	
Queen's Park: Baird, Sillars, Sellar, Gillespie, Robertson, Stewart, Waddell, Lambie, Gulliland, Hamilton, Scott	
Referee: G. Sneddon, SFA	20,000
Following a game on 12 March that was won 1–0 by Celtic, but declared a friendly following repeated encroachment of the 40,000 crowd at 1st Ibrox	

1893	11 March	Queen's Park	2	1	Celtic	1st Ibrox
		Sellar (2)			Blessington	

Queen's Park: Baird, Sillars, Smellie, Gillespie, McFarlane, Stewart, Gulliland, Waddell, Hamilton, Lambie, Sellar	
Celtic: Cullen, Reynolds, Doyle, Maley, Kelly, Dunbar, Towie, Blessington, Madden, McMahon, Campbell	
Referee: R. Harrison, Kilmarnock	15,000
Following a game on 25 February that was won 1–0 by Celtic, but declared a friendly because of a frozen pitch at 1st Ibrox. The game was not postponed for fear of upsetting the 20,000 crowd.	

1894	17 February	Rangers	3	1	Celtic	2nd Hampden Park
		H. McCreadie Barker McPherson			Maley	

Rangers: Haddow, Smith, Drummond, Marshall, A. McCreadie, Mitchell, Steel, H. McCreadie, Gray, McPherson, Barker	
Celtic: Cullen, Reynolds, Doyle, Curran, Kelly, Maley, Blessington, Madden, Cassidy, Campbell, McMahon	
Referee: J. Marshall, Third Lanark	15,000

1895	20 April	St Bernard's	2	1	Renton	1st Ibrox
		Clelland (2)			Duncan	
St Bernard's: Sneddon, Hall, Foyers, McManus, Robertson, Murdoch, Laing, Paton, Oswald, Crossan, Clelland						
Renton: Dickie, Ritchie, McCall, Glen, McColl, Tait, McLean, Murray, Price, Gilfillan, Duncan						
Referee: J. Robertson, Glasgow						13,500

1896	14 March	Hearts	3	1	Hibernian	Logie Green
		Baird King Michael			O'Neill	
Hearts: Fairbairn, McCartney, Mirk, Begbie, Russell, Hogg, McLaren, Baird, Michael, King, Walker						
Hibernian: McColl, Robertson, McFarlane, Breslin, Neill, Murphy, Murray, Kennedy, Groves, Smith, O'Neill						
Referee: W. McLeod, Cowlairs						16,034

1897	20 March	Rangers	5	1	Dumbarton	2nd Hampden Park
		Miller (2) Hyslop McPherson A. Smith			W. Thomson	
Rangers: Dickie, N. Smith, Drummond, Gibson, McCreadie, Mitchell, Low, McPherson, Miller, Hyslop, A. Smith						
Dumbarton: Docherty, D. Thomson, Mauchlan, Miller, Gillan, Sanderson, Mackie, Speedie, Hendry, W. Thomson, Fraser						
Referee: Mr. Simpson, Aberdeen						15,000

1898	26 March	Rangers	2	0	Kilmarnock	2nd Hampden Park
		A. Smith Hamilton				
Rangers: Dickie, N. Smith, Drummond, Gibson, Neil, Mitchell, Miller, McPherson, Hamilton, Hyslop, A. Smith						
Kilmarnock: McAllan, Busby, Brown, McPherson, Anderson, Johnstone, Muir, Maitland, Campbell, Reid, Finlay						
Referee: Mr. Colville, Inverness						14,000

1899	22 April	Celtic	2	0	Rangers	2nd Hampden Park
		McMahon Hodge				
Celtic: McArthur, Welford, Storrier, Battles, Marshall, King, Hodge, Campbell, Divers, McMahon, Bell						
Rangers: Dickie, N. Smith, Crawford, Gibson, Neill, Mitchell, Campbell, McPherson, Hamilton, Miller, A. Smith						
Referee: T. Robertson, Queen's Park						25,000

1900	14 April	Celtic	4	3	Queen's Park	2nd Ibrox
		McMahon Divers (2) Bell			Christie W. Stewart Battles o.g.	
Celtic: McArthur, Storrier, Battles, Russell, Marshall, Orr, Hodge, Campbell, Divers, McMahon, Bell							
Queen's Park: Gourlay, D. Stewart, Swan, Irons, Christie, Templeton, W. Stewart, Wilson, McColl, Kennedy, Hay							
Referee: J. Walker, Kilmarnock						17,000	

1901	6 April	Hearts	4	3	Celtic	Ibrox
		Bell (2) Walker Thomson			McOustra (2) McMahon	
Hearts: Philip, Allan, Baird, Key, Buick, Hogg, Porteous, Walker, Thomson, Houston, Bell							
Celtic: McArthur, Davidson, Battles, Russell, Loney, Orr, McOustra, Divers, Campbell, McMahon, Quinn							
Referee: A. Jackson, Rangers						15,000	

1902	26 April	Hibernian	1	0	Celtic	Celtic Park
		McGeachen				
Hibernian: Rennie, Gray, Glen, Breslin, Harrower, Robertson, McCall, McGeachen, Divers, Callaghan, Atherton							
Celtic: McFarlane, Watson, Battles, Loney, Marshall, Orr, McCafferty, McDermott, McMahon, Livingstone, Quinn							
Referee: R.T. Murray, Stenhousemuir						16,000	

1903	11 April	Rangers	1	1	Hearts	Celtic Park
		Stark			Walker	
Rangers: Dickie, Fraser, Drummond, Gibson, Stark, Robertson, McDonald, Speedie, Hamilton, Walker, Smith							
Hearts: McWattie, Thomson, Orr, Key, Buick, Hogg, Dalrymple, Walker, Porteous, Hunter, Baird							
Referee: T. Robertson, Queen's Park						28,000	

1903	18 April	Rangers	0	0	Hearts	Celtic Park
Rangers: As per first game							
Hearts: As per first game							
Referee: T. Robertson, Queen's Park						16,000	

1903	25 April	Rangers	2	0	Hearts	Celtic Park
		Mackie Hamilton				
Rangers: Henderson and Mackie for Gibson and Walker						
Hearts: Anderson for Buick						
Referee: T. Robertson, Queen's Park						32,000

1904	16 April	Celtic	3	2	Rangers	3rd Hampden Park
		Quinn (3)			Speedie (2)	
Celtic: Adams, McLeod, Orr, Young, Loney, Hay, Muir, McMenemy, Quinn, Somers, Hamilton						
Rangers: Watson, N. Smith, Drummond, Henderson, Stark, Robertson, Walker, Speedie, Mackie, Donnachie, A. Smith						
Referee: T. Robertson, Queen's Park						64,323

1905	8 April	Third Lanark	0	0	Rangers	Hampden Park
Third Lanark: Raeside, Barr, McIntosh, Comrie, Sloan, Neilson, Johnstone, Kidd, McKenzie, Wilson, Munro						
Rangers: Sinclair, Fraser, Craig, Henderson, Stark, Robertson, Hamilton, Speedie, McColl, Kyle, Smith						
Referee: J. Deans, Dalkeith						55,000

1905	15 April	Third Lanark	3	1	Rangers	Hampden Park
		Wilson (2) Johnstone			Smith	
Third Lanark: As per first game						
Rangers: Low for Hamilton						
Referee: J. Deans, Dalkeith						40,000

1906	28 April	Hearts	1	0	Third Lanark	Ibrox
		G. Wilson				
Hearts: G. Philip, McNaught, D. Philip, McLaren, Thomson, Dickson, Cooper, Walker, Menzies, D. Wilson, G. Wilson						
Third Lanark: Raeside, Barr, Hill, Cross, Neilson, Comrie, Johnstone, Graham, Reid, Wilson, Munro						
Referee: R. T. Murray, Stenhousemuir						30,000

1907	20 April	Celtic	3	0	Hearts	Hampden Park
		Somers (2) Orr pen				
Celtic: Adams, McLeod, Orr, Young, McNair, Hay, Bennett, McMenemy, Quinn, Somers, Templeton						
Hearts: Allan, Reid, Collins, Philip, McLaren, Henderson, Bauchope, Walker, Axford, Yates, Wombwell						
Referee: D. Philp, Dunfermline						50,000

1908	18 April	Celtic	5	1	St Mirren	Hampden Park
		Bennett (2) Hamilton Somers Quinn			Cunningham	

Celtic: Adams, McNair, Weir, Young, Loney, Hay, Bennett, McMenemy, Quinn, Somers, Hamilton

St Mirren: Grant, Gordon, White, Key, Robertson, McAvoy, Clements, Cunningham, Wylie, Paton, Anderson

Referee: J. R. W. Ferguson, Falkirk	55,000

1909	10 April	Celtic	2	2	Rangers	Hampden Park
		Quinn Munro			Gilchrist Bennett	

Celtic: Adams, McNair, Weir, Young, Dodds, Hay, Munro, McMenemy, Quinn, Somers, Hamilton

Rangers: Rennie, Law, Craig, May, Stark, Galt, Bennett, Gilchrist, Campbell, McPherson, Smith

Referee: J. B. Stark, Airdrie	70,000

1909	17 April	Celtic	1	1	Rangers	Hampden Park
		Quinn			Gordon	

Celtic: Kivlichan for Munro

Rangers: Gordon, McDonald and Reid for May, Gilchrist and Campbell

Referee: J. B. Stark, Airdrie	60,000

Cup withheld after a riot when spectators expected extra time after second game.

1910	9 April	Dundee	2	2	Clyde	Ibrox
		Own goal Langlands			Chalmers Booth	

Dundee: Crumley, Lawson, Chaplin, Lee, Dainty, Comrie, Bellamy, Langlands, Hunter, McFarlane, Fraser

Clyde: McTurk, Watson, Blair, Walker, McAteer, Robertson, Stirling, McCartney, Chalmers, Jackson, Booth

Referee: T. Dougray, Bellshill	60,000

1910	16 April	Dundee	0	0	Clyde	Ibrox
						a.e.t.

Dundee: Neal for Lawson

Clyde: As per first game

Referee: T. Dougray, Bellshill	20,000

1910	20 April	Dundee	2	1	Clyde	Ibrox
		Bellamy Hunter			Chalmers	
Dundee: McEwan for Chaplin						
Clyde: Wyllie and Wyse for Stirling and Jackson						
Referee: T. Dougray, Bellshill						24,000

1911	8 April	Celtic	0	0	Hamilton Ac.	Ibrox
Celtic: Adams, McNair, Dodds, Young, McAteer, Hay, Kivlichan, McMenemy, Quinn, Hastie, Hamilton						
Hamilton Academical: J. Watson, Davie, Miller, P. Watson, W. McLaughlin, Eglinton, J. McLaughlin, Waugh, Hunter, Hastie, McNeil						
Referee: T. Dougray, Bellshill						45,000

1911	15 April	Celtic	2	0	Hamilton Ac.	Ibrox
		Quinn McAteer				
Celtic: McAtee for Hastie						
Hamilton Academical: As per first game						
Referee: T. Dougray, Bellshill						25,000

1912	6 April	Celtic	2	0	Clyde	Ibrox
		McMenemy Gallacher				
Celtic: Mulrooney, McNair, Dodds, Young, Loney, Johnstone, McAtee, Gallacher, Quinn, McMenemy, Brown						
Clyde: Grant, Gilligan, Blair, Walker, McAndrew, Collins, Hamilton, Jackson, Morrison, Carmichael, Stevens						
Referee: T. Dougray, Bellshill						45,000

1913	12 April	Falkirk	2	0	Raith Rovers	Celtic Park
		Robertson Logan				
Falkirk: Stewart, Orrock, Donaldson, McDonald, Logan, McMillan, McNaught, Gibbons, Robertson, Croal, Terris						
Raith Rovers: McLeod, Morrison, Cumming, J. Gibson, Logan, Anderson, Cranston, Graham, Martin, Gourlay, F. Gibson						
Referee: T. Robertson, Glasgow						45,000

1914	11 April	Celtic	0	0	Hibernian	Ibrox

Celtic: Shaw, McNair, Dodds, Young, Johnstone, McMaster, McAtee, Gallacher, Owers, McMenemy, Browning						

| Hibernian: Allan, Girdwood, Templeton, Kerr, Paterson, Grossert, Wilson, Fleming, Hendren, Wood, Smith |||||||

Referee: T. Dougray, Bellshill	55,000

1914	16 April	Celtic	4	1	Hibernian	Ibrox
		McColl (2) Browning (2)		Smith		

Celtic: McColl for Owers						

| Hibernian: As per first game |||||||

Referee: T. Dougray, Bellshill	45,000

Competition suspended between 1915 and 1919 because of First World War

1920	17 April	Kilmarnock	3	2	Albion Rovers	Hampden Park
		Culley Shortt J. Smith		Watson Hillhouse		

Kilmarnock: Blair, Hamilton, Gibson, Bagan, Shortt, Neave, McNaught, M. Smith, J. Smith, Culley, McPhail						

| Albion Rovers: Short, Penman, Bell, Wilson, Black, Ford, Ribchester, James White, John White, Watson, Hillhouse |||||||

Referee: W. Bell, Hamilton	95,000

1920: Kilmarnock on the attack as Albion's Penman attempts a tackle in this first post-war Scottish Cup final

1921	16 April	Partick Thistle	1	0	Rangers	Celtic Park
		Blair				
Partick Thistle: Campbell, Crichton, Bulloch, Harris, Wilson, Borthwick, Blair, Kinloch, Johnston, McMenemy, Salisbury						
Rangers: Robb, Manderson, McCandless, Meiklejohn, Dixon, Bowie, Archibald, Cunningham, Henderson, Cairns, Morton						
Referee: H. Humphreys, Greenock						28,294

1922	15 April	Morton	1	0	Rangers	Hampden Park
		Gourlay				
Morton: Edwards, McIntyre, R. Brown, Gourlay, Wright, McGregor, McNab, McKay, Buchanan, A. Brown, McMinn						
Rangers: Robb, Manderson, McCandless, Meiklejohn, Dixon, Muirhead, Archibald, Cunningham, Henderson, Cairns, Morton						
Referee: T. Dougray, Bellshill						75,000

1923	31 March	Celtic	1	0	Hibernian	Hampden Park
		Cassidy				
Celtic: Shaw, McNair, W. McStay, J. McStay, Cringan, McFarlane, McAtee, Gallacher, Cassidy, McLean, Connolly						
Hibernian: Harper, McGinnigle, Dornan, Kerr, Miller, Shaw, Ritchie, Dunn, McColl, Halligan, Walker						
Referee: T. Dougray, Bellshill						80,100

1924	19 April	Airdrieonians	2	0	Hibernian	Ibrox
		Russell (2)				
Airdrieonians: Ewart, Dick, McQueen, Preston, McDougall, Bennie, Reid, Russell, Gallacher, McPhail, Sommerville						
Hibernian: Harper, McGinnigle, Dornan, Kerr, Miller, Shaw, Ritchie, Dunn, McColl, Halligan, Walker						
Referee: T. Dougray, Bellshill						59,214

1925	11 April	Celtic	2	1	Dundee	Hampden Park
		Gallacher McGrory			McLean	
Celtic: Shevlin, W. McStay, Hilley, Wilson, J. McStay, McFarlane, Connolly, Gallacher, McGrory, Thomson, McLean						
Dundee: Britton, Brown, Thomson, Ross, W. Rankine, Irving, Duncan, McLean, Halliday, J. Rankine, Gilmour						
Referee: T. Dougray, Bellshill						75,137

1926	10 April	St Mirren	2	0	Celtic	Hampden Park
		McCrae Howieson				
St Mirren: Bradford, Findlay, Newbiggin, Morrison, Summers, McDonald, Morgan, Gebbie, McCrae, Howieson, Thomson						
Celtic: Shevlin, W. McStay, Hilley, Wilson, J. McStay, McFarlane, Connolly, Thomson, McGrory, McInally, Leitch						
Referee: P. Craigmyle, Aberdeen						98,620

1927	16 April	Celtic	3	1	East Fife	Hampden Park
		Robertson o.g. McLean Connolly			Wood	
Celtic: J. Thomson, W. McStay, Hilley, Wilson, J. McStay, McFarlane, Connolly, A. Thomson, McInally, McMenemy, McLean							
East Fife: Gilfillan, Robertson, Gillespie, Hope, Brown, Russell, Weir, Paterson, Wood, Barrett, Edgar							
Referee: T. Dougray, Bellshill						80,070	

1928	14 April	Rangers	4	0	Celtic	Hampden Park
		Meiklejohn McPhail Archibald (2)				
Rangers: T. Hamilton, Gray, R. Hamilton, Buchanan, Meiklejohn, Craig, Archibald, Cunningham, Fleming, McPhail, Morton							
Celtic: J. Thomson, W. McStay, Donoghue, Wilson, J. McStay, McFarlane, Connolly, A. Thomson, McGrory, McInally, McLean							
Referee: W. Bell, Motherwell						118,115	

1929	6 April	Kilmarnock	2	0	Rangers	Hampden Park
		Aitken Williamson				
Kilmarnock: Clemie, Robertson, Nibloe, Morton, McLaren, McEwan, Connell, Smith, Cunningham, Williamson, Aitken							
Rangers: T. Hamilton, Gray, R. Hamilton, Buchanan, Meiklejohn, Craig, Archibald, Muirhead, Fleming, McPhail, Morton							
Referee: T. Dougray, Bellshill						114,708	

1930	12 April	Rangers	0	0	Partick Thistle	Hampden Park
Rangers: T. Hamilton, Gray, R. Hamilton, Buchanan, Meiklejohn, Craig, Archibald, Marshall, Fleming, McPhail, Nicholson							
Partick Thistle: Jackson, Calderwood, Rae, Elliot, Lambie, McLeod, Ness, Grove, Boardman, Ballantyne, Torbet							
Referee: W. Bell, Motherwell						107,475	

1930	16 April	Rangers	2	1	Partick Thistle	Hampden Park
		Marshall Craig			Torbet	
Rangers: McDonald and Morton for Buchanan and Nicholson							
Partick Thistle: As per first game							
Referee: W. Bell, Motherwell						103,686	

1931	11 April	Celtic	2	2	Motherwell	Hampden Park
		McGrory Craig o.g.			Stevenson McMenemy	
Celtic: J. Thomson, Cook, McGonagle, Wilson, McStay, Geatons, R. Thomson, A. Thomson, McGrory, Scarff, Napier							
Motherwell: McClory, Johnman, Hunter, Wales, Craig, Telfer, Murdoch, McMenemy, McFadyen, Stevenson, Ferrier							
Referee: P. Craigmyle, Aberdeen						105,000

1931	15 April	Celtic	4	2	Motherwell	Hampden Park
		R. Thomson (2) McGrory (2)			Murdoch Stevenson	
Celtic: As per first game							
Motherwell: As per first game							
Referee: P. Craigmyle, Aberdeen						98,579

1932	16 April	Rangers	1	1	Kilmarnock	Hampden Park
		McPhail			Maxwell	
Rangers: Hamilton, Gray, McAuley, Meiklejohn, Simpson, Brown, Archibald, Marshall, English, McPhail, Morton							
Kilmarnock: Bell, Leslie, Nibloe, Morton, Smith, McEwan, Connell, Muir, Maxwell, Duncan, Aitken							
Referee: P. Craigmyle, Aberdeen						111,982

1932: Rangers stars McPhail, English, Meiklejohn, and Fleming pictured the day after the club beat Kilmarnock 3–0 in the replayed final at Hampden

1932	20 April	Rangers	3	0	Kilmarnock	Hampden Park
		Fleming McPhail English				
Rangers: Fleming for Morton						
Kilmarnock: As per first game						
Referee: P. Craigmyle, Aberdeen					104,695	

1933	15 April	Celtic	1	0	Motherwell	Hampden Park
		McGrory				
Celtic: Kennaway, Hogg, McGonagle, Wilson, McStay, Geatons, R. Thomson, A. Thomson, McGrory, Napier, O'Donnell						
Motherwell: McClory, Crapnell, Ellis, Wales, Blair, McKenzie, Murdoch, McMenemy, McFadyen, Stevenson, Ferrier						
Referee: T. Dougray, Bellshill					102,339	

1934	21 April	Rangers	5	0	St Mirren	Hampden Park
		Nicholson (2) McPhail Main Smith				
Rangers: Hamilton, Gray, McDonald, Meiklejohn, Simpson, Brown, Main, Marshall, Smith, McPhail, Nicholson						
St Mirren: McCloy, Hay, Ancell, Gebbie, Wilson, Miller, Knox, Latimer, McGregor, McCabe, Phillips						
Referee: M. Hutton, Glasgow					113,403	

1935	20 April	Rangers	2	1	Hamilton Acad.	Hampden Park
		Smith (2)			Harrison	
Rangers: Dawson, Gray, McDonald, Kennedy, Simpson, Brown, Main, Venters, Smith, McPhail, Gillick						
Hamilton Academical: Morgan, Wallace, Bulloch, Cox, McStay, Murray, King, McLaren, Wilson, Harrison, Reid						
Referee: H. Watson, Glasgow					87,286	

1936	18 April	Rangers	1	0	Third Lanark	Hampden Park
		McPhail				
Rangers: Dawson, Gray, Cheyne, Meiklejohn, Simpson, Brown, Fiddes, Venters, Smith, McPhail, Turnbull						
Third Lanark: Muir, Carabine, Hamilton, Blair, Denmark, McInnes, Howe, Gallacher, Hay, Kennedy, Kinnaird						
Referee: J. Martin, Ladybank					88,859	

1937: Celtic's Jimmy McGrory and Aberdeen's Willie Cooper chase the ball

1937	24 April	Celtic	2	1	Aberdeen	Hampden Park
		Crum Buchan			Armstrong	
Celtic: Kennaway, Hogg, Morrison, Geatons, Lyon, Paterson, Delaney, Buchan, McGrory, Crum, Murphy							
Aberdeen: Johnstone, Cooper, Temple, Dunlop, Falloon, Thomson, Benyon, McKenzie, Armstrong, Mills, Laing							
Referee: M. Hutton, Glasgow						147,365	

1938	23 April	East Fife	1	1	Kilmarnock	Hampden Park
		McLeod			McAvoy	
East Fife: Milton, Laird, Tait, Russell, Sneddon, Herd, Adams, McLeod, McCartney, Miller, McKerrell							
Kilmarnock: Hunter, Fyfe, Milloy, Robertson, Stewart, Ross, Thomson, Reid, Collins, McAvoy, McGrogan							
Referee: H. Watson, Glasgow						80,091	

1938	27 April	East Fife	4	2	Kilmarnock	Hampden Park
		McKerrell (2) McLeod Miller			Thomson McGrogan	a.e.t.
East Fife: Harvey for Herd							
Kilmarnock: as per first game							
Referee: H. Watson, Glasgow						92,716	

1939	22 April	Clyde	4	0	Motherwell	Hampden Park
		Martin (2) Wallace Noble				

Clyde: Brown, Kirk, Hickie, Beaton, Falloon, Weir, Robertson, Noble, Martin, Wallace, Gillies

Motherwell: Murray, Wales, Ellis, McKenzie, Blair, Telfer, Ogilvie, Bremner, Mathie, Stevenson, McCulloch

Referee: W. Webb, Glasgow	94,799

Competition suspended between 1940 and 1946 because of Second World War

1947	19 April	Aberdeen	2	1	Hibernian	Hampden Park
		Hamilton Williams		Cuthbertson		

Aberdeen: Johnstone, McKenna, Taylor, McLaughlin, Dunlop, Waddell, Harris, Hamilton, Williams, Baird, McCall

Hibernian: Kerr, Govan, Shaw, Howie, Aird, Kean, Smith, Finnigan, Cuthbertson, Turnbull, Ormond

Referee: R. Calder, Glasgow	82,140

1948	17 April	Rangers	1	1	Morton	Hampden Park
		Gillick			Whyte	a.e.t.

Rangers: Brown, Young, Shaw, McColl, Woodburn, Cox, Rutherford, Gillick, Thornton, Findlay, Duncanson

Morton: Cowan, Mitchell, Whigham, Campbell, Miller, Whyte, Hepburn, Murphy, Cupples, Orr, Liddell

Referee: J. Martin, Blairgowrie	129,176

1948	21 April	Rangers	1	0	Morton	Hampden Park
		Williamson				a.e.t.

Rangers: Williamson for Findlay

Morton: As per first game

Referee: J. Martin, Blairgowrie	131,975

1949	23 April	Rangers	4	1	Clyde	Hampden Park
		Young (2) Williamson Duncanson			Galletly	

Rangers: Brown, Young, Shaw, McColl, Woodburn, Cox, Waddell, Duncanson, Thornton, Williamson, Rutherford

Clyde: Cullan, Gibson, Mennie, Campbell, Milligan, Long, Davies, Wright, Linwood, Galletly, Bootland

Referee: R. Benzie, Irvine	108,435

1949: Willie Woodburn heads clear from a Clyde attack in the Scottish Cup final, which Rangers won 4–1. Rangers became the first club to win the League Championship, the Scottish Cup and the League Cup in the same season

1950	22 April	Rangers	3	0	East Fife	Hampden Park
		Findlay Thornton (2)				
Rangers: Brown, Young, Shaw, McColl, Woodburn, Cox, Rutherford, Findlay, Thornton, Duncanson, Rae						
East Fife: Easson, Laird, Stewart, Philp, Finlay, Aitken, Black, Fleming, Morris, Brown, Duncan						
Referee: J. Mowat, Glasgow						118,262

1951	21 April	Celtic	1	0	Motherwell	Hampden Park
		McPhail				
Celtic: Hunter, Fallon, Rollo, Evans, Boden, Baillie, Weir, Collins, McPhail, Peacock, Tully						
Motherwell: Johnstone, Kilmarnock, Shaw, McLeod, Paton, Redpath, Humphries, Forrest, Kelly, Watson, Aitkenhead						
Referee: J. Mowat, Glasgow						131,943

1952	19 April	Motherwell	4	0	Dundee	Hampden Park
		Watson Redpath Humphries Kelly				
Motherwell: Johnstone, Kilmarnock, Shaw, Cox, Paton, Redpath, Sloan, Humphries, Kelly, Watson, Aitkenhead							
Dundee: Henderson, Fallon, Cowan, Gallacher, Cowie, Boyd, Hill, Patillo, Flavell, Steel, Christie							
Referee: J. Mowat, Glasgow						136,304	

1953	25 April	Rangers	1	1	Aberdeen	Hampden Park
		Prentice			Yorston	
Rangers: Niven, Young, Little, McColl, Stanners, Pryde, Waddell, Greirson, Paton, Prentice, Hubbard							
Aberdeen: Martin, Mitchell, Shaw, Harris, Young, Allister, Rodger, Yorston, Buckley, Hamilton, Hather							
Referee: J. Mowat, Glasgow						129,861	

1953	29 April	Rangers	1	0	Aberdeen	Hampden Park
		Simpson				
Rangers: Woodburn and Simpson for Stanners and Prentice							
Aberdeen: As per first game							
Referee: J. Mowat, Glasgow						112,619	

1954	24 April	Celtic	2	1	Aberdeen	Hampden Park
		Young o.g. Fallon			Buckley	
Celtic: Bonnar, Haughney, Meechan, Evans, Stein, Peacock, Higgins, Fernie, Fallon, Tully, Mochan							
Aberdeen: Martin, Mitchell, Caldwell, Allister, Young, Glen, Leggat, Hamilton, Buckley, Clunie, Hather							
Referee: C. Faultless, Giffnock						129,926	

1955	23 April	Clyde	1	1	Celtic	Hampden Park
		Robertson			Walsh	
Clyde: Hewkins, Murphy, Haddock, Granville, Anderson, Laing, Divers, Robertson, Hill, Brown, Ring							
Celtic: Bonnar, Haughney, Meechan, Evans, Stein, Peacock, Collins, Fernie, McPhail, Walsh, Tully							
Referee: C. Faultless, Giffnock						106,111	

1955: It is the last minute of the Scottish Cup final and Clyde have just equalised direct from a corner kick against Celtic

1955	27 April	Clyde	1	0	Celtic	Hampden Park
		Ring				
Clyde: As per first game						
Celtic: Fallon for Collins						
Referee: C. Faultless, Giffnock					68,735	

1956	21 April	Hearts	3	1	Celtic	Hampden Park
		Crawford (2) Conn			Haughney	
Hearts: Duff, Kirk, McKenzie, Mackay, Glidden, Cumming, Young, Conn, Bauld, Wardhaugh, Crawford						
Celtic: Beattie, Meechan, Fallon, Smith, Evans, Peacock, Craig, Haughney, Mochan, Fernie, Tully						
Referee: R. Davidson, Airdrie					133,399	

1957	20 April	Falkirk	1	1	Kilmarnock	Hampden Park
		Prentice			Curlett	
Falkirk: Slater, Parker, Rae, Wright, Irvine, Prentice, Murray, Greirson, Merchant, Moran, O'Hara						
Kilmarnock: Brown, Collins, J. Stewart, R. Stewart, Toner, Mackay, Mays, Harvey, Curlett, Black, Burns						
Referee: J. Mowat, Glasgow					81,057	

1957	24 April	Falkirk	2	1	Kilmarnock	Hampden Park
		Merchant Moran			Curlett	a.e.t.
Falkirk: As per first game						
Kilmarnock: As per first game						
Referee: J. Mowat, Glasgow					79,785	

1956: Hearts won 3–1 and the Scottish Cup went back to Tynecastle for the first time in fifty years. The trophy is held by Freddie Glidden

1958	26 April	Clyde	1	0	Hibernian	Hampden Park
		Coyle				
Clyde: McCulloch, Murphy, Haddock, Walters, Finlay, Clinton, Herd, Currie, Coyle, Robertson, Ring						
Hibernian: Leslie, Grant, McClelland, Turnbull, Plenderleith, Baxter, Fraser, Aitken, Baker, Preston, Ormond						
Referee: J. Mowat, Glasgow						95,123

1959	25 April	St Mirren	3	1	Aberdeen	Hampden Park
		Bryceland Miller Baker			Baird	
St Mirren: Walker, Lapsley, Wilson, Neilson, McGugan, Leishman, Rodger, Bryceland, Baker, Gemmell, Miller						
Aberdeen: Martin, Caldwell, Hogg, Brownlie, Clunie, Glen, Ewan, Davidson, Baird, Wishart, Hather						
Referee: J. Mowat, Glasgow						108,591

1959: This commemorative tankard was produced when St Mirren won the Scottish Cup for the first time since 1926. They beat Aberdeen 3–1 in the final

1960	23 April	Rangers	2	0	Kilmarnock	Hampden Park
		Millar (2)				
Rangers: Niven, Caldow, Little, McColl, Paterson, Stevenson, Scott, McMillan, Millar, Brand, Wilson						
Kilmarnock: Brown, Richmond, Watson, Beattie, Toner, Kennedy, Stewart, McInally, Kerr, Black, Muir						
Referee: R. Davidson, Airdrie					108,017	

1961	22 April	Dunfermline	0	0	Celtic	Hampden Park
Dunfermline: Connachan, Fraser, Cunningham, Mailer, Williamson, Miller, Peebles, Smith, Dickson, McAlindon, Melrose						
Celtic: Haffey, McKay, Kennedy, Crerand, McNeill, Clark, Gallagher, Fernie, Hughes, Chalmers, Byrne						
Referee: H. Phillips, Wishaw					113,618	

1961	26 April	Dunfermline	2	0	Celtic	Hampden Park
		Thomson Dickson				
Dunfermline: Sweeney and Thomson for Williamson and McAlindon						
Celtic: O'Neill for Kennedy						
Referee: H. Phillips, Wishaw					87,866	

1962	21 April	Rangers	2	0	St Mirren	Hampden Park
		Brand Wilson				
Rangers: Ritchie, Shearer, Caldow, Davis, McKinnon, Baxter, Henderson, McMillan, Millar, Brand, Wilson						
St Mirren: Williamson, Campbell, Wilson, Stewart, Clunie, McLean, Henderson, Bryceland, Kerrigan, Fernie, Beck						
Referee: T. Wharton, Clarkston					126,930	

1963	4 May	Rangers	1	1	Celtic	Hampden Park
		Brand		Murdoch		
Rangers: Ritchie, Shearer, Caldow, Greig, McKinnon, Baxter, Henderson, McLean, Miller, Brand, Wilson						
Celtic: Haffey, McKay, Kennedy, McNamee, McNeill, Price, Johnstone, Murdoch, Hughes, Divers, Brogan						
Referee: T. Wharton, Clarkston					129,527	

1963	15 May	Rangers	3	0	Celtic	Hampden Park
		Brand (2) Wilson				
Rangers: McMillan for McLean						
Celtic: Craig and Chalmers for Johnstone and Brogan						
Referee: T. Wharton, Clarkston						120,263

1964	25 April	Rangers	3	1	Dundee	Hampden Park
		Millar (2) Brand			Cameron	
Rangers: Ritchie, Shearer, Caldow, Greig, McKinnon, Baxter, Henderson, McLean, Millar, Brand, Wilson						
Dundee: Slater, Hamilton, Cox, Seith, Ryden, Stuart, Penman, Cousin, Cameron, Gilzean, Robertson						
Referee: H. Phillips, Wishaw						120,982

1965	24 April	Celtic	3	2	Dunfermline	Hampden Park
		Auld (2) McNeill			Melrose McLaughlin	
Celtic: Fallon, Young, Gemmell, Murdoch, McNeill, Clark, Chalmers, Gallagher, Hughes, Lennox, Auld						
Dunfermline: Herriot, W. Callaghan, Lunn, Thomson, McLean, T. Callaghan, Edwards, Smith, McLaughlin, Melrose, Sinclair						
Referee: H. Phillips, Wishaw						108,800

1966	23 April	Rangers	0	0	Celtic	Hampden Park
Rangers: Ritchie, Johansen, Provan, Greig, McKinnon, Millar, Henderson, Watson, Forrest, Johnston, Wilson						
Celtic: Simpson, Young, Gemmell, Murdoch, McNeill, Clark, Johnstone, McBride, Chalmers, Gallagher, Hughes						
Referee: T. Wharton, Clarkston						126,552

1966	27 April	Rangers	1	0	Celtic	Hampden Park
		Johansen				
Rangers: McLean for Forrest						
Celtic: Craig and Auld for Young and Gallagher						
Referee: T. Wharton, Clarkston						98,202

1967	29 April	Celtic	2	0	Aberdeen	Hampden Park
		Wallace (2)				
Celtic: Simpson, Craig, Gemmell, Murdoch, McNeill, Clark, Johnstone, Wallace, Chalmers, Auld, Lennox						
Aberdeen: Clark, Whyte, Shewan, Munro, McMillan, Petersen, Wilson, Smith, Storrie, Melrose, Johnston						
Referee: W. Syme, Glasgow						127,117

1968	27 April	Dunfermline	3	1	Hearts	Hampden Park
		Gardner (2) Lister			Lunn o.g.	
Dunfermline: Martin, W. Callaghan, Lunn, McGarty, Barry, T. Callaghan, Lister, Paton, Gardner, Robertson, Edwards						
Hearts: Cruickshank, Sneddon, Mann, Anderson, Thomson, Miller, Jensen (Moller), Townsend, Ford, Irvine, Traynor						
Referee: W. Anderson, East Kilbride						56,366

1969	26 April	Celtic	4	0	Rangers	Hampden Park
		McNeill Lennox Connelly Chalmers				
Celtic: Fallon, Craig, Gemmell, Murdoch, McNeill, Brogan (Clark), Connelly, Chalmers, Wallace, Lennox, Auld						
Rangers: Martin, Johansen, Mathieson, Greig, McKinnon, Smith, Henderson, Penman, Ferguson, Johnston, Persson						
Referee: J. Callaghan, Glasgow						132,870

1970	11 April	Aberdeen	3	1	Celtic	Hampden Park
		Harper McKay (2)			Lennox	
Aberdeen: Clark, Boel, Murray, Hermiston, McMillan, Buchan, McKay, Robb, Forrest, Harper, Graham						
Celtic: Williams, Hay, Gemmell, Murdoch, McNeill, Brogan, Johnstone, Wallace, Connelly, Lennox, Hughes (Auld)						
Referee: R. Davidson, Airdrie						108,244

1971	8 May	Celtic	1	1	Rangers	Hampden Park
		Lennox			D. Johnstone	
Celtic: Williams, Craig, Brogan, Connelly, McNeill, Hay, Johnstone, Lennox, Wallace, Callaghan, Hood						
Rangers: McCloy, Miller, Mathieson, Greig, McKinnon, Jackson, Henderson, Penman (D. Johnstone), Stein, MacDonald, W. Johnston						
Referee: T. Wharton, Clarkston						120,027

1971	12 May	Celtic	2	1	Rangers	Hampden Park
		Macari Hood pen			Craig o.g.	
Celtic: Macari for Wallace, who substituted for Hood						
Rangers: Denny for Miller. D. Johnstone again substituted for Penman.						
Referee: T. Wharton, Clarkston						103,297

1972	6 May	Celtic	6	1	Hibernian	Hampden Park
		Deans (3) Macari (2) McNeill			Gordon	
Celtic: Williams, Craig, Brogan, Murdoch, McNeill, Connelly, Johnstone, Deans, Macari, Dalglish, Callaghan						
Hibernian: Herriot, Brownlie, Schaedler, Stanton, Black, Blackley, Edwards, Hazel, Gordon, O'Rourke, Duncan (Auld)						
Referee: A. MacKenzie, Larbert						105,909

1973	5 May	Rangers	3	2	Celtic	Hampden Park
		Parlane Conn Forsyth			Dalglish Connelly	
Rangers: McCloy, Jardine, Mathieson, Greig, Johnstone, MacDonald, McLean, Forsyth, Parlane, Conn, Young						
Celtic: Hunter, McGrain, Brogan (Lennox), Murdoch, McNeill, Connelly, Johnstone, Deans, Dalglish, Hay, Callaghan						
Referee: J.R.P. Gordon, Tayport						122,714

1974	4 May	Celtic	3	0	Dundee United	Hampden Park
		Hood Murray Deans				
Celtic: Connaghan, McGrain (Callaghan), Brogan, Murray, McNeill, McCluskey, Johnstone, Hood, Deans, Hay, Dalglish						
Dundee United: Davie, Gardner, Kopel, Copland, D. Smith (Traynor), W. Smith, Payne (Rolland), Knox, Gray, Fleming, Houston						
Referee: W. Black, Glasgow						75,959

1975	3 May	Celtic	3	1	Airdrieonians	Hampden Park
		Wilson (2) McCluskey			McCann	
Celtic: Latchford, McGrain, Lynch, Murray, McNeill, McCluskey, Hood, Glavin, Dalglish, Lennox, Wilson						
Airdrieonians: McWilliams, Jonquin, Cowan, Menzies, Black, Whiteford, McCann, Walker, McCulloch (March), Lapsley (Reynolds), Wilson						
Referee: I. Foote, Glasgow						75,457

1976	1 May	Rangers	3	1	Hearts	Hampden Park
		Johnstone (2) MacDonald			Shaw	
Rangers: McCloy, Miller, Greig, Forsyth, Jackson, MacDonald, McKean, Hamilton (Jardine), Henderson, McLean, Johnstone							
Hearts: Cruickshank, Brown, Burrell (Aird), Jefferies, Gallagher, Kay, Gibson (Park), Busby, Shaw, Callachan, Prentice							
Referee: R. Davidson, Airdrie						85,250	

1977	7 May	Celtic	1	0	Rangers	Hampden Park
		Lynch				
Celtic: Latchford, McGrain, Lynch, Stanton, McDonald, Aitken, Dalglish, Edvaldsson, Craig, Conn, Wilson							
Rangers: Kennedy, Jardine, Greig, Forsyth, Jackson, Watson (Robertson), McLean, Hamilton, Parlane, MacDonald, Johnstone							
Referee: R. Valentine, Dundee						54,252	

1978	6 May	Rangers	2	1	Aberdeen	Hampden Park
		MacDonald Johnstone			Ritchie	
Rangers: McCloy, Jardine, Greig, Forsyth, Jackson, MacDonald, McLean, Russell, Johnstone, Smith, Cooper (Watson)							
Aberdeen: Clark, Kennedy, Ritchie, McMaster, Garner, Miller, Sullivan, Fleming (Scanlon), Harper, Jarvie, Davidson							
Referee: B. McGinlay, Balfron						61,563	

1979	12 May	Rangers	0	0	Hibernian	Hampden Park
Rangers: McCloy, Jardine, Dawson, Johnstone, Jackson, MacDonald (Miller), McLean, Russell, Parlane, Smith, Cooper							
Hibernian: McArthur, Brazil, Duncan, Bremner, Stewart, McNamara, Hutchison (Rae), McLeod, Campbell, Callachan, Higgins							
Referee: B. McGinlay, Balfron						50,260	

1979	16 May	Rangers	0	0	Hibernian	Hampden Park
						a.e.t.
Rangers: As per first game. Miller substituted for McLean							
Hibernian: Rae for Hutchison. Brown substituted for Higgins							
Referee: B. McGinlay, Balfron						33,508	

1979	28 May	Rangers	3	2	Hibernian	Hampden Park
		Johnstone (2) Duncan o.g.			Higgins McLeod	a.e.t.
Rangers: Watson for Smith. Miller and Smith substituted for Watson and McLean						
Hibernian: Rae for Hutchison. Brown and Hutchison substituted for Callachan and Higgins						
Referee: I. Foote, Glasgow						30,602

1980	10 May	Celtic	1	0	Rangers	Hampden Park
		McCluskey				a.e.t.
Celtic: Latchford, Sneddon, McGrain, Aitken, Conroy, MacLeod, Provan, Doyle (Lennox), McCluskey, Burns, McGarvey						
Rangers: McCloy, Jardine, Dawson, Forsyth (Miller), Jackson, Stevens, Cooper, Russell, Johnstone, Smith, MacDonald (McLean)						
Referee: G. Smith, Edinburgh						70,303

1981	9 May	Rangers	0	0	Dundee United	Hampden Park
						a.e.t.
Rangers: Stewart, Jardine, Dawson, Stevens, Forsyth, Bett, McLean, Russell, McAdam (Cooper), Redford, W. Johnston						
Dundee United: McAlpine, Holt, Kopel, Phillip (Stark), Hegarty, Narey, Bannon, Milne (Pettigrew), Kirkwood, Sturrock, Dodds						
Referee: I. Foote, Glasgow						53,000

1981	12 May	Rangers	4	1	Dundee United	Hampden Park
		Cooper Russell MacDonald (2)			Dodds	
Rangers: Cooper, D. Johnstone and MacDonald for McLean, McAdam and W. Johnston						
Dundee United: As per first game, with Stark again substituting for Phillip						
Referee: I. Foote, Glasgow						43,099

1982	22 May	Aberdeen	4	1	Rangers	Hampden Park
		McLeish McGhee Strachan Cooper			MacDonald	a.e.t.
Aberdeen: Leighton, Kennedy, Rougvie, McMaster (Bell), McLeish, Miller, Strachan, Cooper, McGhee, Simpson, Hewitt (Black)						
Rangers: Stewart, Jardine (McAdam), Dawson, McClelland, Jackson, Bett, Cooper, Russell, Dalziel (McLean), Miller, MacDonald						
Referee: B. McGinlay, Balfron						53,788

1983	21 May	Aberdeen	1	0	Rangers	Hampden Park
		Black				a.e.t.

Aberdeen: Leighton, Rougvie (Watson), McMaster, Cooper, McLeish, Miller, Strachan, Simpson, McGhee, Black, Weir

Rangers: McCloy, Dawson, McClelland, McPherson, Paterson, Bett, Cooper (Davis), McKinnon, Clark, Russell, MacDonald (Dalziel)

Referee: D. Syme, Rutherglen	62,979

1984	19 May	Aberdeen	2	1	Celtic	Hampden Park
		Black McGhee			P. McStay	a.e.t.

Aberdeen: Leighton, McKimmie, Rougvie (Stark), Cooper, McLeish, Miller, Strachan, Simpson, McGhee, Black, Weir (Bell)

Celtic: Bonner, McGrain, Reid (Melrose), Aitken, W. McStay, MacLeod, Provan, P. McStay, McGarvey, Burns, McClair (Sinclair)

Referee: R. Valentine, Dundee	58,900

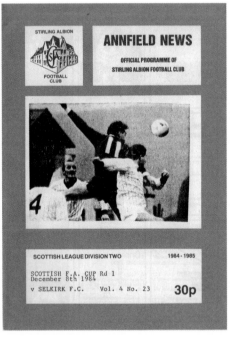

1984: Stirling Albion scored twenty goals without reply against Selkirk in the first round of the Scottish Cup on 8 December 1984

1985	18 May	Celtic	2	1	Dundee United	Hampden Park
		Provan McGarvey			Beedie	

Celtic: Bonner, W. McStay, McGrain, Aitken, McAdam, MacLeod, Provan, P. McStay (O'Leary), Johnston, Burns (McClair), McGarvey

Dundee United: McAlpine, Malpas, Beedie (Holt), Gough, Hegarty, Narey, Bannon, Milne, Kirkwood, Sturrock, Dodds

Referee: B. McGinlay, Balfron	60,346

1986	10 May	Aberdeen	3	0	Hearts	Hampden Park
		Hewitt (2) Stark				

Aberdeen: Leighton, McKimmie, McQueen, McMaster (Stark), McLeish, W. Miller, Hewitt (J. Miller), Cooper, McDougall, Bett, Weir

Hearts: Smith, Kidd, Whittaker, Jardine, Berry, Levein, Colquhoun, Black, Clark, Mackay, Robertson

Referee: H. Alexander, Irvine	62,841

1987	16 May	St Mirren	1	0	Dundee United	Hampden Park
		Ferguson				a.e.t.

St Mirren: Money, Wilson, D. Hamilton, Abercromby, Winnie, Cooper, McGarvey, Ferguson, McDowall (Cameron), B. Hamilton, Lambert (Fitzpatrick)

Dundee United: Thomson, Holt, Malpas, McInally, Clark, Narey, Ferguson, Bowman, Bannon, Sturrock (Gallacher), Redford (Hegarty)

Referee: K. Hope, Clarkston	51,782

1988	14 May	Celtic	2	1	Dundee United	Hampden Park
		McAvennie (2)			Gallacher	

Celtic: McKnight, Morris, Rogan, Aitken, McCarthy, Whyte (Stark), Miller, McStay, McAvennie, Walker (McGhee), Burns

Dundee United: Thomson, Bowman, Malpas, McInally, Hegarty, Narey, Bannon, Gallacher, Paatelainen (Clark), Ferguson, McKinlay

Referee: G. Smith, Edinburgh	74,000

1989	20 May	Celtic	1	0	Rangers	Hampden Park
		Miller				

Celtic: Bonner, Morris, Rogan, Aitken, McCarthy, Whyte, Grant, McStay, Miller, McGhee, Burns

Rangers: Woods, Stevens, Munro (Souness), Gough, Sterland (Cooper), Butcher, Drinkell, Ferguson, McCoist, Brown, Walters

Referee: R. Valentine, Dundee	72,069

1990	12 May	Aberdeen	0	0	Celtic	Hampden Park
						a.e.t.

Aberdeen won 9–8 on penalties

Aberdeen: Snelders, McKimmie, Robertson, Grant, McLeish, Irvine, Nicholas, Bett, Mason (Watson), Connor, Gilhaus

Celtic: Bonner, Wdowczyk, Rogan, Grant, Elliott, Whyte, Stark (Galloway), McStay, Dziekanowski, Walker (Coyne), Miller

Referee: G. Smith, Edinburgh	60,493

1991	18 May	Motherwell	4	3	Dundee United	Hampden Park
		Ferguson O'Donnell Angus Kirk			Bowman O'Neil Jackson	a.e.t.

Motherwell: Maxwell, Nijholt, Boyd, Griffin, Paterson, McCart, Arnott, Angus, Ferguson (Kirk), O'Donnell, Cooper (O'Neill)

Dundee United: Main, Clark, Malpas, McInally, Krivokapic, Bowman, van der Hoorn, McKinnon (McKinlay), French, Ferguson (O'Neil), Jackson

Referee: D. Syme, Rutherglen — 57,319

1992	9 May	Rangers	2	1	Airdrieonians	Hampden Park
		Hateley McCoist			Smith	

Rangers: Goram, Stevens, Robertson, Gough, Spackman, Brown, Durrant (Gordon), McCall, McCoist, Hateley, Mikhailichenko

Airdrieonians: Martin, Kidd, Stewart, Honor, Caesar, Jack, Boyle, Balfour, Lawrence (Smith), Coyle, Kirkwood (Reid)

Referee: D. Hope, Linburn — 44,045

1993	29 May	Rangers	2	1	Aberdeen	Celtic Park
		Murray Hateley			Richardson	

Rangers: Goram, McCall, Robertson, Gough, McPherson, Brown, Murray, Ferguson, Durrant, Hateley, Huistra (Pressley)

Aberdeen: Snelders, McKimmie, Wright (Smith), Grant, Irvine, McLeish, Richardson, Mason, Booth, Shearer (Jess), Paatelainen

Referee: J. McCluskey, Stewarton — 50,715

1994	21 May	Dundee United	1	0	Rangers	Hampden Park
		Brewster				

Dundee United: Van de Kamp, Cleland, Malpas, McInally, Petric, Welsh, Bowman, Hannah, McLaren (Nixon), Brewster, Dailly

Rangers: Maxwell, Stevens (Mikhailichenko), Robertson, McPherson, Gough, McCall, Murray, I. Ferguson, McCoist (D. Ferguson), Hateley, Durie

Referee: D. Hope, Erskine — 37,450

1995	27 May	Celtic	1	0	Airdrieonians	Hampden Park
		Van Hooijdonk				

Celtic: Bonner, Boyd, McKinlay, Vata, McNally, Grant, McLaughlin, McStay, van Hooijdonk (Falconer), Donnelly (O'Donnell), Collins

Airdrieonians: Martin, Stewart, Jack, Sandison, Hay (McIntyre), Black, Boyle, A. Smith, Cooper, Harvey (T. Smith), Lawrence

Referee: L. Mottram, Wilsontown — 36,915

1996	18 May	Rangers	5	1	Hearts	Hampden Park
		Laudrup (2) Durie (3)			Colquhoun	
Rangers: Goram, Cleland, Robertson, Gough, McLaren, Brown, Durie, Gascoigne, Ferguson (Durrant), McCall, Laudrup							
Hearts: Rousset, Locke (Lawrence), Ritchie, McManus, McPherson, Bruno (Robertson), Johnston, Mackay, Colquhoun, Fulton, Pointon							
Referee: H. Dallas, Motherwell						37,730	

1997	24 May	Kilmarnock	1	0	Falkirk	Ibrox
		Wright				
Kilmarnock: Lekovic, MacPherson, Kerr, Montgomerie, McGowne, Reilly, Bagen (Mitchell), Burke, Wright (Henry), McIntyre (Brown), Holt							
Falkirk: Nelson, McGowan, Seaton, Oliver, James, Gray, McAllister, McKenzie, Crabbe (Craig), Hagen, McGrillen (Fellner)							
Referee: H. Dallas, Motherwell						48,953	

1998	16 May	Hearts	2	1	Rangers	Celtic Park
		Cameron Adam			McCoist	
Hearts: Rousset, McPherson, Naysmith, Weir, Salvatori, Ritchie, McCann, Fulton, Adam (Hamilton), Cameron, Flogel							
Rangers: Goram, Porrini, Stensaas (McCoist), Gough, Amoruso, Bjorklund, Gattuso, Ferguson, Durie, McCall (Durrant), Laudrup							
Referee: W. Young, Clarkston						48,946	

1999	29 May	Rangers	1	0	Celtic	Hampden Park
		Wallace				
Rangers: Klos, Porrini (Kanchelskis), Amoruso, Hendry, Vidmar, McCann (Ferguson), McInnes, van Bronckhorst, Wallace, Amato (Wilson), Albertz							
Celtic: Gould, Boyd, Mahe (O'Donnell), Mjallby, Stubbs, Annoni (Johnson), Lambert, Wieghorst, Larsson, Moravcik, Blinker							
Referee: H. Dallas, Motherwell						51,746	

2000	27 May	Rangers	4	0	Aberdeen	Hampden Park
		Van Bronckhorst Vidmar Dodds Albertz				
Rangers: Klos, Reyna, Moore (Porrini), Vidmar, Numan, Kanchelskis, Ferguson, Albertz, van Bronckhorst (Kerimoglu), Wallace (McCann), Dodds							
Aberdeen: Leighton (Winters), Solberg, McAllister, Whyte, Anderson (Belabed), Dow, Bernard, Jess, Rowson, Guntweit, Stavrum (Zerouali)							
Referee: J. McCluskey, Stewarton						50,685	

2001	26 May	Celtic	3	0	Hibernian	Hampden Park
		McNamara Larsson (2)				

Celtic: Douglas, Mjallby, Valgaeren, Vega, Thompson (Johnson), Agathe, Lennon, Lambert (Boyd), Moravcik (McNamara), Larsson, Sutton

Hibernian: Colgan, Fenwick, Smith, Sauzee, Jack, Laursen, Murray, Brebner (Arpinon) (Lovell), O'Neill, Paatelainen (Zitelli), Libbra

Referee: K. Clark, Paisley — 51,284

2002	4 May	Rangers	3	2	Celtic	Hampden Park
		Lovenkrands (2) Ferguson			Hartson Balde	

Rangers: Klos, Ricksen, Amoruso, Moore, Numan, Ross, Ferguson, Lovenkrands, de Boer, Caniggia (Arveladze), McCann

Celtic: Douglas, Mjallby, Sutton, Balde, Thompson, Petrov, Lennon, Lambert (McNamara), Agathe, Larsson, Hartson

Referee: H. Dallas, Motherwell — 51,138

2003	31 May	Rangers	1	0	Dundee	Hampden Park
		Amoruso				

Rangers: Klos, Ricksen, Moore, Amoruso, Numan (Muscat), Malcolm, Ferguson, McCann, de Boer, Mols (Ross), Arveladze (Thompson)

Dundee: Speroni, Mackay (Milne), Hernandez, Khizivanishvili, Muir, Smith, Nemsadze, Rae (Brady), Lovell, Caballero, Burchill (Novo)

Referee: K. Clark, Paisley — 47,136

2004	22 May	Celtic	3	1	Dunfermline	Hampden Park
		Larsson (2) Petrov			Skerla	

Celtic: Marshall, Varga, Balde, McNamara, Agathe, Lennon, Petrov, Pearson (Wallace), Thompson, Larsson, Sutton

Dunfermline: Stillie, Labonte, Mason (Grondin), Skerla, Byrne (Tod), Darren Young, Nicholson, Dempsey (Bullen), Derek Young, Crawford, Brewster

Referee: S. Dougall, Burnside — 50,846

2005	28 May	Celtic	1	0	Dundee United	Hampden Park
		Thompson				

Celtic: Douglas, Agathe, Varga, Balde, McNamara, Petrov, Lennon, Thompson (McGeady), Sutton, Hartson (Valgaeren), Bellamy

Dundee United: Bullock, Ritchie, Archibald, Wilson, Kenneth, McInnes (Samuel), Brebner (Duff), Kerr, Robson, Crawford (Grady), Scotland

Referee: J. Rowbotham, Kirkcaldy — 50,635

2006	13 May	Hearts	1	1	Gretna	Hampden Park
		Skacel			McGuffie pen	a.e.t.

Hearts won 4–2 on penalties

Hearts: Gordon, Neilson, Pressley, Tall, Fyssas, Cesnauskas (Mikoliunas), Aguiar (Brellier), Hartley, Skacel, Bednar (Pospisil), Jankauskas

Gretna: Main, Birch, Townsley, Innes, Nicholls (Graham), McGuffie, Tosh, O'Neil, Skelton, Grady, Deuchar (McQuilken)

Referee: D. McDonald, Edinburgh	51,232

2007	26 May	Celtic	1	0	Dunfermline	Hampden Park
		Perrier- Doumbe				

Celtic: Boruc, Perrier-Doumbe, McManus, Pressley, Naylor, Nakamura, Lennon (Caldwell), Hartley, McGeady, Vennegoor of Hesselink, Miller (Beattie)

Dunfermline: de Vries, Shields, Wilson, Bamba, Morrison (Crawford), Hammill, Young, McCunnie, Muirhead, McIntyre (Hamilton), Burchill

Referee: K. Clark, Paisley	49,600

2008	24 May	Rangers	3	2	Queen of the South	Hampden Park
		Boyd (2)			Tosh	
		Beasley			Thomson	

Rangers: Alexander, Whittaker, Cuellar, Weir, Papac, McCulloch, Ferguson, Thomson, Beasley (Davis), Boyd, Darcheville (Fleck)

Queen of the South: MacDonald, McCann (Robertson), Thomson, Aitken, Harris, McQuilken (Stewart), MacFarlane, Tosh, Burns, Dobbie (O'Neill), O'Connor

Referee: S. Dougall, Burnside	48,821

2009	30 May	Rangers	1	0	Falkirk	Hampden Park
		Novo				

Rangers: Alexander, Whittaker, Bougherra, Weir, Papac, Davis, Ferguson, McCulloch, Lafferty (Dailly), Boyd (Novo), Miller (Naismith)

Falkirk: Mallo, McNamara, Barr, Aafjes, Scobbie, Arfield, Cregg (Finnigan), McBride (Higdon), O'Brien, McCann (Stewart), Lovell

Referee: C. Thomson, Paisley	50,956

2010	15 May	Dundee United	3	0	Ross County	Hampden Park
		Goodwillie				
		Conway (2)				

Dundee United: Pernis, Dillon, Webster, Kenneth, Kovacevic (Watson), Conway, Swanson (S. Robertson), Buaben, Gomis, Daly, Goodwillie (D. Robertson)

Ross County: McGovern, Miller, Morrison, Scott (Wood), Boyd, Keddie, Gardyne (Di Giacomo), Craig (Lawson), Brittain, Vigurs, Barrowman

Referee: D. McDonald, Edinburgh	47,122

2011	21 May	Celtic	3	0	Motherwell	Hampden Park
		Ki Sung-Yeung Craigan o.g. Mulgrew				

Celtic: Forster, Wilson, Loovens, Majstorovic, Izaguirre, Commons (Forrest), Brown, Ki Sung-Yeung, Mulgrew, Samaras (Stokes), Hooper (McCourt)

Motherwell: Randolph, Hateley, Craigan, Hutchinson, Gunning, Jennings, Humphrey, Hammell (Jeffers), Lasley, Murphy (Jones), Sutton

Referee: C. Murray, Livingston	49,618

2012	19 May	Hearts	5	1	Hibernian	Hampden Park
		Barr Skacel (2) Grainger McGowan		McPake		

Hearts: MacDonald, McGowan, Webster, Zaliukas, Grainger, Black (Robinson), Barr, Santana (Beattie), Skacel, Driver (Taouil), Elliott

Hibernian: Brown, Doherty, McPake, Hanlon, Kujabi, Soares (Francomb), Osbourne, Claros (Sproule), Stevenson, O'Connor (Doyle), Griffiths

Referee: C. Thomson, Paisley	51,041

2013	26 May	Celtic	3	0	Hibernian	Hampden Park
		Hooper (2) Ledley				

Celtic: F. Forster, Lustig, Wilson, Mulgrew, Izaguirre, Commons (Samaras), Brown (Ambrose), Ledley, Forrest (McCourt), Hooper, Stokes

Hibernian: Williams, Maybury, J. Forster, Hanlon, McGivern, Harris, Taiwo, Claros, Thomson (Caldwell), Doyle (Handling), Griffiths (Stevenson)

Referee: W. Collum, Glasgow	51, 254

2014	17 May	St Johnstone	2	0	Dundee United	Celtic Park
		Anderson MacLean				

St Johnstone: Mannus, Mackay, Easton, Wotherspoon (McDonald), Wright, Anderson, Millar, Dunne, May, MacLean, O'Halloran (Croft)

Dundee United: Cierzniak, Watson, Robertson, Rankin, Dillon, Gunning, Dow, Paton (Graham), Ciftci, Armstrong, Mackay-Steven (Gauld)

Referee: C. Thomson, Paisley	47,345

At the end of the 2013/14 season the trophy had been competed for 129 times, and the winners were as follows:

Celtic	36
Rangers	33
Queen's Park	10
Hearts	8
Aberdeen	7
Clyde	3
Kilmarnock	3
Vale of Leven	3
St Mirren	3
Dundee United	2
Dunfermline	2
Falkirk	2
Hibernian	2
Motherwell	2
Renton	2
Third Lanark	2
Airdrieonians	1
Dumbarton	1
Dundee	1
East Fife	1
Greenock Morton	1
Partick Thistle	1
St Bernard's	1
St Johnstone	1
In 1909 the Scottish Cup was withheld, following the Hampden riot.	

In 2007/08 junior clubs were admitted for the first time and the Scottish Qualifying Cup was discontinued. The format for the competition became:

First Round (36 clubs) (A preliminary round may first be required to reduce the clubs to this number)	The clubs that would have participated in the Scottish Qualifying Cup (North) (does not include top two Highland League clubs); the clubs that would have participated in the Scottish Qualifying Cup (South) (does not include top two Lowland clubs – originally EOSL champions and SOSL champions); winners of the Scottish Junior Cup; winners of the East, North and West junior Super Leagues
Second Round (32 clubs)	Eighteen first-round winners; top two Highland League clubs; top two Lowland clubs; ten League Two clubs
Third Round (32 clubs)	Sixteen second-round winners; ten League One clubs; bottom six clubs in the Championship;
Fourth Round (32 clubs)	Sixteen third-round winners; top four clubs in the Championship; twelve Premiership clubs
Fifth Round (16 clubs)	Sixteen fourth-round winners
Quarter-Finals (8 clubs)	Eight fifth-round winners
Semi-Finals (4 clubs)	Four quarter-final winners (No replays; extra-time and penalties if necessary)
Final (2 clubs)	Two semi-final winners

The draw for the first round of the 2008/09 competition produced the first-ever Scottish Cup-tie between two junior clubs, which resulted in a 3–1 victory for Lochee United at home to Bathgate Thistle on 27 September 2008. Lochee went on to beat Buckie Thistle 3–0, and then drew 1–1 against Ayr United at Thomson Park in the third-round, before the 'Honest Men' won the replay 3–1.

SCOTTISH LEAGUE CUP

- First Scottish League Cup final: Rangers beat Aberdeen 4–0 at Hampden Park on 5 April 1947 (Scorers: Jimmy Duncanson (2), Billy Williamson and Torry Gillick).

- Although the competition was held for the first time in 1946/47, some people regard the 1945/46 Southern League Cup (a wartime competition) as an unofficial Scottish League Cup. Aberdeen beat Rangers 3–2 in the final on 11 May 1946 at Hampden Park.

- 1953/54: East Fife won the trophy for the third time on 24 October 1953, when they beat Partick Thistle 3–0 at Hampden Park after also winning in 1947/48 and 1949/50. On the first occasion they were in the lower of the Scottish Football League's two divisions.

- 1974/75: Joe Harper scored a hat-trick in the final, but still finished on the losing side when Celtic beat Hibernian 6–3 at Hampden Park on 26 October 1974.

- 1977/78: Ayr United beat Queen's Park 4–2 on penalties in the first tie to be decided by a penalty shoot-out. The score in this second round encounter stood at 1–1 on aggregate after the teams had played each other both home and away.

- 1979/80: This was the last occasion on which the final was replayed. Aberdeen and Dundee United drew 0–0 at Hampden Park on 8 December 1979 and played again at Dens Park four days later, when United won 3–0 (there had been penalty shoot-outs in previous rounds, avoiding the need for replays). The replay was the first time that the final had been played at a ground other than Hampden Park.

- 1983/84: A unique format was adopted for this season, with two knockout rounds followed by a group stage, and then semi-finals and a final. The competition had traditionally started with a group stage (except 1977/78, 1978/79, 1979/80 and 1980/81 when there were no groups), but after 1983/84 a group stage was not used again.

- 1987/88: The League Cup final was decided on penalties for the first time when Rangers beat Aberdeen 5–3, following a 3–3 draw at Hampden Park on 25 October 1987.

- 1994/95: Raith Rovers became the first team outside the top flight to win the trophy since East Fife in 1947/48. They beat Celtic 6–5 on penalties at Ibrox after a 2–2 draw. Rovers went on to play in the UEFA Cup, losing to Bayern Munich in the second round.

The name of the competition has changed many times because of sponsorship. It is organised by the Scottish Professional Football League and the format has varied over the years. Between 1946/47 and 1976/77 it was played on a sectional basis followed by a knock-out competition, but since then it has been on a knock-out basis with many variations – e.g. home and away ties, replays allowed, straight knock-out games, and (in 1983/84) a knock-out phase followed by sections and then more knock-out. In recent seasons teams in the top division have been given an exemption from the early rounds, and teams competing in Europe are allowed a further exemption to the quarter-final stage. The final was sometimes played in the autumn, but more recently it has been in the spring; thus it is necessary to give the years of the season concerned (eg 1955/56 rather than just 1956).

1946/47	5 April	Rangers	4	0	Aberdeen	Hampden Park
		Duncanson (2) Williamson Gillick				

Rangers: Brown, Young, Shaw, McColl, Woodburn, Rae, Rutherford, Gillick, Williamson, Thornton, Duncanson

Aberdeen: Johnstone, Cooper, McKenna, McLaughlin, Dunlop, Taylor, Harris, Hamilton, Williams, Baird, McCall

Referee: R. Calder, Rutherglen | 82,584

1947/48	25 October	East Fife	0	0	Falkirk	Hampden Park

East Fife: Niven, Laird, Stewart, Philip, Finlay, Aitken, Adams, D. Davidson, Norris, J. Davidson, Duncan

Falkirk: J. Dawson, Whyte, McPhie, Bolt, R. Henderson, Whitelaw, Fiddes, Fleck, Aikman, J. Henderson, K. Dawson

Referee: P. Craigmyle, Aberdeen | 52,781

1947/48	1 November	East Fife	4	1	Falkirk	Hampden Park
		Duncan (3) Adams			Aikman	

East Fife: As per first game

Falkirk: Gallagher and Alison for Whitelaw and Fleck

Referee: P. Craigmyle, Aberdeen | 30,664

1948/49	12 March	Rangers	2	0	Raith Rovers	Hampden Park
		Gillick Paton				

Rangers: Brown, Young, Shaw, McColl, Woodburn, Cox, Gillick, Paton, Thornton, Duncanson, Rutherford

Raith Rovers: Westland, McClure, McNaught, Young, Colville, Leigh, Hall, Collins, Penman, Brady, Joiner

Referee: W. G. Livingstone, Glasgow | 53,359

1949/50	29 October	East Fife	3	0	Dunfermline Ath.	Hampden Park
		Fleming Duncan Morris				
East Fife: McGarrity, Laird, Stewart, Philip, Finlay, Aitken, Black, Fleming, Morris, Brown, Duncan						
Dunfermline Athletic: Johnstone, Kirk, McLean, McCall, Clarkson, Whyte, Mayes, Cannon, Henderson, McGairy, Smith						
Referee: W. Webb, Glasgow						38,897

1950/51	28 October	Motherwell	3	0	Hibernian	Hampden Park
		Kelly Forrest Waters				
Motherwell: Johnstone, Kilmarnock, Shaw, McLeod, Paton, Redpath, Watters, Forrest, Kelly, Watson, Aitkenhead						
Hibernian: Younger, Govan, Ogilvie, Buchanan, Paterson, Coombe, Smith, Johnstone, Reilly, Ormond, Bradley						
Referee: J. Mowat, Glasgow						63,074

1951/52	27 October	Dundee	3	2	Rangers	Hampden Park
		Flavell Pattillo Boyd			Findlay Thornton	
Dundee: Brown, Fallon, Cowan, Gallacher, Cowie, Boyd, Toner, Pattillo, Flavell, Steel, Christie						
Rangers: Brown, Young, Little, McColl, Woodburn, Cox, Waddell, Findlay, Thornton, Johnson, Rutherford						
Referee: J. Mowat, Glasgow						91,075

1952/53	25 October	Dundee	2	0	Kilmarnock	Hampden Park
		Flavell (2)				
Dundee: R. Henderson, Fallon, Frew, Ziesing, Boyd, Cowie, Toner, A. Henderson, Flavell, Steel, Christie						
Kilmarnock: Niven, Collins, Hood, Russell, Thyne, Middlemass, Henaughan, Harvey, Mayes, Jack, Murray						
Referee: J. Mowat, Glasgow						51,830

1953/54	24 October	East Fife	3	2	Partick Thistle	Hampden Park
		Gardiner ·Fleming Christie			Walker McKenzie	
East Fife: Curran, Emery, S. Stewart, Christie, Finlay, McLennan, J. Stewart, Fleming, Bonthrone, Gardiner, Matthew						
Partick Thistle: Ledgerwood, McGowan, Gibb, Crawford, Davidson, Kerr, McKenzie, Howitt, Sharp, Wright, Walker						
Referee: J. Cox, Rutherglen						88,529

1954/55	23 October	Hearts	4	2	Motherwell	Hampden Park
		Bauld (3) Wardhaugh			Redpath Bain	
Hearts: Duff, Parker, McKenzie, Mackay, Glidden, Cumming, Souness, Conn, Bauld, Wardhaugh, Urquhart							
Motherwell: Weir, Kilmarnock, McSeveney, Cox, Paton, Redpath, Hunter, Aitken, Bain, Humphries, Williams							
Referee: J. Mowat, Glasgow						55,640	

1955/56	22 October	Aberdeen	2	1	St Mirren	Hampden Park
		Mallan o.g. Leggat			Holmes	
Aberdeen: Martin, Mitchell, Caldwell, Wilson, Clunie, Glen, Leggat, Yorston, Buckley, Wishart, Hather							
St Mirren: Lornie, Lapsley, Mallon, Neilson, Telfer, Holmes, Rodger, Laird, Brown, Gemmell, Callan							
Referee: H. Phillips, Wishaw						44,103	

1956/57	27 October	Celtic	0	0	Partick Thistle	Hampden Park
Celtic: Beattie, Haughney, Fallon, Evans, Jack, Peacock, Walsh, Collins, McPhail, Tully, Fernie							
Partick Thistle: Ledgerwood, Kerr, Gibb, Collins, Davidson, Mathers, McKenzie, Smith, Hogan, Wright, Ewing							
Referee: J. Mowat, Glasgow						58,794	

1956/57	31 October	Celtic	3	0	Partick Thistle	Hampden Park
		McPhail (2) Collins				
Celtic: Mochan for Walsh							
Partick Thistle: Crawford and McParland for Davidson and Smith							
Referee: J. Mowat, Glasgow						31,126	

1957/58	19 October	Celtic	7	1	Rangers	Hampden Park
		McPhail (3) Mochan (2) Wilson Fernie			Simpson	
Celtic: Beattie, Donnelly, Fallon, Fernie, Evans, Peacock, Tully, Collins, McPhail, Wilson, Mochan							
Rangers: Niven, Shearer, Caldow, McColl, Valentine, Davis, Scott, Simpson, Murray, Baird, Hubbard							
Referee: J. Mowat, Glasgow						82,293	

1958/59	25 October	Hearts	5	1	Partick Thistle	Hampden Park
		Bauld (2) Murray (2) Hamilton			Smith	

Hearts: Marshall, Kirk, Thomson, Mackay, Glidden, Cumming, Hamilton, Murray, Bauld, Wardhaugh, Crawford
Partick Thistle: Ledgerwood, Hogan, Donlevy, Mathers, Davidson, Wright, McKenzie, Thomson, Smith, McParland, Ewing

Referee: R. H. Davidson, Airdrie	59,960

1959/60	24 October	Hearts	2	1	Third Lanark	Hampden Park
		Hamilton Young			Gray	

Hearts: Marshall, Kirk, Thomson, Bowman, Cumming, Higgins, Smith, Crawford, Young, Blackwood, Hamilton
Third Lanark: Robertson, Lewis, Brown, Reilly, McCallum, Cunningham, McInnes, Craig, D. Hilley, Gray, L. Hilley

Referee: R. H. Davidson, Airdrie	57,974

Eric Caldow of Rangers and Bertie Peacock of Celtic lead their teams out for a game in Section Two of the League Cup in August 1960. Rangers won the section and went on to lift the trophy

1960/61	29 October	Rangers	2	0	Kilmarnock	Hampden Park
		Brand Scott				
Rangers: Niven, Shearer, Caldow, Davis, Paterson, Baxter, Scott, McMillan, Millar, Brand, Wilson						
Kilmarnock: J. Brown, Richmond, Watson, Beattie, Toner, Kennedy, H. Brown, McInally, Kerr, Black, Muir						
Referee: T. Wharton, Clarkston						82,063

1961/62	28 October	Rangers	1	1	Hearts	Hampden Park
		Millar			Cumming	a.e.t.
Rangers: Ritchie, Shearer, Caldow, Davis, Paterson, Baxter, Scott, McMillan, Millar, Brand, Wilson						
Hearts: Marshall, Kirk, Holt, Cumming, Polland, Higgins, Ferguson, Elliott, Wallace, Gordon, Hamilton						
Referee: R. H. Davidson, Airdrie						88,635

1961/62	18 December	Rangers	3	1	Hearts	Hampden Park
		Millar Brand McMillan			Davidson	
Rangers: Baillie for Paterson						
Hearts: Cruickshank, Davidson, Bauld and Blackwood for Marshall, Elliott, Wallace and Gordon						
Referee: R. H. Davidson, Airdrie						47,552

1962/63	27 October	Hearts	1	0	Kilmarnock	Hampden Park
		Davidson				
Hearts: Marshall, Polland, Holt, Cumming, Barry, Higgins, Wallace, Paton, Davidson, W. Hamilton, J. Hamilton						
Kilmarnock: McLaughlin, Richmond, Watson, O'Connor, McGrory, Beattie, Brown, Black, Kerr, McInally, McIlroy						
Referee: T. Wharton, Clarkston						51,280

1963/64	26 October	Rangers	5	0	Morton	Hampden Park
		Forrest (4) Willoughby				
Rangers: Ritchie, Shearer, Provan, Greig, McKinnon, Baxter, Henderson, Willoughby, Forrest, Brand, Watson						
Morton: Brown, Boyd, Mallan, Reilly, Keirman, Strachan, Adamson, Campbell, Stevenson, McGraw, Wilson						
Referee: H. Phillips, Wishaw						105,907

1964/65	24 October	Rangers	2	1	Celtic	Hampden Park
		Forrest (2)			Divers	
Rangers: Ritchie, Provan, Caldow, Greig, McKinnon, Wood, Brand, Millar, Forrest, Baxter, Johnston						
Celtic: Fallon, Young, Gemmell, Clark, Cushley, Kennedy, Johnstone, Murdoch, Chalmers, Divers, Hughes						
Referee: H. Phillips, Wishaw						91,423

Jim Baxter and Eric Caldow celebrate the League Cup victory over Celtic in October 1964

1965/66	23 October	Celtic	2	1	Rangers	Hampden Park
		Hughes (2 pens)			Young o.g.	
Celtic: Simpson, Young, Gemmell, Murdoch, McNeill, Clark, Johnstone, Gallagher, McBride, Lennox, Hughes						
Rangers: Ritchie, Johansen, Provan, Wood, McKinnon, Greig, Henderson, Willoughby, Forrest, Wilson, Johnston						
Referee: H. Phillips, Wishaw						107,600

1966/67	29 October	Celtic	1	0	Rangers	Hampden Park
		Lennox				
Celtic: Simpson, Gemmell, O'Neill, Murdoch, McNeill, Clark, Johnstone, Lennox, McBride, Auld, Hughes (Chalmers)						
Rangers: Martin, Johansen, Provan, Greig, McKinnon, D. Smith, Henderson, Watson, McLean, A. Smith, Johnston						
Referee: T. Wharton, Clarkston						94,532

1967/68	28 October	Celtic	5	3	Dundee	Hampden Park
		Chalmers (2) Hughes Lennox Wallace			G. McLean (2) J. McLean	

Celtic: Simpson, Craig, Gemmell, Murdoch, McNeill, Clark, Chalmers, Lennox, Wallace, Auld (O'Neill), Hughes

Dundee: Arrol, Wilson, Houston, Murray, Stewart, Stuart, Campbell, J. McLean, Wilson, G. McLean, Bryce

Referee: R. H. Davidson, Airdrie — 66,600

1968/69	5 April	Celtic	6	2	Hibernian	Hampden Park
		Lennox (3) Wallace Auld Craig			O'Rourke Stevenson	

Celtic: Fallon, Craig, Gemmell (Clark), Murdoch, McNeill, Brogan, Johnstone, Wallace, Chalmers, Auld, Lennox

Hibernian: Allan, Shevlane, Davis, Stanton, Madsen, Blackley, Marinello, Quinn, Cormack, O'Rourke, Stevenson

Referee: W. Syme, Airdrie — 74,000

1969/70	25 October	Celtic	1	0	St Johnstone	Hampden Park
		Auld				

Celtic: Fallon, Craig, Hay, Murdoch, McNeill, Brogan, Callaghan, Hood, Hughes, Chalmers (Johnstone), Auld

St Johnstone: Donaldson, Lambie, Coburn, Gordon, Rooney, McPhee, Aird, Hall, McCarry (Whitelaw), Connolly, Aitken

Referee: J. Paterson, Bothwell — 73,067

1970/71	24 October	Rangers	1	0	Celtic	Hampden Park
		D. Johnstone				

Rangers: McCloy, Jardine, Miller, Conn, McKinnon, Jackson, Henderson, MacDonald, D. Johnstone, Stein, W. Johnston

Celtic: Williams, Craig, Quinn, Murdoch, McNeill, Hay, Johnstone, Connelly, Wallace, Hood (Lennox), Macari

Referee: T. Wharton, Clarkston — 106,263

1971/72	23 October	Partick Thistle	4	1	Celtic	Hampden Park
		Rae Lawrie McQuade Bone			Dalglish	

Partick Thistle: Rough, Hansen, Forsyth, Glavin (Gibson), Campbell, Strachan, McQuade, Coulston, Bone, Rae, Lawrie

Celtic: Williams, Hay, Gemmell, Murdoch, Connelly, Brogan, Johnstone (Craig), Dalglish, Hood, Callaghan, Macari

Referee: W. Mullan, Dalkeith — 62,740

1972/73	9 December	Hibernian	2	1	Celtic	Hampden Park
		Stanton O'Rourke			Dalglish	

Hibernian: Herriot, Brownlie, Schaedler, Stanton, Black, Blackley, Edwards, O'Rourke, Gordon, Cropley, Duncan

Celtic: Williams, McGrain, Brogan, McCluskey, McNeill, Hay, Johnstone (Callaghan), Connelly, Dalglish, Hood, Macari

Referee: A. MacKenzie, Larbert	71,696

Action in the 1972/73 League Cup final between Celtic and Hibernian, which Hibs won 2–1

1973/74	15 December	Dundee	1	0	Celtic	Hampden Park
		Wallace				

Dundee: Allan, Wilson, Gemmell, Ford, Stewart, Phillip, Duncan, Robinson, Wallace, Scott, Lambie

Celtic: Hunter, McGrain, Brogan, McCluskey, McNeill, Murray, Hood (Johnstone), Hay (Connelly), Wilson, Callaghan, Dalglish

Referee: R. H. Davidson, Airdrie	27,974

1974/75	26 October	Celtic	6	3	Hibernian	Hampden Park
		Deans (3) Johnstone Wilson Murray			Harper (3)	

Celtic: Hunter, McGrain, Brogan, Murray, McNeill, McCluskey, Johnstone, Dalglish, Deans, Hood, Wilson

Hibernian: McArthur, Brownlie (Smith), Bremner, Stanton, Spalding, Blackley, Edwards, Cropley, Harper, Munro, Duncan (Murray)

Referee: J. R. P. Gordon, Newport on Tay	53,848

1975/76	25 October	Rangers	1	0	Celtic	Hampden Park
		MacDonald				
Rangers: Kennedy, Jardine, Greig, Forsyth, Jackson, MacDonald, McLean, Stein, Parlane, Johnstone, Young						
Celtic: Latchford, McGrain, Lynch, McCluskey, MacDonald, Edvaldsson, Hood (McNamara), Dalglish, Wilson (Glavin), Callaghan, Lennox						
Referee: W. Anderson, East Kilbride						50,806

1976/77	6 November	Aberdeen	2	1	Celtic	Hampden Park
		Jarvie Robb			Dalglish	a.e.t.
Aberdeen: Clark, Kennedy, Williamson, Smith, Garner, Miller, Sullivan, Scott, Harper, Jarvie (Robb), Graham						
Celtic: Latchford, McGrain, Lynch, Edvaldsson, MacDonald, Aitken, Doyle, Glavin, Dalglish, Burns (Lennox), Wilson						
Referee: J. Paterson, Bothwell						69,707

1977/78	18 March	Rangers	2	1	Celtic	Hampden Park
		Cooper Smith			Edvaldsson	a.e.t.
Rangers: Kennedy, Jardine, Jackson, Forsyth, Greig, Hamilton (Miller), MacDonald, Smith, McLean, Johnstone, Cooper (Parlane)						
Celtic: Latchford, Sneddon, Lynch (Wilson), Munro, MacDonald, Dowie, Glavin (Doyle), Edvaldsson, McCluskey, Aitken, Burns						
Referee: D. Syme, Rutherglen						60,168

1978/79	31 March	Rangers	2	1	Aberdeen	Hampden Park
		McMaster o.g. Jackson			Davidson	
Rangers: McCloy, Jardine, Dawson, Johnstone, Jackson, MacDonald, McLean, Russell, Urquhart (Miller), Smith (Parlane), Cooper						
Aberdeen: Clark, Kennedy, McLelland, McMaster, Rougvie, Miller, Strachan, Archibald, Harper, Jarvie (McLeish), Davidson						
Referee: I. Foote, Glasgow						54,000

1979/80	8 December	Dundee United	0	0	Aberdeen	Hampden Park
						a.e.t.
Dundee United: McAlpine, Stark, Kopel, Phillip (Fleming), Hegarty, Narey, Bannon, Sturrock, Pettigrew, Holt, Payne (Murray)						
Aberdeen: Clark, Kennedy, Rougvie, McLeish, Garner, Miller, Strachan, Archibald, McGhee (Jarvie), McMaster (Hamilton), Scanlon						
Referee: B. McGinlay, Balfron						27,173

1979/80	12 December	Dundee United	3	0	Aberdeen	Dens Park
		Pettigrew (2) Sturrock				
Dundee United: Fleming and Kirkwood for Phillip and Payne							
Aberdeen: As per first game. Jarvie substituted for McGhee, and Hamilton for Scanlon							
Referee: B. McGinlay, Balfron						28,933

1980/81	6 December	Dundee United	3	0	Dundee	Dens Park
		Sturrock (2) Dodds				
Dundee United: McAlpine, Holt, Kopel, Phillip, Hegarty, Narey, Bannon, Payne, Pettigrew, Sturrock, Dodds							
Dundee: R. Geddes, Barr, Schaedler, Fraser, Glennie, McGeachie, Mackie, Stephen, Sinclair, Williamson, A. Geddes							
Referee: R. Valentine, Dundee						24,466

1981/82	28 November	Rangers	2	1	Dundee United	Hampden Park
		Cooper Redford		Milne		
Rangers: Stewart, Jardine, Miller, Stevens, Jackson, Bett, Cooper, Johnstone, Russell, MacDonald, Dalziel (Redford)							
Dundee United: McAlpine, Holt, Stark, Narey, Hegarty, Phillip, Bannon, Milne, Kirkwood, Sturrock, Dodds							
Referee: E. Pringle, Edinburgh						53,777

1982/83	4 December	Celtic	2	1	Rangers	Hampden Park
		Nicholas MacLeod		Bett		
Celtic: Bonner, McGrain, Sinclair, Aitken, McAdam, MacLeod, Provan, McStay (Reid), McGarvey, Burns, Nicholas							
Rangers: Stewart, McKinnon, Redford, McClelland, Paterson, Bett, Cooper, Prytz (Dawson), Johnstone, Russell (MacDonald), Smith							
Referee: K. Hope, Clarkston						55,372

1983/84	25 March	Rangers	3	2	Celtic	Hampden Park
		McCoist (3)		McClair Reid	a.e.t.	
Rangers: McCloy, Nicholl, Dawson, McClelland, Paterson, McPherson, Russell, McCoist, Clark (McAdam), MacDonald (Burns), Cooper							
Celtic: Bonner, McGrain, Reid, Aitken, McAdam, MacLeod, Provan (Sinclair), McStay, McGarvey (Melrose), Burns, McClair							
Referee: R. Valentine, Dundee						66,369

1984/85	28 October	Rangers	1	0	Dundee United	Hampden Park
		Ferguson				

Rangers: McCloy, Dawson, McClelland, Fraser, Paterson, McPherson, Russell (Prytz), McCoist, Ferguson (Mitchell), Redford, Cooper

Dundee United: McAlpine, Holt (Clark), Malpas, Gough, Hegarty, Narey, Bannon, Milne (Beedie), Kirkwood, Sturrock, Dodds

Referee: B. McGinlay, Balfron   44,698

1985/86	27 October	Aberdeen	3	0	Hibernian	Hampden Park
		Black (2) Stark				

Aberdeen: Leighton, McKimmie, Mitchell, Stark, McLeish, Miller, Black (Gray), Simpson, McDougall, Cooper, Hewitt

Hibernian: Rough, Sneddon, Munro, Brazil (Harris), Fulton, Hunter, Kane, Chisholm, Cowan, Durie, McBride (Collins)

Referee: R. Valentine, Dundee   40,065

1986/87	26 October	Rangers	2	1	Celtic	Hampden Park
		Durrant Cooper			McClair	

Rangers: Woods, Nicholl, Munro, Fraser (MacFarlane), Dawson, Butcher, Ferguson, McMinn, McCoist (Fleck), Durrant, Cooper

Celtic: Bonner, Grant, MacLeod, Aitken, Whyte, McGhee (Archdeacon), McClair, McStay, Johnston, Shepherd, McInally

Referee: D. Syme, Rutherglen   74,219

1987/88	25 October	Rangers	3	3	Aberdeen	Hampden Park
		Cooper Durrant Fleck			Bett Falconer Hewitt	a.e.t.

Rangers won 5–3 on penalties

Rangers: Walker, Nicholl, Munro, Roberts, Ferguson (Francis), Gough, McGregor (Cohen), Fleck, McCoist, Durrant, Cooper

Aberdeen: Leighton, McKimmie, Connor, Simpson (Weir), McLeish, W. Miller, Hewitt, Bett, J. Miller, Nicholas, Falconer

Referee: R. Valentine, Dundee   71,961

1988/89	23 October	Rangers	3	2	Aberdeen	Hampden Park
		McCoist (2) Ferguson			Dodds (2)	

Rangers: Woods, Stevens, Brown, Gough, Wilkins, Butcher, Drinkell, Ferguson, McCoist, Cooper, Walters

Aberdeen: Snelders, McKimmie, Robertson, Simpson (Irvine), McLeish, Miller, Nicholas, Bett, Dodds, Connor, Hewitt

Referee: G. Smith, Edinburgh   72,122

1989/90	22 October	Aberdeen	2	1	Rangers	Hampden Park
		Mason (2)			Walters	a.e.t.

Aberdeen: Snelders, McKimmie, Robertson, Grant (van der Ark), McLeish, Miller, Nicholas, Bett, Mason, Connor, Jess (Irvine)

Rangers: Woods, Stevens, Munro, Gough, Wilkins, Butcher, Steven, Ferguson, McCoist, Johnston, Walters (McCall)

Referee: G. Smith, Edinburgh	61,190

Aberdeen captain Willie Miller celebrates after the Dons won the 1989/90 League Cup. Paul Mason scored twice in their 2–1 victory over Rangers

1990/91	28 October	Rangers	2	1	Celtic	Hampden Park
		Walters Gough			Elliott	a.e.t.

Rangers: Woods, Stevens, Munro, Gough, Spackman, Brown, Steven, Hurlock (Huistra), McCoist (Ferguson), Hateley, Walters

Celtic: Bonner, Grant, Wdowczyk, Fulton (Hewitt), Elliott, Rogan, Miller (Morris), McStay, Dziekanowski, Creaney, Collins

Referee: J. McCluskey, Stewarton	62,817

1991/92	27 October	Hibernian	2	0	Dunfermline	Hampden Park
		McIntyre Wright				

Hibernian: Burridge, Miller, Mitchell, Hunter, McIntyre, MacLeod, Weir, Hamilton, Wright, Evans, McGinlay

Dunfermline: Rhodes, Wilson, Sharp (Cunnington), McCathie, Moyes, Robertson, McWilliams, Kozma, Leitch, Davies, Sinclair (McCall)

Referee: B. McGinlay, Balfron	40,377

1992/93	25 October	Rangers	2	1	Aberdeen	Hampden Park
		McCall Smith o.g.			Shearer	a.e.t.
Rangers: Goram, McCall, Robertson, Gough (Mikhailichenko), McPherson, Brown, Steven (Gordon), Ferguson, McCoist, Hateley, Durrant						
Aberdeen: Snelders, Wright, Winnie, Grant, McLeish, Smith, Aitken (Richardson), Bett (Booth), Jess, Shearer, Paatelainen						
Referee: D.D. Hope, Erskine						45,298

1993/94	24 October	Rangers	2	1	Hibernian	Celtic Park
		Durrant McCoist			McPherson o.g.	
Rangers: Maxwell, Stevens, Robertson, Gough, McPherson, McCall, Steven, Ferguson, Durrant, Hateley, Huistra (McCoist)						
Hibernian: Leighton, Miller, Mitchell, Farrell, Tweed, Hunter, McAllister, Hamilton, Wright, Jackson (Evans), O'Neill						
Referee: J. McCluskey, Stewarton						47,632

1994/95	27 November	Raith Rovers	2	2	Celtic	Ibrox
		Crawford Dalziel			Walker Nicholas	a.e.t.
Raith Rovers won 6–5 on penalties						
Raith Rovers: Thomson, McAnespie, Broddle (Rowbotham), Narey, Dennis, Sinclair, Crawford, Dalziel (Redford), Graham, Cameron, Dair						
Celtic: Marshall, Galloway, Boyd, McNally, Mowbray, O'Neil, Donnelly (Falconer), McStay, Nicholas (Byrne), Walker, Collins						
Referee: J. McCluskey, Stewarton						45,384

1995/96	26 November	Aberdeen	2	0	Dundee	Hampden Park
		Dodds Shearer				
Aberdeen: Watt, McKimmie, Glass, Grant, Inglis, Smith, Miller (Robertson), Shearer, Bernard, Dodds, Jess (Hetherston)						
Dundee: Pageaud, J. Duffy, McQueen, Manley, Wieghorst, C. Duffy, Shaw, Vrto (Farningham), Tosh (Britton), Hamilton, McCann (Anderson)						
Referee: L. Mottram, Forth						33,096

1996/97	24 November	Rangers	4	3	Hearts	Celtic Park
		McCoist (2) Gascoigne (2)			Fulton Robertson Weir	
Rangers: Goram, Cleland (Robertson), Moore, Gough, Petric, Bjorklund, Miller, Gascoigne, McCoist, Albertz, Laudrup						
Hearts: Rousset, Weir, Pointon, Mackay, Ritchie, Bruno, Paille (Beckford), Fulton, Robertson, Cameron, McCann						
Referee: H. Dallas, Motherwell						48,599

1997/98	30 November	Celtic	3	0	Dundee United	Ibrox
		Rieper Larsson Burley				
Celtic: Gould, Boyd, Mahe, McNamara (Annoni), Rieper, Stubbs, Larsson, Burley, Thom (Donnelly), Wieghorst, Blinker (Lambert)							
Dundee United: Dijkstra, Skoldmark (McSwegan), Malpas, Pressley, Perry, Pedersen, Olofsson, Zetterlund, Winters, Easton, Bowman							
Referee: J. McCluskey, Stewarton						49,305	

1998/99	29 November	Rangers	2	1	St Johnstone	Celtic Park
		Guivarc'h Albertz		Dasovic		
Rangers: Niemi, Porrini, Numan, Amoruso, Hendry, Albertz (I. Ferguson), B. Ferguson, van Bronckhorst, Kanchelskis, Wallace, Guivarc'h (Durie)							
St Johnstone: Main, McQuillan, Dods, Kernaghan, Bollan, Scott, O'Neil (Preston), Kane, O'Boyle (Lowndes), Dasovic, Simao (Grant)							
Referee: H. Dallas, Motherwell						45,533	

1999/00	19 March	Celtic	2	0	Aberdeen	Hampden Park
		Riseth Johnson				
Celtic: Gould, Boyd, Riseth, Mjallby, Mahe, McNamara, Wieghorst, Petrov, Moravcik (Stubbs), Johnson (Berkovic), Viduka							
Aberdeen: Leighton, Perry, McAllister, Solberg, Anderson, Dow, Bernard, Jess (Mayer), Guntweit (Belabed), Zerouali (Winters), Stavrum							
Referee: K. Clark, Paisley						50,073	

2000/01	18 March	Celtic	3	0	Kilmarnock	Hampden Park
		Larsson (3)				
Celtic: Gould, Mjallby, Valgaeren, Vega, Petta (Crainey) (Boyd), Healy, Lennon, Lambert, Moravcik (Smith), Larsson, Sutton							
Kilmarnock: Marshall, MacPherson, McGowne, Dindeleux (Canero), Innes, Hay, Holt, Durrant (Reilly), Mahood, Cocard (McLaren), Dargo							
Referee: H. Dallas, Motherwell						48,830	

2001/02	17 March	Rangers	4	0	Ayr United	Hampden Park
		Flo Ferguson Caniggia (2)				
Rangers: Klos, Ricksen, Vidmar (Hughes), Amoruso, Numan, Konterman, Ferguson, Latapy (Dodds), Caniggia, Flo, Lovenkrands (McCann)							
Ayr United: Nelson, Robertson, Lovering, Duffy, Hughes, Craig, Wilson (Chaplain), McGinlay, McLaughlin (Kean), Grady, Sheerin							
Referee: H. Dallas, Motherwell						50,049	

2002/03	16 March	Rangers	2	1	Celtic	Hampden Park
		Caniggia Lovenkrands			Larsson	

Rangers: Klos, Ricksen, Moore, Amoruso, Bonnisel (Ross), Arteta (Konterman), Ferguson, Caniggia, de Boer (Arveladze), Mols, Lovenkrands

Celtic: Douglas, Mjallby (Petrov), Valgaeren, Balde, Thompson, Lennon, Smith (Sylla), Lambert, Sutton (Maloney), Larsson, Hartson

Referee: K. Clark, Paisley	52,000

2003/04	14 March	Livingston	2	0	Hibernian	Hampden Park
		Lilley McAllister				

Livingston: McKenzie, McNamee (McLaughlin), McAllister, Rubio, Andrews, Dorado, Makel, O'Brien (McGovern), Lovell, Fernandez (Pasquinelli), Lilley

Hibernian: Anderson, Murdock, Smith (McManus), Edge, Doumbe, Caldwell, Thomson, Reid (Dobbie), Riordan, O'Connor, Brown

Referee: W. Young, Clarkston	45,443

2004/05	20 March	Rangers	5	1	Motherwell	Hampden Park
		Kyrgiakos (2) Ross Ricksen Novo			Partridge	

Rangers: Waterreus, Ross, Malcolm, Kyrgiakos, Ball, Ricksen, Ferguson, Vignal (Rae), Buffel, Novo (Thompson), Prso

Motherwell: Marshall, Corrigan, Partridge, Hammell, Craigan, McBride (Quinn), O'Donnell, Leitch, Paterson (Fitzpatrick), Foran (Clarkson), McDonald

Referee: M. McCurry, Glasgow	50,182

2005/06	19 March	Celtic	3	0	Dunfermline	Hampden Park
		Zurawski Maloney Dublin				

Celtic: Boruc, Telfer, Balde, McManus, Wallace, Nakamura, Keane (Dublin), Lennon, Maloney, Zurawski, Petrov

Dunfermline: McGregor, Shields, Wilson, Ross (Donnelly), Campbell (Derek Young), Mason, Thomson, Daquin (Tarachulski), Labonte, Makel, Burchill

Referee: S. Dougal, Burnside	50,090

2006/07	18 March	Hibernian	5	1	Kilmarnock	Hampden Park
		Jones Benjelloun (2) Fletcher (2)			Greer	

Hibernian: McNeil, Whittaker (Martis), Hogg (McCann), Jones, Murphy, Sproule (Zemmama), Brown, Beuzelin, Stevenson, Benjelloun, Fletcher

Kilmarnock: Combe, Wright, Greer, Ford, Hay, Di Giacomo (Locke), Johnston, Fowler, Leven (Wales), Nish, Naismith

Referee: D. McDonald, Edinburgh	50,162

2007/08	16 March	Rangers	2	2	Dundee United	Hampden Park
		Boyd (2)			Hunt De Vries	a.e.t.
Rangers won 3–2 on penalties						
Rangers: McGregor, Broadfoot, Cuellar, Weir, Papac (Boyd), Hemdani (Darcheville), Dailly, Burke (Whittaker), Ferguson, Davis, McCulloch						
Dundee United: Zaluska, Kovacevic, Kenneth, Wilkie, Kalvenes, Buaben (Robertson), Flood, Kerr, Gomis, Hunt (Conway), De Vries						
Referee: K. Clark, Paisley					50,019	

2008/09	15 March	Celtic	2	0	Rangers	Hampden Park
		O'Dea McGeady				a.e.t.
Celtic: Boruc, Hinkel, Loovens, McManus, O'Dea (Wilson), Caldwell, Nakamura, S. Brown, Hartley (Samaras) (Vennegoor of Hesselink), McGeady, McDonald						
Rangers: McGregor, Whittaker, Weir, Broadfoot, Papac, Davis, McCulloch (Dailly), Ferguson, Mendes, Miller (Novo), Lafferty (Boyd)						
Referee: D. McDonald, Edinburgh					51,193	

2009/10	21 March	Rangers	1	0	St Mirren	Hampden Park
		Miller				
Rangers: Alexander, Whittaker, Wilson, Weir, Papac, Davis (Edu), K. Thomson, McCulloch, Novo (Smith), Miller, Boyd (Naismith)						
St Mirren: Gallacher, Barron, Potter, Mair, Ross, S. Thomson, Brady (O'Donnell), Murray (Dorman), Carey, Mehmet (Dargo), Higdon						
Referee: C. Thomson, Paisley					44,538	

2010/11	20 March	Rangers	2	1	Celtic	Hampden Park
		Davis Jelavic			Ledley	a.e.t.
Rangers: Alexander, Whittaker, Bougherra (Hutton), Weir, Papac, Lafferty (Weiss), Davis, Edu, Wylde, Naismith, Jelavic (Diouf)						
Celtic: Forster, Wilson, Rogne (Loovens), Mulgrew, Izaguirre, Brown (Sung-Yueng), Kayal, Ledley, Commons (McCourt), Hooper, Samaras						
Referee: C. Thomson, Paisley					51,181	

2011/12	18 March	Kilmarnock	1	0	Celtic	Hampden Park
		Van Tornhout				
Kilmarnock: Bell, Hay, Fowler, Nelson, Gordon, Sissoko (Kroca), Kelly, Buijs (Johnson), Harkins (van Tornhout), Shiels, Heffernan						
Celtic: Forster, Wilson, Mulgrew, Rogne (Ki Sung-Yeung), Matthews, Brown, Ledley (Commons), Wanyama, Stokes, Forrest, Hooper (Samaras)						
Referee: W. Collum, Glasgow					49,572	

2012/13	17 March	St Mirren	3	2	Hearts	Hampden Park
		Gonçalves Thompson Newton			Stevenson (2)	

St Mirren: Samson, van Zanten, Goodwin, McAusland, Dummett, Newton, McGinn (Carey), Teale, McGowan, Gonçalves (Mair), Thompson (Parkin)

Hearts: MacDonald, McGowan, Webster, Wilson, McHattie, Stevenson, Barr (Holt), Taouil (Carrick), Walker (Novikovas), Ngoo, Sutton

Referee: C. Thomson, Paisley	44,036

2013/14	16 March	Aberdeen	0	0	Inverness CT	Celtic Park
						a.e.t.

Aberdeen won 4–2 on penalties

Aberdeen: Langfield, Logan, Anderson, Reynolds, Considine (Vernon), Jack, Flood, Robson, McGinn, Rooney, Hayes (Smith, Low)

Inverness CT: Brill, Raven, Devine, Meekings, Shinnie, Tansey, Watkins (Ross), Draper, Foran (Christie), Vincent (Doran), McKay

Referee: S. McLean, Newton Mearns	51,143

At the end of the 2013/14 season the trophy had been competed for sixty-eight times and the winners were as follows:

Rangers	27
Celtic	14
Aberdeen	6
Hearts	4
Dundee	3
East Fife	3
Hibernian	3
Dundee United	2
Kilmarnock	1
Livingston	1
Motherwell	1
Partick Thistle	1
Raith Rovers	1
St Mirren	1

SCOTTISH LEAGUE CHALLENGE CUP

- First Challenge Cup final: The tournament was known as the B&Q Centenary Cup in its first season. Dundee beat Ayr United 3–2 after extra time at Fir Park on Sunday 11 November 1990 (the score was 2–2 after ninety minutes). Billy Dodds scored a hat-trick for Dundee, whilst Ian McAllister and David Smyth scored for Ayr United.

- 1995/96: The final was decided by a penalty shoot-out for the first time. The match between Dundee United and Stenhousemuir at McDiarmid Park on Sunday 5th November 1995 finished goalless after extra time, and Stenhousemuir won 5–4 on penalties.

- 1998/99: The tournament was cancelled for one season. There had been no sponsorship in 1995/96, 1996/97 and 1997/98, and the situation proved to be unsustainable. A new sponsor was found for 1999/2000 and the competition resumed.

- 2006/07: The first-round draw was divided into north/east and south/west regional sections for the first time (the regional format was extended to the second-round draw in 2012/13).

- 2009/10: Annan Athletic became the first club from the Third Division (re-named Scottish League Two in 2013) to reach the last four when they beat Elgin City 4–2 in the quarter-finals; they then lost 3–0 to Dundee at Dens Park. They reached the semi-finals again in 2011/12 and 2013/14.

- 2011/12: Falkirk became the first club to win the Challenge Cup four times. They beat Hamilton Academical 1–0 at Livingston on Sunday 1 April 2012, with Darren Dods scoring the only goal.

- 2011/12: Clubs from a league other than the Scottish Football League were admitted for the first time. Highland League champions Buckie Thistle and runners-up Deveronvale took part in the first round, but both fell at the first hurdle.

This knock-out tournament was introduced in the 1990/91 season to celebrate the centenary of the formation of the SFA and proved sufficiently popular to be continued in succeeding years. There are no replays, and matches are decided by a penalty shoot-out if the scores are level after extra-time. Originally designed for just the SFL clubs that were not in the top division, with some receiving a bye in the first round, it was extended in 2011/12 to become a competition for thirty-two clubs, with no byes.

The thirty SPFL (originally SFL) clubs outwith the top flight are joined in the first-round draw by two clubs from a lower level. These were Highland League champions Buckie Thistle and runners-up Deveronvale in 2011/12, but in 2012 it was decided that the competition would be restricted to licensed clubs and the two additional clubs for 2012/13 were Inverurie Loco Works and Wick Academy – the two highest licensed clubs in the Highland League at the end of the previous season.

The opportunity to take part was further extended in 2013/14, when Spartans and Threave Rovers, the highest licensed clubs in the EOSL and SOSL, met in a preliminary round. Spartans won 4–3 on aggregate and went on to play holders Queen of the South in the first round. The Highland League was represented by its highest licensed club, Formartine United.

This table shows the result of each final, together with the venue:

1990/91	Dundee	3	Ayr United	2	Fir Park	a.e.t.
1991/92	Hamilton Ac.	1	Ayr United	0	Fir Park	
1992/93	Hamilton Ac.	3	Morton	2	Love Street	
1993/94	Falkirk	3	St Mirren	0	Fir Park	
1994/95	Airdrieonians	3	Dundee	2	McDiarmid Park	a.e.t.
1995/96	Stenhousemuir	0	Dundee United	0	McDiarmid Park	a.e.t.
	Stenhousemuir won 5–4 on penalties					
1996/97	Stranraer	1	St Johnstone	0	Broadwood Stadium	
1997/98	Falkirk	1	Queen of the South	0	Fir Park	
1998/99	No competition					
1999/00	Alloa Athletic	4	Inverness CT	4	Excelsior Stadium	a.e.t.
Alloa Athletic won 5–4 on penalties						
2000/01	Airdrieonians	2	Livingston	2	Broadwood Stadium	a.e.t.
	Airdrieonians won 4–3 on penalties					
2001/02	Airdrieonians	2	Alloa Athletic	1	Broadwood Stadium	
2002/03	Queen of the South	2	Brechin City	0	Broadwood Stadium	
2003/04	Inverness CT	2	Airdrie United	0	McDiarmid Park	
2004/05	Falkirk	2	Ross County	1	McDiarmid Park	
2005/06	St Mirren	2	Hamilton Ac.	1	Excelsior Stadium	
2006/07	Ross County	1	Clyde	1	McDiarmid Park	a.e.t.
	Ross County won 5–4 on penalties					
2007/08	St Johnstone	3	Dunfermline	2	Dens Park	
2008/09	Airdrie United	2	Ross County	2	McDiarmid Park	a.e.t.
	Airdrie United won 3–2 on penalties					
2009/10	Dundee	3	Inverness Cal. Thistle	2	McDiarmid Park	
2010/11	Ross County	2	Queen of the South	0	McDiarmid Park	
2011/12	Falkirk	1	Hamilton Ac.	0	Almondvale Stadium	
2012/13	Queen of the South	1	Partick Thistle	1	Almondvale Stadium	a.e.t.
	Queen of the South won 6–5 on penalties					
2013/14	Raith Rovers	1	Rangers	0	Easter Road	a.e.t.

CLUB FOOTBALL IN EUROPE

EUROPEAN CUP (1955–92)

- First Scottish (and British) club to participate: Hibernian beat Rot-Weiss Essen 4–0 in West Germany on 14 September 1955 in the first leg of their first-round match (Scorers: Eddie Turnbull 2, Lawrie Reilly and Willie Ormond) and won 5–1 on aggregate.

- 1966/67: Celtic became the first British club to win the European Cup when they beat Inter Milan 2–1 in Lisbon on 25 May 1967 (Scorers: Tommy Gemmell and Steve Chalmers).

- 1969/70: Celtic reached the final for a second time, only to lose 1–2 to Feyenoord Rotterdam in Milan on 6 May 1970 (Scorer: Tommy Gemmell).

- As well as Celtic's two appearances in the final, Scottish clubs reached the semi-finals on six occasions: Hibernian (1955/56), Rangers (1959/60), Dundee (1962/63), Celtic (1971/72; 1973/74) and Dundee United (1983/84).

The brainchild of French journalist Gabriel Hanot in the 1950s, this was a knockout competition between the league champions of each European country. It was played on a home and away basis, with the final being a single game at a neutral venue. It first saw Scottish participation in 1955/56, when Hibs were invited to take part (even though they had only finished fifth in the Scottish League). To Hibs thus belongs the honour of kicking the first ball for Scotland in the

European Cup, and to Eddie Turnbull belongs the honour of scoring the first goal. Jock Buchanan scored the first home goal at Easter Road.

After that it was always the league champions of the previous season who played in this tournament, and Scotland's record was good considering that it is a small nation – one win, one runner-up and six semi-final appearances. Hampden Park hosted the final in 1960, when Real Madrid beat Eintracht Frankfurt 7–3 in a classic match. In 1992/93 it was re-branded as the Champions League, formalising the mini-league system that had been used in 1991/92.

The record of Scottish teams is as follows:

Season	Scottish Club	Opposition	Aggregate	Round
1955/56	Hibernian	Rot-Weiss Essen	5–1	First
		Djugarden	4–1	Quarter-final
		Reims	0–3	Semi-final
1956/57	Rangers	Nice	3–3	First
			1–3	Play-off
1957/58	Rangers	St Etienne	4–3	Preliminary
		AC Milan	1–6	First
1958/59	Hearts	Standard Liege	3–6	Preliminary
1959/60	Rangers	Anderlecht	7–2	Preliminary
		Red Star Bratislava	5–4	First
		Sparta Rotterdam	3–3	Quarter-Final
			3–2	Play-off
		Eintracht Frankfurt	4–12	Semi-final
1960/61	Hearts	Benfica	1–5	Preliminary
1961/62	Rangers	Monaco	6–4	Preliminary
		Vorwaerts	6–2	First
		Standard Liege	3–4	Quarter-final
1962/63	Dundee	FC Cologne	8–5	Preliminary
		Sporting Lisbon	4–2	First
		Anderlecht	6–2	Quarter-final
		AC Milan	2–5	Semi-final
1963/64	Rangers	Real Madrid	0–7	Preliminary

Season	Scottish Club	Opposition	Aggregate	Round
1964/65	Rangers	Red Star Belgrade	5–5	Preliminary
			3–1	Play-off
		Rapid Vienna	3–0	First
		Inter Milan	2–3	Quarter-final
1965/66	Kilmarnock	Nendori Tirana	1–0	Preliminary
		Real Madrid	3–8	First
1966/67	Celtic	Zurich	5–0	First
		Nantes	6–2	Second
		Vojvodina	2–1	Quarter-final
		Dukla Prague	3–1	Semi-final
		Inter Milan	2–1	Final
Played in Lisbon on 25 May 1967. Celtic's team was: Simpson; Craig; Gemmell; Murdoch; McNeill; Clark; Johnstone; Wallace; Chalmers; Auld; Lennox. Scorers: Gemmell and Chalmers				

Steve Chalmers' goal hits the back of the Inter Milan net and Celtic are now 2–1 up in Lisbon and on their way to the club's greatest triumph, victory in the 1967 European Cup final

The Celtic squad that won the 1967 European Cup. Back row, left to right: Willie O'Neil, Billy McNeill, Jim Craig, Tommy Gemmell, Ronnie Simpson, John Hughes, Bobby Murdoch, John Clark. Front row: Jimmy Johnstone, Bobby Lennox, Willie Wallace, Steve Chalmers, Charlie Gallagher, Joe McBride and Bertie Auld

Season	Scottish Club	Opposition	Aggregate	Round
1967/68	Celtic	Dinamo Kiev	2–3	First
1968/69	Celtic	St Etienne	4–2	First
		Red Star Belgrade	6–2	Second
		AC Milan	0–1	Quarter-final
1969/70	Celtic	Basle	2–0	First
		Benfica	3–3	Second
Celtic won on the toss of a coin				
		Fiorentina	3–1	Quarter-final
		Leeds United	3–1	Semi-final
		Feyenoord	1–2	Final
1970/71	Celtic	KPV Kokkola	14–0	First
		Waterford	10–2	Second
		Ajax	1–3	Quarter-final
1971/72	Celtic	BK 1903 Copenhagen	4–2	First
		Sliema Wanderers	7–1	Second
		Ujpest Dozsa	3–2	Quarter-final

Season	Scottish Club	Opposition	Aggregate	Round
1971/72 Celtic—*contd*		Inter Milan	0–0	Semi-final
Celtic lost on penalties				
1972/73	Celtic	Rosenborg	5–2	First
		Ujpest Dozsa	2–4	Second
1973/74	Celtic	Turku	9–1	First
		Vejle	1–0	Second
		Basle	6–5	Quarter-final
		Atletico Madrid	0–2	Semi-final
1974/75	Celtic	Olympiakos	1–3	First
1975/76	Rangers	Bohemians	5–2	First
		St Etienne	1–4	Second
1976/77	Rangers	Zurich	1–2	First
1977/78	Celtic	Jeunesse D'Esch	11–1	First
		SW Innsbruck	2–4	Second
1978/79	Rangers	Juventus	2–1	First
		PSV Eindhoven	3–2	Second
		FC Cologne	1–2	Quarter-final
1979/80	Celtic	Partizan Tirana	4–2	First
		Dundalk	3–2	Second
		Real Madrid	2–3	Quarter-final
1980/81	Aberdeen	Austria Vienna	1–0	First
		Liverpool	0–5	Second
1981/82	Celtic	Juventus	1–2	First
1982/83	Celtic	Ajax	4–3	First
		Real Sociedad	2–3	Second
1983/84	Dundee United	Hamrun Spartans	6–0	First
		Standard Liege	4–0	Second
		Rapid Vienna	2–2	Quarter-final
Dundee United won on away goals				
		AS Roma	2–3	Semi-final

Season	Scottish Club	Opposition	Aggregate	Round
1984/85	Aberdeen	Dinamo Berlin	3–3	First
Aberdeen lost on penalties				
1985/86	Aberdeen	Akranes	7–2	First
		Servette	1–0	Second
		IKF Gothenburg	2–2	Quarter-final
Aberdeen lost on away goals				
1986/87	Celtic	Shamrock Rovers	3–0	First
		Dinamo Kiev	2–5	Second
1987/88	Rangers	Dinamo Kiev	2–1	First
		Gornik Zabrze	4–2	Second
		Steaua Bucharest	2–3	Quarter-final
1988/89	Celtic	Honved	4–1	First
		Werder Bremen	0–2	Second
1989/90	Rangers	Bayern Munich	1–3	First
1990/91	Rangers	Valletta	10–0	First
		Red Star Belgrade	1–4	Second
1991/92	Rangers	Sparta Prague	2–2	First
Rangers lost on away goals				

The following table summarises the performance of Scottish clubs by showing which round they reached each year:

1955/56	Hibernian	semi-final
1956/57	Rangers	1st
1957/58	Rangers	1st
1958/59	Hearts	1st
1959/60	Rangers	semi-final
1960/61	Hearts	1st
1961/62	Rangers	quarter-final
1962/63	Dundee	semi-final
1963/64	Rangers	preliminary round
1964/65	Rangers	quarter-final
1965/66	Kilmarnock	1st
1966/67	Celtic	winners
1967/68	Celtic	1st
1968/69	Celtic	quarter-final
1969/70	Celtic	runners-up
1970/71	Celtic	quarter-final
1971/72	Celtic	semi-final
1972/73	Celtic	2nd
1973/74	Celtic	semi-final
1974/75	Celtic	1st
1975/76	Rangers	2nd
1976/77	Rangers	1st
1977/78	Celtic	2nd
1978/79	Rangers	quarter-final
1979/80	Celtic	quarter-final
1980/81	Aberdeen	2nd
1981/82	Celtic	1st
1982/83	Celtic	2nd
1983/84	Dundee United	semi-final
1984/85	Aberdeen	1st
1985/86	Aberdeen	quarter-final
1986/87	Celtic	2nd
1987/88	Rangers	quarter-final
1988/89	Celtic	2nd
1989/90	Rangers	1st
1990/91	Rangers	2nd
1991/92	Rangers	1st

CHAMPIONS LEAGUE

- First Scottish club to participate: Rangers beat Lyngby of Denmark 2–0 at Ibrox on 16 September 1992 in the first leg of their first round match (Scorers: Mark Hateley and Pieter Huistra)

- 2005/06: Rangers became the first Scottish club to reach the Round of 16 and played Villarreal both home and away. They drew 2–2 at Ibrox on 22 February (Scorers: Peter Løvenkrands and an own goal) and then drew 1–1 in Spain on 7 March 2006 (scorer: Peter Løvenkrands). Villarreal went through on the away goals rule.

- 2006/07: Celtic reached the Round of 16 and played AC Milan both home and away. They drew 0–0 at Celtic Park on 20 February and then lost 0–1 in Milan on 7 March after extra time.

- 2007/08: Celtic reached the Round of 16 for a second time and played Barcelona both home and away. They lost 2–3 at Celtic Park on 20 February (Scorers: Jan Vennegoor of Hesselink and Barry Robson) and then lost 0–1 in Spain on 4 March 2008.

- 2012/13: Celtic reached the Round of 16 for a third time and played Juventus both home and away. They lost 0–3 at Celtic Park on 12 February and then lost 0–2 in Italy on 6 March 2013.

In 1992/93 the European Cup, the top club competition in Europe, was re-branded as the UEFA Champions League and this formalised the mini-league system that had been used in 1991/92. The format has changed several times, with either one or two group stages providing varying numbers of clubs for a knockout competition. In recent times there have, on occasion, been two places offered to Scottish teams, although there is usually at least one qualifying round to negotiate first. In 2002 Hampden Park hosted the final for the second time and Real Madrid were the victors, just as they had been in 1960. This time they beat Bayer Leverkusen 2–1.

When the Europa League was introduced in 2009/10, it was linked to the Champions League as follows, so that clubs eliminated from certain stages of the CL are able to continue to participate in European competition:

Champions League	1st QR	2 n d QR	3rd QR (*)	Play-offs (**)	Group Stage (8 gps. of 4) (***)		Rnd. of 16	QFs	SFs	F
Europa League	1st QR	2 n d QR	3rd QR	Play-offs	Group Stage (12 gps. of 4)	Round of 32	Rnd. of 16	QFs	SFs	F

(*) 15 clubs eliminated in the 3rd QR of the CL admitted to play-offs for the EL
(**) 10 clubs eliminated in the play-offs for the CL admitted to the GS of the EL
(***) 8 clubs which finish the GS of the CL in third place are admitted to the EL round of 32

The record of Scottish teams in the Champions League is as follows:

Season	Scottish Club	Opposition	Aggregate	Round
1992/93	Rangers	Lyngby	3–0	First
		Leeds United	4–2	Second
		Marseille (H)	2–2	Group Stage
		CSKA Moscow (A)	1–0	
		FC Bruges (A)	1–1	
		FC Bruges (H)	2–1	
		Marseille (A)	1–1	
		CSKA Moscow (H)	0–0	
1993/94	Rangers	Levski Sofia	4–4	First
	Rangers lost on away goals			
1994/95	Rangers	AEK Athens	0–3	Qualifying
1995/96	Rangers	Anorthosis	1–0	Qualifying
		Steaua Bucharest (A)	0–1	Group Stage
		Borussia Dortmund (H)	2–2	
		Juventus (A)	1–4	
		Juventus (H)	0–4	
		Steaua Bucharest (H)	1–1	
		Borussia Dortmund (A)	2–2	
1996/97	Rangers	Vladikavkaz	10–3	Qualifying
		Grasshopper Zur. (A)	0–3	Group Stage

Season	Scottish Club	Opposition	Aggregate	Round
1996/97 Rangers—*contd*		Auxerre (H)	1–2	
		Ajax (A)	1–4	
		Ajax (H)	0–1	
		Grasshopper Zur. (H)	2–1	
		Auxerre (A)	1–2	
1997/98	Rangers	Gotu	11–0	1st Qualifying
		Gothenburg	4–1	2nd Qualifying
1998/99	Celtic	St Patrick's	2–0	1st Qualifying
		Croatia Zagreb	1–3	2nd Qualifying
1999/00	Rangers	FC Haka	7–1	2nd Qualifying
		Parma	2–1	3rd Qualifying
		Valencia (A)	2–0	1st Group Stage
		Bayern Munich (H)	1–1	
		PSV Eindhoven (A)	1–0	
		PSV Eindhoven (H)	4–1	
		Valencia (H)	1–2	
		Bayern Munich (A)	0–1	
2000/01	Rangers	Zalgiris Kaunas	4–1	2nd Qualifying
		Herfolge BK	6–0	3rd Qualifying
		Sturm Graz (H)	5–0	1st Group Stage
		Monaco (A)	1–0	
		Galatasaray (A)	2–3	
		Galatasaray (H)	0–0	
		Sturm Graz (A)	0–2	
		Monaco (H)	2–2	
2001/02	Celtic	Ajax	3–2	3rd Qualifying
		Juventus (A)	2–3	1st Group Stage
		Porto (H)	1–0	
		Rosenborg (H)	1–0	

Season	Scottish Club	Opposition	Aggregate	Round
2001/02 Celtic—contd		Porto (A)	0–3	
		Rosenborg (A)	0–2	
		Juventus (H)	4–3	
	Rangers	NK Maribor	6–1	2nd Qualifying
		Fenerbahce	1–2	3rd Qualifying
2002/03	Celtic	FC Basel	3–3	3rd Qualifying
Celtic lost on away goals				
2003/04	Celtic	FBK Kaunas	5–0	2nd Qualifying
		MTK Hungaria	5–0	3rd Qualifying
		Bayern Munich (A)	1–2	Group Stage
		Lyon (H)	2–0	
		Anderlecht (A)	0–1	
		Anderlecht (H)	3–1	
		Bayern Munich (H)	0–0	
		Lyon (A)	2–3	
	Rangers	FC Copenhagen	3–2	3rd Qualifying
		VfB Stuttgart (H)	2–1	Group Stage
		Panathinaikos (A)	1–1	
		Manchester United (H)	0–1	
		Manchester United (A)	0–3	
		VfB Stuttgart (A)	0–1	
		Panathinaikos (H)	1–3	
2004/05	Celtic	Barcelona (H)	1–3	Group Stage
		AC Milan (A)	1–3	
		Shakhtar Donetsk (A)	0–3	
		Shakhtar Donetsk (H)	1–0	
		Barcelona (A)	1–1	
		AC Milan (H)	0–0	
	Rangers	CSKA Moscow	2–3	3rd Qualifying

Season	Scottish Club	Opposition	Aggregate	Round
2005/06	Celtic	Artmedia Bratislava	4–5	2nd Qualifying
	Rangers	Anorthosis Famagusta	4–1	3rd Qualifying
		Porto (H)	3–2	Group Stage
		Inter Milan (A)	0–1	
		Artmedia Bratislava (H)	0–0	
		Artmedia Bratislava (A)	2–2	
		Porto (A)	1–1	
		Inter Milan (H)	1–1	
		Villarreal	3–3	1st Knockout
Rangers lost on away goals				
2006/07	Celtic	Manchester United (A)	2–3	Group Stage
		FC Copenhagen (H)	1–0	
		Benfica (H)	3–0	
		Benfica (A)	0–3	
		Manchester United (H)	1–0	
		FC Copenhagen (A)	1–3	
		AC Milan	0–1a.e.t.	1st Knockout
	Hearts	Siroki Brijeg	3–0	2nd Qualifying
		AEK Athens	1–5	3rd Qualifying
2007/08	Celtic	Spartak Moscow	2–2	3rd Qualifying
Celtic won on penalties				
		Shakhtar Donetsk (A)	0–2	Group Stage
		AC Milan (H)	2–1	
		Benfica (A)	0–1	
		Benfica (H)	1–0	
		Shakhtar Donetsk (H)	2–1	
		AC Milan (A)	0–1	
		Barcelona	2–4	1st Knockout
	Rangers	Zeta	3–0	2nd Qualifying

Season	Scottish Club	Opposition	Aggregate	Round
2007/08 Rangers—*contd*		Crvena Zvezda	1–0	3rd Qualifying
		VfB Stuttgart (H)	2–1	Group Stage
		Lyon (A)	3–0	
		Barcelona (H)	0–0	
		Barcelona (A)	0–2	
		VfB Stuttgart (A)	2–3	
		Lyon (H)	0–3	
2008/09	Celtic	Aalborg (H)	0–0	Group Stage
		Villarreal (A)	0–1	
		Manchester United (A)	0–3	
		Manchester United (H)	1–1	
		Aalborg (A)	1–2	
		Villarreal (H)	2–0	
	Rangers	FBK Kaunas	1–2	2nd Qualifying
2009/10	Celtic	Dinamo Moscow	2–1	3rd Qualifying
		Arsenal	1–5	Play-off Round
	Rangers	VfB Stuttgart (A)	1–1	Group Stage
		Sevilla (H)	1–4	
		Unirea Urziceni (H)	1–4	
		Unirea Urziceni (A)	1–1	
		VfB Stuttgart (H)	0–2	
		Sevilla (A)	0–1	
2010/11	Celtic	SC Braga	2–4	3rd Qualifying
	Rangers	Manchester United (A)	0–0	Group Stage
		Bursaspor (H)	1–0	
		Valencia (H)	1–1	
		Valencia (A)	0–3	
		Manchester United (H)	0–1	
		Bursaspor (A)	1–1	

Season	Scottish Club	Opposition	Aggregate	Round
2011/12	Rangers	Malmö	1–2	3rd Qualifying
2012/13	Celtic	HJK Helsinki	4–1	3rd Qualifying
		Helsingborgs IF	4–0	Play-off Round
		Benfica (H)	0–0	Group Stage
		Spartak Moscow (A)	3–2	
		Barcelona (A)	1–2	
		Barcelona (H)	2–1	
		Benfica (A)	1–2	
		Spartak Moscow (H)	2–1	
		Juventus	0–5	Round of 16
	Motherwell	Panathinaikos	0–5	3rd Qualifying
2013/14	Celtic	Cliftonville	5–0	2nd Qualifying
		Elfsborg	1–0	3rd Qualifying
		Shakhter Karagandy	3–2	Play-off Round
		AC Milan (A)	0–2	Group Stage
		Barcelona (H)	0–1	
		Ajax (H)	2–1	
		Ajax (A)	0–1	
		AC Milan (H)	0–3	
		Barcelona (A)	1–6	

The following table summarises the performance of Scottish clubs by showing which round/stage they reached each year. It also shows how the format of the competition has changed several times.

One group stage, followed by the final				
1992/93	Rangers	2nd in group		
One group stage, followed by semi-finals				
1993/94	Rangers	1st round		
One group stage, followed by quarter-finals				
1994/95	Rangers	QR		
1995/96	Rangers	4th in group		
1996/97	Rangers	4th in group		
1997/98	Rangers	2nd QR		
1998/99	Celtic	2nd QR		
Two group stages, followed by quarter-finals				
1999/2000	Rangers	3rd in 1st GS		
2000/01	Rangers	3rd in 1st GS		
2001/02	Rangers	3rd QR	Celtic	3rd in 1st GS
2002/03	Celtic	3rd QR		
One group stage, followed by first knockout round with sixteen clubs				
2003/04	Rangers	4th in group	Celtic	3rd in group
2004/05	Rangers	3rd QR	Celtic	4th in group
2005/06	Celtic	2nd QR	Rangers	1st KR
2006/07	Hearts	3rd QR	Celtic	1st KR
2007/08	Rangers	GS	Celtic	1st KR
2008/09	Rangers	2nd QR	Celtic	GS
2009/10	Celtic	POR	Rangers	GS
2010/11	Celtic	3rd QR	Rangers	GS
2011/12	Rangers	3rd QR		
2012/13	Motherwell	3rd QR	Celtic	Round of 16
2013/14	Celtic	GS		

QR-Qualifying round; POR - play-off round (twenty clubs; ten winners join twenty-two others in GS); GS-Group stage; 1st KR- First Knockout Round (sixteen clubs)

EUROPEAN CUP-WINNERS' CUP

- First Scottish club to participate: Rangers beat Ferencvaros of Hungary 4–2 at Ibrox on 28 September 1960 in the first leg of their qualifying-round match (Scorers: Harold Davis, Jimmy Millar 2 and Ralph Brand) and won 5–4 on aggregate.

- 1960/61: Rangers became the first British club to contest the final of a major European club competition when they reached the two-legged final of the European Cup-Winners' Cup in its inaugural season (17 and 27 May 1961). They lost 0–2 to Fiorentina in the first leg at Ibrox and then lost 1–2 in Florence (Scorer: Alex Scott).

- 1966/67: Rangers reached the final again, but lost 0–1 to Bayern Munich in Nuremberg on 31 May 1967 after extra time.

- 1971/72: Rangers reached the final for a third time and beat Moscow Dynamo 3–2 in Barcelona on 24 May 1972 (Scorers: Colin Stein and Willie Johnston 2).

- 1982/83: Aberdeen became the second Scottish club to reach the final, beating Real Madrid 2–1 in Gothenburg on 11 May 1983 after extra time (Scorers: Eric Black and John Hewitt).

- In addition to these four finals, Scottish clubs reached the semi-finals on four occasions: Celtic (1963/64 and 1965/66), Dunfermline (1968/69) and Aberdeen (1983/84).

This tournament is now defunct, but was once held in great esteem. As the name suggests, the winners of each domestic cup competition competed for it. On occasion, when the same team won the league and the cup, the defeated finalist would enter the competition. It would thus be possible to win the European Cup-Winners' Cup without winning the domestic cup. Scotland did well, winning the trophy on two occasions, reaching the final on another two and on many other occasions having a team in the semi-final. The trophy began to lose its value when it became apparent that other nations did not always hold their cup competition in such high regard as British nations did. Cup winners now qualify for the Europa League. The results of Scottish clubs were as follows:

Season	Scottish Club	Opposition	Aggregate	Round
1960/61	Rangers	Ferencvaros	5–4	Preliminary
		Borussia Mönchengladbach	11–0	Quarter-final
		Wolves	3–1	Semi-final
		Fiorentina	1–4	Final
1961/62	Dunfermline	St Patrick's Athletic	8–1	First
		Vardar Skopje	5–2	Second
		Ujpest Dozsa	3–5	Quarter-final
1962/63	Rangers	Seville	4–2	First
		Tottenham Hotspur	4–8	Second
1963/64	Celtic	Basle	10–1	First
		Dinamo Zagreb	4–2	Second
		Slovan Bratislava	2–0	Quarter-final
		MTK	3–4	Semi-final
1964/65	Dundee	Real Zaragoza	3–4	Second
1965/66	Celtic	Go Ahead Deventer	7–0	First
		Aarhus	3–0	Second
		Dinamo Kiev	4–1	Quarter-final
		Liverpool	1–2	Semi-final
1966/67	Rangers	Glentoran	5–1	First
		Borussia Dortmund	2–1	Second
		Real Zaragoza	2–2	Quarter-final
Rangers won on toss of a coin				
		Slavia Sofia	2–0	Semi-final
		Bayern Munich	0–1 a.e.t.	Final
1967/68	Aberdeen	KR Reykjavik	14–2	First
		Standard Liege	2–3	Second
1968/69	Dunfermline	Apoel Nicosia	12–1	First
		Olympiakos Piraeus	4–3	Second
		West Bromwich Alb.	1–0	Quarter-final
		Slovan Bratislava	1–2	Semi-final

Colin Stein celebrates his goal in Rangers' 3–2 win over Moscow Dynamo in the 1972 European Cup-Winners' Cup final in Barcelona. The Rangers team was McCloy, Jardine, Mathieson, Greig, Johnstone, Smith, McLean, Conn, Stein, MacDonald, and Johnston

Season	Scottish Club	Opposition	Aggregate	Round
1969/70	Rangers	Steaua Bucharest	2–0	First
		Gornik Zabrze	2–6	Second
1970/71	Aberdeen	Honved	4–4	First
Aberdeen lost on penalties				
1971/72	Rangers	Rennes	2–1	First
		Sporting Lisbon	6–6	Second
Rangers won on away goals				
		Torino	2–1	Quarter-final
		Bayern Munich	3–1	Semi-final
		Moscow Dynamo	3–2	Final
Played in Barcelona on 24 May 1972. Rangers' team was: McCloy; Jardine; Mathieson; Greig; D. Johnstone; Smith; McLean; Conn; Stein; MacDonald; W. Johnston. Scorers: Stein; W. Johnston (2)				
1972/73	Hibernian	Sporting Lisbon	7–3	First
		Besa	8–2	Second
		Hajduk Split	4–5	Quarter-final

Season	Scottish Club	Opposition	Aggregate	Round
1973/74	Rangers	Ankaragucu	6–0	First
		Borussia Mönchengladbach	3–5	Second
1974/75	Dundee United	Jiul Petrosani	3–2	First
		Bursaspor	0–1	Second
1975/76	Celtic	Valur	9–0	First
		Boavista	3–1	Second
		Zwickau	1–2	Quarter-final
1976/77	Hearts	Lokomotiv Leipzig	5–3	First
		SV Hamburg	3–8	Second
1977/78	Rangers	Young Boys	3–2	Preliminary
		Twente Enschede	0–3	First
1978/79	Aberdeen	Marek Stanke	5–3	First
		Fortuna Dusseldorf	2–3	Second
1979/80	Rangers	Lillestrom	3–0	First
		Fortuna Dusseldorf	2–1	Second
		Valencia	2–4	Quarter-final
1980/81	Celtic	Diosgyor	7–2	First
		Poli Timosarara	2–2	Second
Celtic lost on away goals				
1981/82	Rangers	Dukla Prague	2–4	First
1982/83	Aberdeen	Sion	11–1	Preliminary
		Dinamo Tirana	1–0	First
		Lech Poznan	3–0	Second
		Bayern Munich	3–2	Quarter-final
		Waterschei	5–2	Semi-final
		Real Madrid	2–1	Final

Played in Gothenburg on 11 May 1983. Aberdeen's team was: Leighton; Rougvie; McMaster; Cooper; McLeish; Miller; Strachan; Simpson; McGhee; Black (Hewitt); Weir. Scorers: Black; Hewitt

Aberdeen have just won the European Cup-Winners' Cup in Gothenburg in 1983, beating Real Madrid 2–1. The Aberdeen team was Leighton, Rougvie, Miller, McLeish, McMaster, Cooper, Strachan, Simpson, Weir, McGhee, Black (Hewitt)

Season	Scottish Club	Opposition	Aggregate	Round
1983/84	Aberdeen	Akranes	3–2	First
		Beveren	4–1	Second
		Ujpest Dozsa	3–2	Quarter-final
		Porto	0–2	Semi-final
	Rangers	Valletta	18–0	First
		Porto	2–2	Second
Rangers lost on away goals				
1984/85	Celtic	Gent	3–1	First
		Rapid Vienna	4–3	Second
Home leg ordered to be replayed at Old Trafford, and Celtic lost 0–1 (Instead of 3–0 win).				
1985/86	Celtic	Atletico Madrid	2–3	First
1986/87	Aberdeen	Sion	2–4	First

Season	Scottish Club	Opposition	Aggregate	Round
1987/88	St Mirren	Tromso	1–0	First
		Mechelen	0–2	Second
1988/89	Dundee United	Floriana	1–0	First
		Dinamo Bucharest	1–2	Second
1989/90	Celtic	Partizan Belgrade	6–6	First
Celtic lost on away goals				
1990/91	Aberdeen	Salamis	5–0	First
		Legia Warsaw	0–1	Second
1991/92	Motherwell	Katowice	3–3	First
Motherwell lost on away goals				
1992/93	Airdrieonians	Sparta Prague	1–3	First
1993/94	Aberdeen	Valur	7–0	First
		Torino	3–6	Second
1994/95	Dundee United	Tatran Presov	4–5	First
1995/96	Celtic	Dinamo Batumi	7–2	First
		Paris St Germain	0–4	Second
1996/97	Hearts	Red Star Belgrade	1–1	First
Hearts lost on away goals				
1997/98	Kilmarnock	Shelbourne	3–2	Qualifying
		Nice	2–4	First
1998/99	Hearts	Lantana	6–0	Qualifying
		Real Mallorca	1–2	First

The following table summarises the performance of Scottish clubs by showing which round they reached each year:

1960/61	Rangers	runners-up		
1961/62	Dunfermline	quarter-final		
1962/63	Rangers	2nd		
1963/64	Celtic	semi-final		
1964/65	Dundee	2nd		
1965/66	Celtic	semi-final		
1966/67	Rangers	runners-up		
1967/68	Aberdeen	2nd		
1968/69	Dunfermline	semi-final		
1969/70	Rangers	2nd		
1970/71	Aberdeen	1st		
1971/72	Rangers	winners		
1972/73	Hibernian	quarter-final		
1973/74	Rangers	2nd		
1974/75	Dundee United	2nd		
1975/76	Celtic	quarter-final		
1976/77	Hearts	2nd		
1977/78	Rangers	1st		
1978/79	Aberdeen	2nd		
1979/80	Rangers	2nd		
1980/81	Celtic	1st		
1981/82	Rangers	1st		
1982/83	Aberdeen	winners		
1983/84	Rangers	2nd	Aberdeen	semi-final
1984/85	Celtic	2nd		
1985/86	Celtic	1st		
1986/87	Aberdeen	1st		
1987/88	St Mirren	2nd		

1988/89	Dundee United	2nd		
1989/90	Celtic	1st		
1990/91	Aberdeen	2nd		
1991/92	Motherwell	1st		
1992/93	Airdrieonians	1st		
1993/94	Aberdeen	2nd		
1994/95	Dundee United	1st		
1995/96	Celtic	2nd		
1996/97	Hearts	qualifying round		
1997/98	Kilmarnock	1st		
1998/99	Hearts	1st		

INTER-CITIES FAIRS CUP

- First Scottish club to participate: Hibernian drew 4–4 with Barcelona in Spain on 27 December 1960 in the first leg of their quarter-final tie (Scorers: Joe Baker 2, Tommy Preston and Johnny MacLeod) and won 7–6 on aggregate. Hibs had been awarded a 2–0 victory over Lausanne in the previous round after their Swiss opponents withdrew.

- 1960/61: Hibernian reached the two-legged semi-final and played AS Roma both home and away. They drew 2–2 at Easter Road on 19 April (Scorers: Joe Baker and Johnny McLeod) and then drew 3–3 in Italy on 26 April 1961 (Scorers: Joe Baker 2 and Bobby Kinloch). This was before the introduction of the away-goals rule and Hibs had to take part in a replay in Rome on 27 May. They lost 0–6.

- 1966/67: Kilmarnock became the second Scottish club to reach the semi-finals and played Leeds United both home and away. They lost 2–4 at Leeds on Friday 19 May (Scorer: Brian McIlroy 2) and then drew 0–0 at home on 24 May 1967.

- 1967/68: Dundee became the third Scottish club to reach the semi-finals and played Leeds United home and away. They drew 1–1 at Dens Park on 1 May (Scorer: Bobby Wilson) and then lost 0–1 at Leeds on 15 May 1968.

- 1968/69: Rangers became the fourth Scottish club to reach the semi-finals and played Newcastle United home and away. They drew 0–0 at Ibrox on 14 May and then lost 0–2 at Newcastle on 21 May 1969.

The 'International Inter-City Industrial Fairs Cup', which was usually shortened to the 'Inter-Cities Fairs Cup', was the original name of the tournament that became the UEFA Cup in 1971. It was created for cities that hosted trade fairs and was designed so that each participating city would be represented by a single team. At first there was no qualification system based on league performance, which explains why a London representative side was invited to take part in the first tournament, which lasted from 1955 to 1958. By the mid 1960s, however, clubs were only invited after taking into account their performance the previous season.

Entry was denied to Clyde in 1967/68, even though they had finished the 1966/67 season in third place, because Rangers had finished second and only one club per city was allowed to enter. Hibernian took their place. The results of Scottish clubs are as follows:

Season	Scottish Club	Opposition	Aggregate	Round
1960/61	Hibernian	Barcelona	7–6	Quarter-final
		AS Roma	5–5	Semi-final
			0–6	Play-off
1961/62	Hearts	Union St Gilloise	5–1	First
		Inter Milan	0–5	Second
	Hibernian	Belenenses	6–4	First
		Red Star Belgrade	0–5	Second
1962/63	Celtic	Valencia	4–6	First
	Dunfermline	Everton	2–1	First
		Valencia	6–6	Second
			0–1	Play-off
	Hibernian	Stavenet	7–2	First
		DOS Utrecht	3–1	Second
		Valencia	2–6	Quarter-final
1963/64	Hearts	Lausanne	4–4	First
			2–3	Play-off
	Partick Thistle	Glentoran	7–1	First
		Spartak Brno	3–6	Second
1964/65	Celtic	Leixoes	4–1	First
		Barcelona	1–3	Second
	Dunfermline	Örgryte	4–2	First
		Stuttgart	1–0	Second
		Athletic Bilbao	1–1	Quarter-final
			1–2	Play-off
	Kilmarnock	Eintracht Frankfurt	5–4	First
		Everton	1–6	Second
1965/66	Dunfermline	KB Copenhagen	9–2	Second
		Spartak Brno	2–0	Third
		Real Zaragoza	3–4	Quarter-final

Season	Scottish Club	Opposition	Aggregate	Round
1965/66 *contd*	Hearts	Valerengen	4–1	Second
		Real Zaragoza	5–5	Third
			0–1	Play-off
	Hibernian	Valencia	2–2	First
			0–3	Play-off
1966/67	Dundee United	Barcelona	4–1	Second
		Juventus	1–3	Third
	Dunfermline	Frigg Oslo	6–2	First
		Dinamo Zagreb	4–4	Second
Dinamo Zagreb won on away goals				
	Kilmarnock	Antwerp	8–2	Second
		La Gantoise	3–1	Third
		Lokomotiv Leipzig	2–1	Quarter-final
		Leeds United	2–4	Semi-final
1967/68	Dundee	DWS Amsterdam	4–2	First
		FC Liege	7–2	Second
		Zurich	2–0	Quarter-final
		Leeds United	1–3	Semi-final
	Hibernian	Porto	4–3	First
		Napoli	6–4	Second
		Leeds United	1–2	Third
	Rangers	Dinamo Dresden	3–2	First
		FC Cologne	4–3	Second
		Leeds United	0–2	Quarter-final
1968/69	Aberdeen	Slavia Sofia	2–0	First
		Real Zaragoza	2–4	Second
	Hibernian	Ljubljana	5–1	First
		Lokomotiv Leipzig	4–1	Second
		SV Hamburg	2–2	Third
SV Hamburg won on away goals				

Season	Scottish Club	Opposition	Aggregate	Round
1968/69 contd	Morton	Chelsea	3–9	First
	Rangers	Vojvodina	2–1	First
		Dundalk	9–1	Second
		DWS Amsterdam	4–1	Third
		Athletic Bilbao	4–3	Quarter-final
		Newcastle United	0–2	Semi-final
1969/70	Dundee United	Newcastle United	1–3	First
	Dunfermline	Bordeaux	4–2	First
		Gwardia Warsaw	3–1	Second
		Anderlecht	3–3	Third
Anderlecht won on away goals				
	Kilmarnock	Zurich	5–4	First
		Slavia Sofia	4–3	Second
		Dinamo Bacau	1–3	Third
1970/71	Dundee United	Grasshoppers	3–2	First
		Sparta Prague	2–3	Second
	Hibernian	Malmö	9–2	First
		Vitoria Guimares	3–2	Second
		Liverpool	0–3	Quarter-final
	Kilmarnock	Coleraine	3–4	First
	Rangers	Bayern Munich	1–2	First

(see UEFA CUP for seasons 1971/72 onwards)

When Dundee United visited Czechoslovakia in 1970 for the first leg of their second-round tie against Sparta Prague, the players required visas to enter the country. Striker Dennis Gillespie didn't play in the 3–1 defeat, but played in the second leg at Tannadice, which United won 1–0

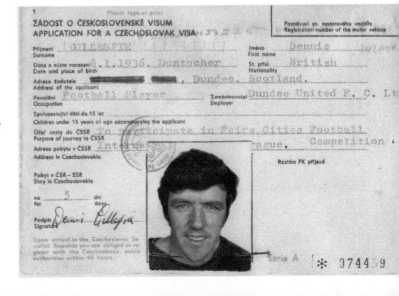

The following table summarises the performance of Scottish clubs by showing which round they reached each year:

1960/61	Hibernian	SF							
1961/62	Hearts	2nd	Hibernian	2nd						
1962/63	Celtic	1st	Dunfermline	2nd	Hibernian	QF				
1963/64	Hearts	1st	Partick Thistle	2nd						
1964/65	Celtic	2nd	Kilmarnock	2nd	Dunfermline	3rd				
1965/66	Hibernian	1st	Hearts	3rd	Dunfermline	QF				
1966/67	Dunfermline	2nd	Dundee Utd.	3rd	Kilmarnock	SF				
1967/68	Hibernian	3rd	Rangers	QF	Dundee	SF				
1968/69	Morton	1st	Aberdeen	2nd	Hibernian	3rd	Rangers	SF		
1969/70	Dundee Utd.	1st	Dunfermline	3rd	Kilmarnock	3rd				
1970/71	Kilmarnock	1st	Rangers	1st	Dundee Utd.	2nd	Hibernian	3rd		

QF- Quarter-final; SF- Semi-final

UEFA CUP

- First Scottish clubs to participate: Aberdeen, Dundee and St Johnstone all played first round (first leg) matches on the evening of 15 September 1971. Aberdeen beat Celta Vigo 2–0 in Spain (Scorers: Joe Harper and Jim Forrest), Dundee beat Akademisk of Denmark 4–2 at Dens Park (Scorers: Alexander Bryce 2, Ian Wallace and Duncan Lambie) and St Johnstone lost 1–2 to Hamburg in West Germany (Scorer: James Pearson). All three clubs progressed to the next round after the second leg.

- 1986/87: Dundee United reached the two-legged final and played IFK Gothenburg both home and away. They lost 0–1 in Sweden on 6 May and then drew 1–1 at Tannadice on 20 May 1987 (Scorer: John Clark).

- 2002/03: Celtic reached the final, which had now become a single match at a neutral venue. They lost 2–3 to Porto after extra time in Seville on 21 May 2003 (Scorer: Henrik Larsson 2).

- 2007/08: Rangers became the third Scottish club to reach the final, losing 0–2 to Zenit St Petersburg in Manchester on 14 May 2008.

This was the name given to the tournament that was previously known as the Inter-Cities Fairs Cup when it was re-branded in 1971 and the link to trade fairs was dropped. Four years later the 'one club per city' rule was also dropped. Qualification was based on a club's league position at the end of the previous season, with some countries being allocated more places than others according to their ranking. It was often regarded as the 'consolation' trophy for clubs that had not managed to reach the Champions League.

Following the demise of the European Cup-Winners' Cup in 1999, a place was also provided for the winners of the Scottish Cup, and from 1996/97 there was a 'parachute' for clubs eliminated from the Champions League after finishing the group stages in third place. Places were also earned via the Intertoto Cup and the UEFA fair play rankings.

The final was changed to a single game at a neutral venue in 1998, and in 2004/05 the format was changed so that clubs progressed to a group stage after the first round. Scotland had its moments in this tournament, although no Scottish team ever won it. The closest were Dundee United, Celtic and Rangers, who all reached the final.

In September 2008 UEFA announced that, with effect from the 2009/10 season, the competition would be re-launched as 'The Europa League'. The last UEFA Cup match was the 2008/09 final in Istanbul on 20 May 2009; Shakhtar Donetsk, from the Ukraine, beat Germans Werder Bremen 2–1 after extra time.

The results of Scottish clubs are as follows:

Season	Scottish Club	Opposition	Aggregate	Round
1971/72	Aberdeen	Celta Vigo	3–0	First
		Juventus	1–3	Second
	Dundee	Akademisk	5–2	First
		Cologne	5–4	Second
		AC Milan	2–3	Third
	St Johnstone	SV Hamburg	4–2	First
		Vasas Budapest	2–1	Second
		Zeljeznicar	2–5	Third
1972/73	Aberdeen	Borussia Mönchengladbach	5–9	First
	Partick Thistle	Honved	0–4	First
1973/74	Aberdeen	Finn Harps	7–2	First
		Tottenham Hotspur	2–5	Second
	Dundee	Twente Enschede	3–7	First
	Hibernian	Keflavik	3–1	First
		Leeds United	0–0	Second
Leeds United won 5–4 on penalties				
1974/75	Dundee	RWD Molenbeek	2–5	First
	Hibernian	Rosenborg	12–3	First
		Juventus	2–8	Second
1975/76	Dundee United	Keflavik	6–0	First
		Porto	2–3	Second
	Hibernian	Liverpool	2–3	First
1976/77	Celtic	Wisla Krakow	2–4	First
	Hibernian	Sochaux	1–0	First
		Osters Vaxjo	3–4	Second
1977/78	Aberdeen	RWD Molenbeek	1–2	First
	Dundee United	KB Copenhagen	1–3	First

Season	Scottish Club	Opposition	Aggregate	Round
1978/79	Dundee United	Standard Liege	0–1	First
	Hibernian	Norrkoping	3–2	First
		Strasbourg	1–2	Second
1979/80	Aberdeen	Eintracht Frankfurt	1–2	First
	Dundee United	Anderlecht	1–1	First
Dundee United won on away goals				
		Diosgyor	1–4	Second
1980/81	Dundee United	Slask Wroclaw	7–2	First
		Lokeren	1–1	Second
Lokeren won on away goals				
	St Mirren	Elfsborg	2–1	First
		St Etienne	0–2	Second
1981/82	Aberdeen	Ipswich Town	4–2	First
		Arges Pitesti	5–2	Second
		SV Hamburg	4–5	Third
	Dundee United	Monaco	6–4	First
		Borussia Mönchengladbach	5–2	Second
		Winterslag	5–0	Third
		Radnicki Nis	2–3	Quarter-final
1982/83	Dundee United	PSV Eindhoven	3–1	First
		Viking Stavanger	3–1	Second
		Werder Bremen	3–2	Third
		Bohemians	0–1	Quarter-final
	Rangers	Borussia Dortmund	2–0	First
		FC Cologne	2–6	Second
1983/84	Celtic	Aarhus	5–1	First
		Sporting Lisbon	5–2	Second
		Nottingham Forest	1–2	Third
	St Mirren	Feyenoord	0–3	First

Season	Scottish Club	Opposition	Aggregate	Round
1984/85	Dundee United	AIK Stockholm	3–1	First
		ASK Linz	7–2	Second
		Manchester United	4–5	Third
	Hearts	Paris St Germain	2–6	First
	Rangers	Bohemians	4–3	First
		Inter Milan	3–4	Second
1985/86	Dundee United	Bohemians	7–4	First
		Vardar Skopje	3–1	Second
		Neuchatel Xamax	3–4	Third
	Rangers	Osasuna	1–2	First
	St Mirren	Slavia Prague	3–1	First
		Hammarby	4–5	Second
1986/87	Dundee United	Lens	2–1	First
		Universitaria Craiova	3–1	Second
		Hajduk Split	2–0	Third
		Barcelona	3–1	Quarter-final
		Borussia Mönchengladbach	2–0	Semi-final
		IFK Gothenburg	1–2	Final
	Hearts	Dukla Prague	3–3	First
Dukla Prague won on away goals				
	Rangers	Ilves	4–2	First
		Boavista	3–1	Second
		Borussia Mönchengladbach	1–1	Third
Borussia Mönchengladbach won on away goals				
1987/88	Aberdeen	Bohemians	1–0	First
		Feyenoord	2–2	Second
Feyenoord won on away goals				
	Celtic	Borussia Dortmund	2–3	First
	Dundee United	Coleraine	4–1	First
		Vitkovice	2–3	Second

Season	Scottish Club	Opposition	Aggregate	Round
1988/89	Aberdeen	Dinamo Dresden	0–2	First
	Hearts	St Patrick's Athletic	4–0	First
		FK Austria	1–0	Second
		Velez Mostar	4–2	Third
		Bayern Munich	1–2	Quarter-final
	Rangers	Katowice	5–2	First
		FC Cologne	1–3	Second
1989/90	Aberdeen	Rapid Vienna	2–2	First
Rapid Vienna won on away goals				
	Dundee United	Glentoran	5–1	First
		Antwerp	3–6	Second
	Hibernian	Videoton	4–0	First
		FC Liege	0–1	Second
1990/91	Dundee United	FH Hafnafjordur	5–3	First
		Arnhem	1–4	Second
	Hearts	Dnepr	4–2	First
		Bologna	3–4	Second
1991/92	Aberdeen	BK Copenhagen	0–3	First
	Celtic	Germinal Ekeren	3–1	First
		Neuchatel Xamax	2–5	Second
1992/93	Celtic	FC Cologne	3–2	First
		Borussia Dortmund	1–3	Second
	Hearts	Slavia Prague	4–3	First
		Standard Liege	0–2	Second
	Hibernian	Anderlecht	3–3	First
Anderlecht won on away goals				
1993/94	Celtic	Young Boys	1–0	First
		Sporting Lisbon	1–2	Second
	Dundee United	Brondby	3–3	First
Brondby won on away goals				
	Hearts	Atletico Madrid	2–4	First

Season	Scottish Club	Opposition	Aggregate	Round
1994/95	Aberdeen	Skonto Riga	1–1	Preliminary
		Skonto Riga won on away goals		
	Motherwell	Hanvar	7–1	Preliminary
		Borussia Dortmund	0–3	First
1995/96	Motherwell	My-Pa 47	3–3	Preliminary
		My-Pa 47 won on away goals		
	Raith Rovers	Gotu	6–4	Preliminary
		Akranes	3–2	First
		Bayern Munich	1–4	Second
1996/97	Aberdeen	FK Zalgiris	5–4	Qualifying
		Barry Town	6–4	First
		Brondby	0–2	Second
	Celtic	Kosice	1–0	Qualifying
		Hamburg	0–4	First
1997/98	Celtic	Inter Cable Tel	8–0	1st Qualifying
		FC Tirol Innsbruck	7–5	2nd Qualifying
		Liverpool	2–2	First
		Liverpool won on away goals		
	Dundee United	CE Principat	17–0	1st Qualifying
		Trabzonspor	1–2	2nd Qualifying
	Rangers	Strasbourg	2–4	First
1998/99	Celtic	Vitoria Guimares	4–2	First
		FC Zurich	3–5	Second
	Kilmarnock	Zeljeznicar	2–1	1st Qualifying
		Sigma Olomouc	0–4	2nd Qualifying
	Rangers	Shelbourne	7–3	1st Qualifying
		PAOK Salonika	2–0	2nd Qualifying
		Beitar	5–3	First
		Bayer Leverkusen	3–2	Second
		Parma	2–4	Third

Season	Scottish Club	Opposition	Aggregate	Round
1999/00	Celtic	Cwmbran Town	10–0	Qualifying
		Hapoel Tel Aviv	3–0	First
		Lyon	0–2	Second
	Kilmarnock	KR Reykjavik	2–1	Qualifying
		Kaiserslautern	0–5	First
	Rangers	Borussia Dortmund	2–2	Third
Borussia Dortmund won 3–1 on penalties				
	St Johnstone	VPS Vaasa	3–1	Qualifying
		Monaco	3–6	First
2000/01	Aberdeen	Bohemians	2–2	Qualifying
Bohemians won on away goals				
	Celtic	Jeunesse Esch	11–0	Qualifying
		HJK Helsinki	3–2	First
		Bordeaux	2–3 a.e.t.	Second
	Hearts	IBV	5–0	Qualifying
		VFB Stuttgart	3–3	First
Stuttgart won on away goals				
	Rangers	Kaiserslautern	1–3	Third
2001/02	Celtic	Valencia	1–1 a.e.t.	Third
Valencia won 5–4 on penalties				
	Hibernian	AEK Athens	3–4 a.e.t.	First
	Kilmarnock	Glenavon	2–0	Qualifying
		Viking Stavanger	1–3	First
	Rangers	Anzhi	1–0	First
		Moscow Dynamo	7–2	Second
		Paris St Germain	0–0 a.e.t.	Third
Rangers won 4–3 on penalties				
		Feyenoord	3–4	Fourth

Season	Scottish Club	Opposition	Aggregate	Round
2002/03	Aberdeen	Nistru Otaci	1–0	Qualifying
		Hertha Berlin	0–1	First
	Celtic	FK Suduva	10–1	First
		Blackburn Rovers	3–0	Second
		Celta Vigo	3–1	Third
		VFB Stuttgart	5–4	Fourth
		Liverpool	3–1	Quarter-final
		Boavista	2–1	Semi-final
		Porto	2–3 a.e.t.	Final
	Livingston	Vaduz	1–1	Qualifying
Livingston won on away goals				
		Sturm Graz	6–8	First
	Rangers	Viktoria Zizkov	3–3 a.e.t.	First
Viktoria Zizkov won on away goals				
2003/04	Celtic	Teplice	3–1	Third
		Barcelona	1–0	Fourth
		Villarreal	1–3	Quarter-final
	Dundee	Vllaznia Shkoder	6–0	Qualifying
		Perugia	1–3	First
	Hearts	Zeljeznicar	2–0	First
		Bordeaux	1–2	Second
2004/05	Dunfermline	FH Hafnarfjordur	3–4	2nd Qualifying
	Hearts	Sporting Braga	5–3	First
		Feyenoord (A)	0–3	Group Stage
		Schalke 04 (H)	0–1	
		FC Basel (A)	2–1	
		Ferencvaros (H)	0–1	
	Rangers	Maritimo	1–1 a.e.t.	First
Rangers won 4–2 on penalties				
		Amica Wronki (A)	5–0	Group Stage
		Grazer AZ (H)	3–0	
		AZ Alkmaar (A)	0–1	
		Auxerre (H)	0–2	

Season	Scottish Club	Opposition	Aggregate	Round
2005/06	Dundee United	My-Pa 47	2–2	2nd Qualifying
My-Pa 47 won on away goals				
	Hibernian	Dnipro	1–5	First
2006/07	Gretna	Derry City	3–7	2nd Qualifying
	Hearts	Sparta Prague	0–2	First
	Rangers	Molde	2–0	First
		Livorno (A)	3–2	Group Stage
		Maccabi Haifa (H)	2–0	
		Auxerre (A)	2–2	
		Partizan Belgrade (H)	1–0	
		Hapoel Tel Aviv	5–2	Round of 32
		Osasuna	1–2	Round of 16
2007/08	Aberdeen	Dnipro	1–1	First
Aberdeen won on away goals				
		Panathinaikos (A)	0–3	Group Stage
		Lokomotiv Moscow (H)	1–1	
		Atletico Madrid (A)	0–2	
		FC Copenhagen (H)	4–0	
		Bayern Munich	3–7	Round of 32
	Dunfermline	BK Hacken	1–2	2nd Qualifying
	Rangers	Panathinaikos	1–1	Round of 32
Rangers won on away goals				
		Werder Bremen	2–1	Round of 16
		Sporting Lisbon	2–0	Quarter-final
		Fiorentina	0–0 a.e.t.	Semi-final
Rangers won 4–2 on penalties				
		Zenit St Petersburg	0–2	Final
2008/09	Motherwell	Nancy	0–3	First
	Queen of the South	Nordsjaelland	2–4	2nd Qualifying

The following table summarises the progress of Scottish clubs by showing which round/stage they reached each year:

1971/72	Aberdeen	2nd	Dundee	3rd	St Johnstone	3rd				
1972/73	Aberdeen	1st	Partick Thistle	1st						
1973/74	Dundee	1st	Aberdeen	2nd	Hibernian	2nd				
1974/75	Dundee	1st	Hibernian	2nd						
1975/76	Hibernian	1st	Dundee Utd.	2nd						
1976/77	Celtic	1st	Hibernian	2nd						
1977/78	Aberdeen	1st	Dundee Utd.	1st						
1978/79	Dundee Utd.	1st	Hibernian	2nd						
1979/80	Aberdeen	1st	Dundee Utd.	2nd						
1980/81	Dundee Utd.	2nd	St Mirren	2nd						
1981/82	Aberdeen	3rd	Dundee Utd	QF						
1982/83	Rangers	2nd	Dundee Utd.	QF						
1983/84	St Mirren	1st	Celtic	3rd						
1984/85	Hearts	1st	Rangers	2nd	Dundee Utd.	3rd				
1985/86	Rangers	1st	St Mirren	2nd	Dundee Utd.	3rd				
1986/87	Hearts	1st	Rangers	3rd	Dundee Utd.	RU				
1987/88	Celtic	1st	Aberdeen	2nd	Dundee Utd.	2nd				
1988/89	Aberdeen	1st	Rangers	1st	Hearts	QF				
1989/90	Aberdeen	1st	Hibernian	2nd						
1990/91	Dundee Utd.	2nd	Hearts	2nd						
1991/92	Aberdeen	1st	Celtic	2nd						
1992/93	Hibernian	1st	Celtic	2nd	Hearts	2nd				
1993/94	Dundee Utd.	1st	Hearts	1st	Celtic	2nd				
1994/95	Aberdeen	1st	Motherwell	1st						
1995/96	Motherwell	PR	Raith Rovers	2nd						
1996/97	Celtic	1st	Aberdeen	2nd						
1997/98	Dundee Utd.	2QR	Celtic	1st	*Rangers	1st				
1998/99	Kilmarnock	2QR	*Celtic	2nd	Rangers	3rd				
1999/00	Kilmarnock	1st	St Johnstone	1st	Celtic	2nd	*Rangers	3rd		
2000/01	Aberdeen	QR	Hearts	1st	Celtic	2nd	*Rangers	3rd		
2001/02	Hibernian	1st	Kilmarnock	1st	*Celtic	3rd	Rangers	4th		

2002/03	Aberdeen	1st	Livingston	1st	Rangers	1st	*Celtic	RU
2003/04	Dundee	1st	Hearts	2nd	*Celtic	QF		
2004/05	Dunfermline	2QR	Hearts	GS	*Rangers	GS		
2005/06	Dundee Utd.	2QR	Hibernian	1st				
2006/07	Gretna	2QR	*Hearts	1st	Rangers	16		
2007/08	Dunfermline	2QR	Aberdeen	32	*Rangers	RU		
2008/09	Queen of the S.	2QR	Motherwell	1st				

*Denotes qualified via Champions League

PR-Preliminary round; QR-Qualifying round; GS-Group stage; 32-Round of 32; 16-Round of 16; QF-Quarter-final; RU-Runners-up. The terms 'Round of 32' and 'Round of 16' were introduced for season 2004/05.

EUROPA LEAGUE

- First Scottish club to participate: Motherwell lost 0–1 to Llanelli at the Excelsior Stadium on 2 July 2009 in the first leg of their first qualifying round match, but won 3–1 on aggregate.

- 2010/11: Rangers reached the Round of 16 and played PSV Eindhoven both home and away. They drew 0–0 in Holland on 10 March and then lost 0–1 at Ibrox on 17 March 2011.

UEFA's Europa League was launched in the summer of 2009, and the competition replaced both the UEFA Cup and the Intertoto Cup. Four years later UEFA decided that, from 2015 onwards, the winners will be rewarded with a place in the play-off round of the following season's Champions League. The Europa League winners could even be given a place in the group stage if the Champions League winners also qualify via their domestic league and thus free up a place in the group stages.

The format of the Europa League is based on forty-eight clubs in twelve groups of four, with teams playing each other both home and away. The top two in each group then join the eight third-placed clubs from the Champions League to form a knockout competition for thirty-two clubs.

Champions League	1st QR	2nd QR	3rd QR (b)	Play-offs (c)	Group Stage (8 gps. of 4) (d)		Rnd. of 16	QFs	SFs	F
Europa League (a)	1st QR	2nd QR	3rd QR	Play-offs	Group Stage (12 gps. of 4)	Round of 32	Rnd. of 16	QFs	SFs	F

(a) 3 clubs admitted to the 1st QR of the EL on the basis of the fair play assessment
(b) 15 clubs eliminated in the 3rd QR of the CL admitted to play-offs for the EL
(c) 10 clubs eliminated in the play-offs for the CL admitted to the GS of the EL
(d) 8 clubs which finish the GS of the CL in third place are admitted to the EL round of 32

The 144 matches in the group stage of the 2009/10 tournament were selected by FIFA for an experiment that introduced 'Additional Assistant Referees' to the senior professional game, with two extra officials being provided to help the referee. The first such match to involve a Scottish club was Celtic's game against Hapoel Tel-Aviv on 17 September 2009, when Belgians Johan Verbist and Peter Vervecken were the AARs. The experiment was later extended.

Season	Scottish Club	Opposition	Aggregate	Round
2009/10	Aberdeen	SK Sigma Olomouc	1–8	3rd Qualifying
	Celtic	Hapoel Tel-Aviv (A)	1–2	Group Stage
		Rapid Vienna (H)	1–1	
		Hamburg (H)	0–1	
		Hamburg (A)	0–0	
		Hapoel Tel-Aviv (H)	2–0	
		Rapid Vienna (A)	3–3	
	Falkirk	FC Vaduz	1–2	2nd Qualifying
	Hearts	NK Dinamo Zagreb	2–4	Play-off Round
	Motherwell	Llanelli	3–1	1st Qualifying
		KS Flamurtari	8–2	2nd Qualifying
		Steaua Bucharest	1–6	3rd Qualifying
2010/11	Celtic	FC Utrecht	2–4	Play-off Round
	Dundee United	AEK Athens	1–2	Play-off Round
	Hibernian	NK Maribor	2–6	3rd Qualifying
	Motherwell	Breidablik UBK	2–0	2nd Qualifying
		Aalesunds FK	4–1	3rd Qualifying
		Odense BK	1–3	Play-off Round
	Rangers	Sporting Lisbon	3–3	Round of 32
		Rangers won on away goals		
		PSV Eindhoven	0–1	Round of 16
2011/12	Celtic	FC Sion	1–3	Play-off Round
		FC Sion expelled for fielding ineligible players		
		Atletico Madrid (A)	0–2	Group Stage
		Udinese (H)	1–1	
		Rennes (A)	1–1	
		Rennes (H)	3–1	
		Atletico Madrid (H)	0–1	
		Udinese (A)	1–1	

Season	Scottish Club	Opposition	Aggregate	Round
2011/12 contd	Dundee United	Slask Wroclaw	3–3	2nd Qualifying
		Slask Wroclaw won on away goals		
	Hearts	Paks	5–2	3rd Qualifying
		Tottenham H.	0–5	Play-off Round
	Rangers	NK Maribor	2–3	Play-off Round
2012/13	Dundee United	Dynamo Moscow	2–7	3rd Qualifying
	Hearts	Liverpool	1–2	Play-off Round
	Motherwell	Levante	0–3	Play-off Round
	St Johnstone	Eskisehirspor	1–3	2nd Qualifying
2013/14	Hibernian	Malmö	0–9	2nd Qualifying
	Motherwell	Kuban Krasnodar	0–3	3rd Qualifying
	St Johnstone	Rosenborg	2–1	2nd Qualifying
		FC Minsk	1–1	3rd Qualifying
		Minsk won 3–2 on penalties		

The following table summarises the progress of Scottish clubs by showing which round/stage they reached each year:

2009/10	Falkirk	2QR	Aberdeen	3QR	Motherwell	3QR		
	Hearts	POR	*Celtic	GS				
2010/11	Hibernian	3QR	*Celtic	POR	Dundee United	POR		
	Motherwell	POR	*Rangers	16				
2011/12	Dundee United	2QR	Hearts	POR	*Rangers	POR		
	Celtic	GS						
2012/13	St Johnstone	2QR	Dundee Utd.	3QR	Hearts	POR		
	*Motherwell	POR						
2013/14	Hibernian	2QR	Motherwell	3QR	St Johnstone	3QR		

*Denotes qualified via Champions League

QR-Qualifying Round; POR-Play-off Round; GS-Group Stage; 16-Round of 16

INTERNATIONAL FOOTBALL

INTERNATIONAL OPPONENTS

- First Scottish international match: Scotland drew 0–0 against England on 30 November 1872 with a team that was made up entirely of amateurs from Queen's Park FC. This was the world's first international football match and it took place at the West of Scotland Cricket Club's ground at Hamilton Crescent in Partick (Hamilton Crescent was renamed Fortrose Street in 1931).

- First Scottish international goal: The first goal came in Scotland's second international match, which was a 2–4 defeat to England at Kennington Oval, London on 8 March 1873. It was scored by Henry Renny-Tailyour of The Royal Engineers.

- Scotland beat England 7–2 on 2 March 1878 in the first international match to be held at the first Hampden Park (Scorers: John McDougall 3, John McGregor, Henry McNeil 2 and William MacKinnon). Five Scotland players came from Queen's Park, three from Vale of Leven, and one each from Clydesdale, Rangers and Third Lanark.

- The 'Wembley Wizards' beat England 5–1 at Wembley on 31 March 1928 (Scorers: Alex Jackson 3 and Alex James 2).

- Scotland beat England 3–2 at Wembley on 15 April 1967. England were holders of the World Cup at the time and Jim Baxter played 'keepie uppie' on the Wembley turf (Scorers: Law, Lennox and McCalliog).

A Scotland cap awarded in 1922 is part of the Scottish Football Museum's collection at Hampden Park

Kenny Dalglish won a record 102 Scottish caps between 1971 and 1987 and scored thirty goals for Scotland

ARGENTINA

Argentina is a name that still sends a shiver down Scottish spines, following the events at the World Cup finals in 1978. The fixture between Scotland and Argentina themselves has twice provided a special occasion for Diego Maradona. In 1979 he scored his first international goal at Hampden Park, and in 2008 he celebrated his first match as head coach of the Argentine national team with a victory.

1977	18 June	Buenos Aires	1–1	Masson (pen)	Passarella (pen)
1979	2 June	Hampden Park	1–3	Graham	Luque (2) Maradona
1990	28 Mar	Hampden Park	1–0	McKimmie	
2008	19 Nov	Hampden Park	0–1		Rodriguez

AUSTRALIA

A Scotland eleven played Australia three times in the course of a world tour in 1967, but these are not recognised as full international matches. The Scots won all three games: 1–0 in Sydney, 2–1 in Adelaide and 2–0 in Melbourne. Since then the countries have met on five occasions, with Scotland winning three, drawing once and losing once. The 1985 games were play-offs for the World Cup finals.

1985	20 Nov	Hampden Park	2–0	Cooper McAvennie	
1985	4 Dec	Melbourne	0–0		
1996	27 Mar	Hampden Park	1–0	McCoist	
2000	15 Nov	Hampden Park	0–2		Emerton Zdrilic
2012	15 Aug	Easter Road	3–1	Rhodes Davidson o.g. McCormack	Bresciano

AUSTRIA

Austria is a country with which Scotland has a few similarities, in that they are both under the shadow of a larger country which speaks the same language (England, Germany) and both have in the past entered into Union or Anschluss with the other country (1707, 1938). Relations between the Scottish and Austrian teams have not always been good, notably in the 1963 friendly, when the game was abandoned by English referee Jim Finney in the face of Austria's dirty tactics after two Austrians had been sent off. In the game in 1951, Billy Steel was sent off, being the first man to receive this penalty in an international match for Scotland. The previous December, Austria had become the first foreign team to beat Scotland at Hampden Park.

1931	16 May	Vienna	0–5		Zischek (2) Schall Vogel Sindelar
1933	29 Nov	Hampden Park	2–2	Meiklejohn McFadyen	Zischek Schall
1937	9 May	Vienna	1–1	O'Donnell	Jerusalem
1950	13 Dec	Hampden Park	0–1		Melchior
1951	27 May	Vienna	0–4		Hanappi (2) Wagner (2)
1954	16 June	Zurich	0–1		Probst
1955	19 May	Vienna	4–1	Robertson Smith Liddell Reilly	Ocwirk
1956	2 May	Hampden Park	1–1	Conn	Wagner
1960	29 May	Vienna	1–4	Mackay	Hanappi (2) Hof (2)
1963	8 May	Hampden Park	4–1	Wilson (2) Law (2)	Linhart
Match abandoned after 79 minutes					
1968	6 Nov	Hampden Park	2–1	Law Bremner	Starek
1969	5 Nov	Vienna	0–2		Redl (2)
1978	20 Sep	Vienna	2–3	McQueen Gray	Pezzey Schachner Kreuz
1979	17 Oct	Hampden Park	1–1	Gemmill	Krankl
1994	20 Apr	Vienna	2–1	McGinlay McKinlay	Hutter
1996	31 Aug	Vienna	0–0		
1997	2 Apr	Celtic Park	2–0	Gallacher (2)	
2003	30 Apr	Hampden Park	0–2		Kirchler Haas
2005	17 Aug	Graz	2–2	Miller O'Connor	Iberstberger Standfest
2007	30 May	Vienna	1–0	O'Connor	

BELARUS

Belarus is a landlocked country in Eastern Europe which gained its independence in 1991, and Scotland's first four games against them resulted in two wins, one draw and one defeat.

1997	8 June	Minsk	1–0	McAllister (pen)	
1997	7 Sep	Pittodrie	4–1	Gallacher (2) Hopkin (2)	Kachuro (pen)
2005	8 June	Minsk	0–0		
2005	8 Oct	Hampden Park	0–1		Kutuzov

BELGIUM

Belgium has Flemish speakers in the north (Flemings) and French speakers in the south (Walloons) and there are sometimes tensions between the two groups. Scotland has played Belgium sixteen times, with four wins, two draws and ten defeats.

1947	18 May	Brussels	1–2	Steel	Anoul (2)
1948	28 Apr	Hampden Park	2–0	Combe Duncan	
1951	20 May	Brussels	5–0	Hamilton (3) Mason Waddell	
1971	3 Feb	Liege	0–3		Van Himst (2) (1 pen) McKinnon o.g.
1971	10 Nov	Pittodrie	1–0	O'Hare	
1974	1 June	Bruges	1–2	Johnstone	Henrotay Lambert (pen)
1979	21 Nov	Brussels	0–2		Van der Elst Voordeckers
1979	19 Dec	Hampden Park	1–3	Robertson	Van der Elst (2) Vandenbergh
1982	15 Dec	Brussels	2–3	Dalglish (2)	Van der Elst (2) Vandenbergh
1983	12 Oct	Hampden Park	1–1	Nicholas	Vercauteren
1987	1 Apr	Brussels	1–4	McStay	Claesen (3) Vercauteren
1987	14 Oct	Hampden Park	2–0	McCoist McStay	
2001	24 Mar	Hampden Park	2–2	Dodds (2) (1 pen)	Wilmots Van Buyten

2001	5 Sep	Brussels	0–2		Van Kerckhoven Goor
2012	16 Oct	Brussels	0–2		Benteke Kompany
2013	6 Sep	Hampden Park	0–2		Defour Mirallas

BOSNIA-HERZEGOVINA

This country in the Balkan Peninsula declared its independence in 1992 following the collapse of Yugoslavia, but was only preserved as a single state after more than three years of war came to an end in 1995. Scotland played them twice in the qualifying campaign for the 2000 European Championships.

| 1999 | 4 Sep | Sarajevo | 2–1 | Hutchison
Dodds | Bolic |
| 1999 | 5 Oct | Ibrox | 1–0 | Collins (pen) | |

BRAZIL

Scotland have never beaten Brazil in the ten times that they have met (four times in World Cup finals), but they have never been outclassed, and have always enjoyed the respect of their opponents, with the atmosphere at such games being much commented on and praised for its colour and good nature. They have drawn twice, the 0–0 draw in the 1974 World Cup finals being the closest that Scotland have come to beating the nation that is acknowledged to be the best on earth.

1966	25 June	Hampden Park	1–1	Chalmers	Servilio
1972	5 July	Rio de Janeiro	0–1		Jairzinho
1973	30 June	Hampden Park	0–1		Johnstone o.g.
1974	18 June	Frankfurt	0–0		
1977	23 June	Rio de Janeiro	0–2		Zico Toninho Cerezo
1982	18 June	Seville	1–4	Narey	Zico Oscar Eder Falcao
1987	26 May	Hampden Park	0–2		Rai Valdo
1990	20 June	Turin	0–1		Muller

| 1998 | 10 June | Paris | 1–2 | Collins (pen) | Cesar Sampaio
Boyd o.g. |
| 2011 | 27 Mar | Emirates Stadium
London | 0–2 | | Neymar (2)
(1 pen) |

BULGARIA

Scotland has a good record against Bulgaria. They have never lost to them in their six games, having won three and drawn three. The most famous game was the one in 1987 when Gary Mackay's late strike prevented Bulgaria reaching the finals of the European Championship of 1988. Unfortunately it was Eire, not Scotland, who qualified as a result. One of Scotland's best performances was the 5–1 victory over the Bulgarians in Japan in May 2006 in the Kirin Cup.

1978	22 Feb	Hampden Park	2–1	Gemmill Wallace	Mladenov
1986	10 Sep	Hampden Park	0–0		
1987	11 Nov	Sofia	1–0	MacKay	
1990	14 Nov	Sofia	1–1	McCoist	Todorov
1991	27 Mar	Hampden Park	1–1	Collins	Kostadinov
2006	11 May	Kobe	5–1	Boyd (2) Burke (2) McFadden	Todorov

CANADA

Scotland has played Canada on five occasions, and beaten them every time. Canada is not one of the greatest football playing countries on earth, and many Canadians are quite happy to admit that they are Scotland supporters! Canada used to be a favourite destination for Scottish teams on their close-season tour.

1983	12 June	Vancouver	2–0	Strachan (pen) McGhee	
1983	16 June	Edmonton	3–0	Nicholas Gough Souness	
1983	20 June	Toronto	2–0	Gray (2)	
1992	21 May	Toronto	3–1	McAllister (2) McCoist	Catliff
2002	15 Oct	Easter Road	3–1	Crawford (2) Thompson	De Rosario (pen)

CHILE

Scotland did not manage to qualify for the 1962 World Cup finals held in Chile. They might have done well if they had done so, for Czechoslovakia, the team that beat Scotland narrowly in the qualifying section, reached the final. Scotland have played Chile twice and won both times. The game in Santiago in 1977 provoked a certain amount of protest, because that was the stadium used in the repression, torture and murder of the supporters of Salvador Allende after the 'golpe' or coup of 11 September 1973.

| 1977 | 15 June | Santiago | 4–2 | Macari (2)
Dalglish
Hartford | Crisoto (2) |
| 1989 | 30 May | Hampden Park | 2–0 | McInally
MacLeod | |

COLOMBIA

Scotland has never beaten Colombia, nor have they ever played there. Colombia have once been to Hampden Park as part of a triangular tournament with Scotland and England called the Rous Cup, and the other games were played in the USA, when both teams were on tour before major tournaments.

1988	17 May	Hampden Park	0–0		
1996	29 May	Miami	0–1		Asprilla
1998	23 May	New York	2–2	Collins Burley	Valderrama Rincon

COMMONWEALTH OF INDEPENDENT STATES

Scotland has played this team once, and will almost certainly never do so again, for it was the name given to all the states of the former Soviet Union. They had started off playing as the Soviet Union, but as various states achieved independence during the qualification for the European Championships in Sweden in 1992, they refused to play under the Soviet banner and called themselves the CIS instead. Many people believe it was one of Scotland's best-ever performances.

| 1992 | 18 June | Norrkoping | 3–0 | McStay
McClair
McAllister | |

COSTA RICA

It was against this third-world nation that Scotland achieved, in the 1990 World Cup finals, what was one of their worst ever results, plunging the country into gloom and earning worldwide ridicule. It was also a day on which Scotland lost international credibility.

1990	11 June	Genoa	0–1		Cayasso

CROATIA

When Scotland played a World Cup qualifier in Zagreb in June 2013 they already knew that they had failed to qualify for the 2014 finals in Brazil, but they nevertheless recorded their first win of the campaign. Four months later they completed a notable double over the Croats.

2000	11 Oct	Zagreb	1–1	Gallacher	Boksic
2001	1 Sep	Hampden Park	0–0		
2008	26 Mar	Hampden Park	1–1	Miller	Kranjcar
2013	7 Jun	Zagreb	1–0	Snodgrass	
2013	15 Oct	Hampden Park	2–0	Snodgrass Naismith	

CYPRUS

Scotland has a 100% record against Cyprus, having won all five games played against them. The game in February 1989 was a close-run thing however, for Scotland needed six minutes of extra time before they scored the winner.

1968	11 Dec	Nicosia	5–0	Gilzean (2) Stein (2) Murdoch	
1969	17 May	Hampden Park	8–0	Stein (4) Gray McNeill Henderson Gemmell	
1989	8 Feb	Limassol	3–2	Gough (2) Johnston	Koliandris Ioannou
1989	26 Apr	Hampden Park	2–1	Johnston McCoist	Nicolaou
2011	11 Nov	Larnaca	2–1	Miller Mackie	Christofi

CZECHOSLOVAKIA

This country no longer exists, being now divided into the Czech Republic and Slovakia. Scotland and Czechoslovakia were drawn in the same qualifying group for the 1962, 1974 and 1978 World Cup finals and Scotland qualified in both 1974 and 1978. In 1962 the Czechoslovakians qualified after a play-off and then went on to reach the World Cup final. All in all, Scotland has played them ten times, winning five, drawing one and losing four.

1937	15 May	Prague	3–1	Simpson McPhail Gillick	Puc
1937	8 Dec	Hampden Park	5–0	McCulloch (2) Black Buchanan Kinnear	
1961	14 May	Bratislava	0–4		Pospichal (2) Kvasnak Kadraba
1961	26 Sep	Hampden Park	3–2	Law (2) St John	Kvasnak Scherer
1961	29 Nov	Brussels	2–4 a.e.t.	St John (2)	Hledik Scherer Pospichal Kvasnak
1972	2 July	Porto Alegre (Brazil)	0–0		
1973	26 Sep	Hampden Park	2–1	Holton Jordan	Nehoda
1973	17 Oct	Bratislava	0–1		Nehoda (pen)
1976	13 Oct	Prague	0–2		Panenka Petras
1977	21 Sep	Hampden Park	3–1	Jordan Hartford Dalglish	Gajdusek (pen)

CZECH REPUBLIC

The Czech Republic came into being, along with Slovakia, on 1 January 1993 when the former Czechoslovakia split into two sovereign states. Scotland recorded only one victory in their first six fixtures against the Republic – a friendly international in March 2010 that was Craig Levein's first match in charge of the national side.

1999	31 Mar	Celtic Park	1–2	Jess	Elliott (o.g.) Smicer

1999	9 Jun	Prague	2–3	Ritchie Johnston	Repka Kuka Koller
2008	30 May	Prague	1–3	Clarkson	Sionko (2) Kadlec
2010	3 Mar	Hampden Park	1–0	Brown	
2010	8 Oct	Prague	0–1		Hubnik
2011	3 Sep	Hampden Park	2–2	Miller Fletcher	Plasil Kadlec (pen)

DENMARK

Scotland has played Denmark on fifteen occasions, having won nine and lost six. There has never been a draw. Scotland beat them the first four times they played, but after two Scotland victories in 1975 the Danes emerged on top until Scotland won a friendly international in 2011.

1951	12 May	Hampden Park	3–1	Steel Reilly Mitchell	Hansen
1952	25 May	Copenhagen	2–1	Thornton Reilly	Rasmussen
1968	16 Oct	Copenhagen	1–0	Lennox	
1970	11 Nov	Hampden Park	1–0	O'Hare	
1971	9 June	Copenhagen	0–1		F. Laudrup
1972	18 Oct	Copenhagen	4–1	Macari Bone Harper Morgan	F. Laudrup
1972	15 Nov	Hampden Park	2–0	Dalglish Lorimer	
1975	3 Sep	Copenhagen	1–0	Harper	
1975	29 Oct	Hampden Park	3–1	Dalglish Rioch MacDougall	Bastrup
1986	4 June	Nezahualcoyotl	0–1		Elkjaer-Larsen
1996	24 Apr	Copenhagen	0–2		M. Laudrup B. Laudrup
1998	25 Mar	Ibrox	0–1		B. Laudrup
2002	21 Aug	Hampden Park	0–1		Sand
2004	28 Apr	Copenhagen	0–1		Sand
2011	10 Aug	Hampden Park	2–1	Kvist o.g. Snodgrass	Eriksen

ECUADOR

This country on the north-west coast of South America has provided opposition for Scotland just once; Scotland played them in the Kirin Cup in Japan, and won 2–1.

1995	24 May	Toyama	2–1	Robertson Crawford	Hurtado (pen)

EGYPT

Much of Egypt is desert and most of the population lives near the River Nile. Scotland has played Egypt once, and it was a humiliating defeat.

1990	16 May	Pittodrie	1–3	McCoist	Abdelhamid Hassan Youssef

EIRE

See IRELAND, REPUBLIC. The republic's governing body is the Football Association of Ireland (FAI), which is not to be confused with Northern Ireland's Irish Football Association (IFA). The southern part of Ireland broke away from the IFA in 1921, and Scotland's fixture in February of that year was the last occasion on which Scotland played a team that represented the whole of Ireland. Scotland did not play the Republic until 1961.

ENGLAND

England was referred to as Scotland's 'auld enemy', and for many years it was 'the' game of the calendar. The annual game was often referred to as 'the international'. The first international between the two of them on 30 November 1872 was the world's first international match. Yet it might not have been so described had Queen's Park, who supplied all of Scotland's eleven players, not decided to call themselves Scotland rather than Queen's Park. They did this presumably for reasons of attracting a large crowd to Hamilton Crescent, and thereby started the whole concept of international football.

There had been five previous England versus Scotland games, all played at the Oval in London, but Scotland's players were all based in the London area and chosen by the English authorities! In fact they were supplemented by a few Englishmen, including some men who later went on to play for England. These five games played between 1870 and 1872 are therefore rightly deemed unofficial. Of these five games, two were 1–1 draws and the other three were victories for England with the scores of 0–1, 1–2 and 0–1.

It is a matter of some regret that the annual match has now disappeared, a victim of hooliganism and a crowded fixture calendar, for it used to be the most eagerly awaited game of the season. 1928 and 1967 are still etched into the memory of every Scotsman, but perhaps credit should also be given to the mighty men of the early 1880s who won five in a row, or the Scotland teams between the wars who never lost to England at Hampden apart from 1927 (when the whole country was plunged into mourning as a result) and in 1939 when everyone was more concerned about Hitler. Most of these games until the mid 1980s were in the Home International Championship, but the games in 1950 and 1954 were World Cup qualifying games as well, whereas those in 1967 and 1968 doubled as European Nations Cup Qualifying games. The game in 1996 was in the European Championships and those in 1999 were play-offs for the European Championships. 111 games have been played, forty-one won, forty-six lost and twenty-four drawn.

1872	30 Nov	Hamilton Crescent	0–0		
1873	8 Mar	Kennington Oval	2–4	Renny-Tailyour Gibb	Kenyon-Stanley (2) Bonsor Chenery
1874	7 Mar	Hamilton Crescent	2–1	Anderson MacKinnon	Kingsford
1875	6 Mar	Kennington Oval	2–2	McNeil Andrews	Wollaston Alcock
1876	4 Mar	Hamilton Crescent	3–0	MacKinnon McNeil Highet	
1877	3 Mar	Kennington Oval	3–1	Ferguson (2) Richmond	Lyttleton
1878	2 Mar	1st Hampden Park	7–2	McDougall (3) McGregor McNeil (2) MacKinnon	Wyllie Cursham
1879	5 Apr	Kennington Oval	4–5	MacKinnon (2) McDougall Smith	Mosforth Bambridge (2) Goodyer Bailey
1880	13 Mar	1st Hampden Park	5–4	Ker (3) Baird Kay	Bambridge (2) Mosforth Sparks
1881	12 Mar	Kennington Oval	6–1	Smith (3) Ker (2) Hill	Bambridge
1882	11 Mar	1st Hampden Park	5–1	Ker (2) Harrower McPherson Kay	Vaughton

1883	10 Mar	Bramall Lane	3–2	Smith (2) Fraser	Mitchell Cobbold
1884	15 Mar	Cathkin Park	1–0	Smith	
1885	21 Mar	Kennington Oval	1–1	Lindsay	Bambridge
1886	27 Mar	2nd Hampden Park	1–1	Somerville	Lindley
1887	19 Mar	Blackburn	3–2	McCall Keir Allan	Lindley Dewhurst
1888	17 Mar	2nd Hampden Park	0–5		Dewhurst (2) Lindley Hodgetts Goodall
1889	13 April	Kennington Oval	3–2	Munro Oswald McPherson	Bassett Weir
1890	5 April	2nd Hampden Park	1–1	McPherson	Wood
1891	4 April	Blackburn	1–2	Watt	Goodall Chadwick
1892	2 April	Ibrox	1–4	Bell	Goodall (2) Chadwick Southworth
1893	1 April	Richmond	2–5	Sellar (2)	Spiksley (2) Gosling Coterill Reynolds
1894	7 April	Celtic Park	2–2	Lambie McMahon	Goodall Reynolds
1895	6 April	Goodison Park	0–3		Bloomer Gibson o.g. Smith
1896	4 April	Celtic Park	2–1	Lambie Bell	Bassett
1897	3 April	Crystal Palace	2–1	Hyslop Millar	Bloomer
1898	2 April	Celtic Park	1–3	Millar	Bloomer (2) Wheldon
1899	8 April	Villa Park	1–2	Hamilton	Smith Settle
1900	7 April	Celtic Park	4–1	McColl (3) Bell	Bloomer
1901	30 Mar	Crystal Palace	2–2	Campbell Hamilton	Blackburn Bloomer
1902	3 May	Villa Park	2–2	Templeton Orr	Settle Wilkes

Original match played at Ibrox on 5 April, but declared unofficial after collapse of west stand, which led to twenty-six people being killed in what became known as the first Ibrox disaster. The first game was a 1–1 draw.

The Scotland team before the game at Villa Park in 1902

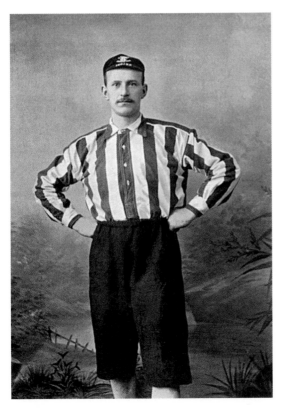

Goalkeepr Ned Doig almost single-handedly defied England in 1903

1903	4 April	Bramall Lane	2–1	Speedie Walker	Woodward
1904	9 April	Celtic Park	0–1		Bloomer
1905	1 April	Crystal Palace	0–1		Bache
1906	7 April	3rd Hampden Park	2–1	Howie (2)	Shepherd
1907	6 April	Newcastle	1–1	Crompton o.g.	Bloomer
1908	4 April	Hampden Park	1–1	Wilson	Windridge
1909	3 April	Crystal Palace	0–2		Wall (2)
1910	2 April	Hampden Park	2–0	McMenemy Quinn	
1911	1 April	Goodison	1–1	Higgins	Stewart
1912	23 Mar	Hampden Park	1–1	Wilson	Holley
1913	5 April	Stamford Bridge	0–1		Hampton
1914	4 April	Hampden Park	3–1	Thomson McMenemy Reid	Fleming
1920	10 April	Hillsborough	4–5	Miller (2) Wilson Donaldson	Kelly (2) Quantrill Cock Morris
1921	9 April	Hampden Park	3–0	Wilson Morton Cunningham	
1922	8 April	Villa Park	1–0	Wilson	
1923	14 April	Hampden Park	2–2	Cunningham Wilson	Kelly Watson
1924	12 April	Wembley	1–1	Cowan	Walker
1925	4 April	Hampden Park	2–0	Gallacher (2)	
1926	17 April	Old Trafford	1–0	Jackson	
1927	2 April	Hampden Park	1–2	Morton	Dean (2)
1928	31 Mar	Wembley	5–1	Jackson (3) James (2)	Kelly
1929	13 April	Hampden Park	1–0	Cheyne	
1930	5 April	Wembley	2–5	Fleming (2)	Watson (2) Rimmer (2) Jack
1931	28 Mar	Hampden Park	2–0	Stevenson McGrory	

Hughie Gallacher scored the two Scotland goals which beat England in 1925. Three years later he became one of the Wembley Wizards

Forfarian Alec Troup was on the winning side in 1926

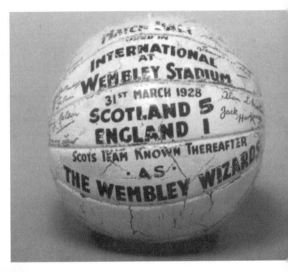

The match ball used by the Wembley Wizards in 1928 – the first Scottish team to win at the new Empire Stadium

Alex Jackson scored a hat-trick for the Wembley Wizards in 1928

1932	9 April	Wembley	0–3		Waring Barclay Crooks
1933	1 April	Hampden Park	2–1	McGrory (2)	Hunt
1934	14 April	Wembley	0–3		Bastin Brook Bowers
1935	6 April	Hampden Park	2–0	Duncan (2)	
1936	4 April	Wembley	1–1	Walker (pen)	Camsell
1937	17 April	Hampden Park	3–1	McPhail (2) O'Donnell	Steele
1938	9 April	Wembley	1–0	Walker	
1939	15 April	Hampden Park	1–2	Dougall	Beasley Lawton
1947	12 April	Wembley	1–1	McLaren	Carter
1948	10 April	Hampden Park	0–2		Finney Mortensen
1949	9 April	Wembley	3–1	Mason Steel Reilly	Milburn
1950	15 April	Hampden Park	0–1		Bentley
1951	14 April	Wembley	3–2	Johnstone Reilly Liddell	Hassall Finney
1952	5 April	Hampden Park	1–2	Reilly	Pearson (2)
1953	18 April	Wembley	2–2	Reilly (2)	Broadis (2)
1954	3 April	Hampden Park	2–4	Brown Ormond	Broadis Nicholls Allen Mullen
1955	2 April	Wembley	2–7	Reilly Docherty	Wilshaw (4) Lofthouse (2) Revie
1956	14 April	Hampden Park	1–1	Leggat	Haynes
1957	6 April	Wembley	1–2	Ring	Kevan Edwards
1958	19 April	Hampden Park	0–4		Kevan (2) Douglas Charlton
1959	11 April	Wembley	0–1		Charlton

Tommy Docherty and Billy Wright at Hampden Park in 1958

1960	9 April	Hampden Park	1–1	Leggat	Charlton (pen)
1961	15 April	Wembley	3–9	Mackay Wilson Quinn	Greaves (3) Smith (2) Haynes (2) Robson Douglas
1962	14 April	Hampden Park	2–0	Wilson Caldow (pen)	
1963	6 April	Wembley	2–1	Baxter (2) (1 pen)	Douglas
1964	11 April	Hampden Park	1–0	Gilzean	
1965	10 April	Wembley	2–2	Law St John	Charlton Greaves
1966	2 April	Hampden Park	3–4	Johnstone (2) Law	Hunt (2) Hurst Charlton
1967	15 April	Wembley	3–2	Law Lennox McCalliog	Charlton Hurst
1968	24 Feb	Hampden Park	1–1	Hughes	Peters

Denis Law scores for Scotland in 1966

Jim Baxter at Wembley after Scotland's 3–2 victory in 1967 alongside Willie Wallace (with his back to the camera), Tommy Gemmell and Eddie McCreadie (in an England shirt!)

Jim McCalliog, who scored in 1967, is congratulated by Ronnie Simpson

ENGLAND—*contd*

1969	10 May	Wembley	1–4	Stein	Peters (2) Hurst (2)
1970	25 April	Hampden Park	0–0		
1971	22 May	Wembley	1–3	Curran	Chivers (2) Peters
1972	27 May	Hampden Park	0–1		Ball
1973	14 Feb	Hampden Park	0–5		Clarke (2) Lorimer o.g. Channon Chivers
		A special game to mark the centenary of the SFA			
1973	19 May	Wembley	0–1		Peters
1974	18 May	Hampden Park	2–0	Jordan Todd o.g.	
1975	24 May	Wembley	1–5	Rioch (pen)	Francis (2) Beattie Bell Johnson
1976	15 May	Hampden Park	2–1	Masson Dalglish	Channon
1977	4 June	Wembley	2–1	McQueen Dalglish	Channon (pen)
1978	20 May	Hampden Park	0–1		Coppell
1979	26 May	Wembley	1–3	Wark	Barnes Coppell Keegan
1980	24 May	Hampden Park	0–2		Brooking Coppell
1981	23 May	Wembley	1–0	Robertson (pen)	
1982	29 May	Hampden Park	0–1		Mariner
1983	1 June	Wembley	0–2		Robson Cowans
1984	26 May	Hampden Park	1–1	McGhee	Woodcock
1985	25 May	Hampden Park	1–0	Gough	
1986	23 April	Wembley	1–2	Souness (pen)	Butcher Hoddle
1987	23 May	Hampden Park	0–0		
1988	21 May	Wembley	0–1		Beardsley
1989	27 May	Hampden Park	0–2		Waddle Bull

1996	15 June	Wembley	0–2		Shearer Gascoigne
1999	13 Nov	Hampden Park	0–2		Scholes (2)
1999	17 Nov	Wembley	1–0	Hutchison	
2013	14 Aug	Wembley	2–3	Morrison Miller	Walcott Welbeck Lambert

ESTONIA

Scotland have played Estonia eight times and drawn twice. They have never lost to them. There were bizarre events on 9 October 1996 in the World Cup when Scotland, having complained about the floodlights, managed to get the game changed from 6.45 pm to an afternoon kick-off at 3.00 pm – or so they thought. The Estonians did not turn up, and thus Scotland, and the referee and linesmen, appeared – but no opposition! Scotland lined up in front of the TV cameras, the referee Miroslav Radoman blew his whistle, Billy Dodds took the kick-off, passed to John Collins who kicked the ball upfield, and the referee blew his whistle again to finish the game. Everyone then shook hands and went away home! Scotland claimed three points, but FIFA rearranged the game in the neutral venue of Monaco the following February. It may well have imperilled Scotland's chances of qualification, but fortunately Scotland, although only drawing in Monaco, managed to qualify for France. When the two countries played an international friendly in 2013, it was Gordon Strachan's first match as manager of the national team.

1993	19 May	Tallinn	3–0	Gallacher Collins Booth	
1993	2 June	Pittodrie	3–1	Nevin (2) (1 pen) McClair	Bragin
1997	11 Feb	Monaco	0–0		
1997	29 Mar	Rugby Park	2–0	Boyd Meet o.g.	
1998	10 Oct	Tynecastle	3–2	Dodds (2) Hohlov-Simson o.g.	Hohlov-Simson Smirnov
1999	8 Sep	Tallinn	0–0		
2004	27 May	Tallinn	1–0	McFadden	
2013	6 Feb	Pittodrie	1–0	Mulgrew	

FAEROE ISLANDS

These small islands have twice held Scotland to a draw, and even Scottish fans conceded that they were unlucky not to win on both occasions. For many followers of the national team it seems that Scotland reserve their worst performances for such fixtures, but they remain undefeated. Nine games have been played, with seven victories and two draws. In November 2010 manager Craig Levein fielded a team in which seven players made their debut for Scotland. Barry Bannon and Danny Wilson were in the starting line-up, whilst Cammy Bell, Craig Bryson, David Goodwillie, James McArthur and Steven Saunders all appeared as substitutes.

1994	12 Oct	Hampden Park	5–1	Collins (2) McGinlay McKinlay Booth	Muller
1995	7 June	Toftir	2–0	McGinlay McKinlay	
1998	14 Oct	Pittodrie	2–1	Burley Dodds	Petersen (pen)
1999	5 June	Toftir	1–1	Johnston	Hansen
2002	7 Sep	Toftir	2–2	Lambert Ferguson	Petersen (2)
2003	6 Sep	Hampden Park	3–1	McCann Dickov McFadden	Johnsson
2006	2 Sep	Celtic Park	6–0	Boyd (2) (1 pen) Miller (pen) Fletcher McFadden O'Connor	
2007	6 June	Toftir	2–0	Maloney O'Connor	
2010	16 Nov	Pittodrie	3–0	Wilson Commons Mackie	

FINLAND

A quarter of Finland lies north of the Arctic Circle, but the capital Helsinki is located in the south of the country. Scotland's record against the Finns is a good one; eight games have been played, six won and two drawn.

1954	25 May	Helsinki	2–1	Ormond Johnstone	Lahtinen
1964	21 Oct	Hampden Park	3–1	Law Chalmers Gibson	Peltonen
1965	27 May	Helsinki	2–1	Wilson Greig	Hyvarinen
1976	8 Sep	Hampden Park	6–0	A. Gray (2) E. Gray Rioch Masson Dalglish	

1992	25 Mar	Hampden Park	1–1	McStay	Litmanen
1994	7 Sep	Helsinki	2–0	Shearer Collins	
1995	6 Sep	Hampden Park	1–0	Booth	
1998	22 Apr	Easter Road	1–1	Jackson	Johansson

FRANCE

Scotland have played France fifteen times, winning eight and losing seven – not a bad performance in the light of the relative populations of the countries – although most of Scotland's successes were in the early years. The victories in 2006 and 2007, in the qualifying section for the 2008 European Football Championships, were tremendous triumphs for the nation, considering that the star-studded French were the beaten World Cup finalists of 2006.

Alan Morton, seen here playing for Queen's Park, was in the Scotland team that beat France 3–1 in Paris in 1932, when Third Lanark's Neil Dewar scored a hat-trick

1930	18 May	Paris	2–0	Gallacher (2)	
1932	8 May	Paris	3–1	Dewar (3)	Langilier (pen)
1948	23 May	Paris	0–3		Bongiorni Flamion Baratte
1949	27 Apr	Hampden Park	2–0	Steel (2)	
1950	27 May	Paris	1–0	Brown	
1951	16 May	Hampden Park	1–0	Reilly	

1958	15 June	Orebro	1–2	Baird	Kopa Fontaine
1984	1 June	Marseilles	0–2		Giresse Lacombe
1989	8 Mar	Hampden Park	2–0	Johnston (2)	
1989	11 Oct	Paris	0–3		Deschamps Cantona Nicol o.g.
1997	12 Nov	St Etienne	1–2	Durie	Laigle Djorkaeff
2000	29 Mar	Hampden Park	0–2		Wiltord Henry
2002	27 Mar	Paris	0–5		Trezeguet (2) Zidane Henry Marlet
2006	7 Oct	Hampden Park	1–0	Caldwell	
2007	12 Sep	Paris	1–0	McFadden	

GEORGIA

Situated on the eastern shore of the Black Sea, Georgia was once part of the Soviet Union. It became an independent state in 1991 and Scotland played them twice in the qualifying campaign for the 2008 European Championship.

2007	24 Mar	Hampden Park	2–1	Boyd Beattie	Arveladze
2007	17 Oct	Tbilisi	0–2		Mchedlidze Siradze
2014	11 Oct	Ibrox			
2015	4 Sep	Tbilisi			

GERMANY

Although Germany was divided between the years of 1945 and 1990, Scotland has played a united Germany seven times, winning twice, drawing twice and losing three times. Allegedly, Scotland's 1936 victory at Ibrox greatly displeased the Fuhrer. Jimmy Delaney scored twice for Scotland, thereby 'putting Hitler aff his tea'.

1929	1 June	Berlin	1–1	Imrie	Ruch
1936	14 Oct	Ibrox	2–0	Delaney (2)	
1992	15 June	Norrkoping	0–2		Riedle Effenberg

1993	24 Mar	Ibrox	0–1		Riedle
1999	28 Apr	Bremen	1–0	Hutchison	
2003	7 June	Hampden Park	1–1	Miller	Bobic
2003	10 Sep	Dortmund	1–2	McCann	Bobic Ballack (pen)
2014	7 Sep	Dortmund			
2015	7 Sep	Hampden Park			

GERMANY (EAST)

Scotland played the German Democratic Republic six times, winning two, drawing one and losing three.

1974	30 Oct	Hampden Park	3–0	Hutchison Burns Dalglish	
1977	7 Sep	East Berlin	0–1		Schade
1982	13 Oct	Hampden Park	2–0	Wark Sturrock	
1983	16 Nov	Halle	1–2	Bannon	Kreer Streich
1985	16 Oct	Hampden Park	0–0		
1990	25 Apr	Hampden Park	0–1		Doll (pen)

GERMANY (WEST)

Scotland played the Federal Republic of Germany eight times before the reunification of Germany on 3 October 1990 – winning two, drawing three and losing three.

1957	22 May	Stuttgart	3–1	Collins (2) Mudie	Siedl
1959	6 May	Hampden Park	3–2	White Weir Leggat	Seeler Juskowiac
1964	12 May	Hanover	2–2	Gilzean (2)	Seeler (2)
1969	16 Apr	Hampden Park	1–1	Murdoch	Muller
1969	22 Oct	Hamburg	2–3	Johnstone Gilzean	Fichtel Muller Libuda
1973	14 Nov	Hampden Park	1–1	Holton	Hoeness
1974	27 Mar	Frankfurt	1–2	Dalglish	Breitner Grabowski
1986	8 June	Queretaro	1–2	Strachan	Voller Allofs

GIBRALTAR

Gibraltar is a rocky promontory on the southern coast of Spain that was ceded to Great Britain in 1713 by the Treaty of Utrecht. The Gibraltar Football Association applied for UEFA membership in April 1999, but this was a sensitive matter in Spain because of Spanish claims to the territory and the GFA was not granted full membership until May 2013. Gibraltar was then able to take part in the 2016 European Championship and was placed in the same qualifying group as Scotland, but their Victoria Stadium was not up to the required standard and 'home' matches were scheduled for the Estadio Algarve in Faro, Portugal.

2015	29 Mar	Hampden Park			
2015	11 Oct	Faro			

GREECE

Scotland has played Greece twice, with the score being 1–0 for the home side on each occasion. Many people have asked, "If Greece can become European champions (as they did in Portugal 2004), why can't Scotland?"

1994	18 Dec	Athens	0–1		Apostolakis (pen)
1995	16 Aug	Hampden Park	1–0	McCoist	

HOLLAND (sometimes called THE NETHERLANDS)

Scotland have played Holland eighteen times, the most famous being the game in Mendoza in Argentina in 1978 when Archie Gemmill scored his wonder goal, praised as 'not without cause, but without end' by a defeated and disgraced nation. On the other hand there was the disgraceful 0–6 defeat in 2003 which knocked Scotland out of the play-off for the 2004 European Championship, a defeat which came all the worse for Scotland as they had won the first leg. Played eighteen, won six, drawn four, lost eight.

1929	4 June	Amsterdam	2–0	Fleming Rankin (pen)	
1938	21 May	Amsterdam	3–1	Black Murphy Walker	Vente
1959	27 May	Amsterdam	2–1	Collins Leggat	Van der Gijp
1966	11 May	Hampden Park	0–3		Van der Kuijlen (2) Nuninga
1968	30 May	Amsterdam	0–0		
1971	1 Dec	Amsterdam	1–2	Graham	Cruijff Hulshott

1978	11 June	Mendoza	3–2	Gemmill (2) (1 pen) Dalglish	Rensenbrink Rep
1982	23 Mar	Hampden Park	2–1	Gray (pen) Dalglish	Kieft
1986	29 Apr	Eindhoven	0–0		
1992	12 June	Gothenburg	0–1		Bergkamp
1994	23 Mar	Hampden Park	0–1		Roy
1994	27 May	Utrecht	1–3	Shearer	Roy Van Vossen Irvine o.g.
1996	10 June	Villa Park	0–0		
2000	26 Apr	Arnhem	0–0		
2003	15 Nov	Hampden Park	1–0	McFadden	
2003	19 Nov	Amsterdam	0–6		Van Nistelrooy (3) Sneider Ooijer De Boer
2009	28 Mar	Amsterdam	0–3		Huntelaar Van Persie Kuyt
2009	9 Sep	Hampden Park	0–1		Elia

HONG KONG

Scotland has played in Hong Kong several times, the most recent being on 23 May 2002 when they beat the home side 4–0. Unfortunately these matches were not recognised by FIFA as official international matches.

2002	23 May	Hong Kong	4–0	Kyle Thompson Dailly Gemmill	

HUNGARY

Scotland has played Hungary eight times, winning two games, drawing twice, and losing four times. The game in December 1954 is often said to be one of the best ever played at Hampden Park, as Scotland did well to hold the World Cup finalists to a 4–2 defeat.

1938	7 Dec	Ibrox	3–1	Walker Black Gillick	Sarosi

1954	8 Dec	Hampden Park	2–4	Ring Johnstone	Bozsik Hidegkuti Sandor Kocsis
1955	29 May	Budapest	1–3	Smith	Hidegkuti Kocsis Fenyvesi
1958	7 May	Hampden Park	1–1	Mudie	Fenyvesi
1960	5 June	Budapest	3–3	Hunter Herd Young	Sandor Gorocs Tichy
1980	31 May	Budapest	1–3	Archibald	Torocsik (2) Kereki
1987	9 Sep	Hampden Park	2–0	McCoist (2)	
2004	18 Aug	Hampden Park	0–3		Huszti (2) (1 pen) Marshall o.g.

ICELAND

Scotland has a perfect record against the men from this volcanic island in the North Atlantic Ocean. The Scots have won all six games that they have played against them.

1984	17 Oct	Hampden Park	3–0	McStay (2) Nicholas	
1985	28 May	Reykjavik	1–0	Bett	
2002	12 Oct	Reykjavik	2–0	Dailly Naysmith	
2003	29 Mar	Hampden Park	2–1	Miller Wilkie	Gudjohnsen
2008	10 Sep	Reykjavik	2–1	Broadfoot McFadden	Gudjohnsen
2009	1 Apr	Hampden Park	2–1	McCormack S. Fletcher	

IRAN

Scotland have played Iran only once, but it was quite a 'once'. This was Scotland's second game of the 1978 World Cup in Argentina, and the match ended in a draw. It is widely regarded as a disastrous game, and possibly their worst-ever, although there is strong competition for that title.

1978	7 June	Cordoba	1–1	Eskandarian o.g.	Danaifar

IRELAND

Scotland has played Ireland since 1884 in the Home International Championship with some fixtures doubling as World Cup or European Championship qualifying games. Ireland has had many troubles since 1884, and this means that games against Ireland before 1922 were against the whole of Ireland, whereas since that date it has been Northern Ireland. For games against southern Ireland see IRELAND, REPUBLIC of. In addition, the troubles of the 1970s meant that all fixtures in that decade had to be played at Hampden Park. After Scotland's victory over Northern Ireland in the Nations Cup tournament of 2011, the statistics were 'Scotland won sixty-two, lost fifteen and drew seventeen'. Ireland were always considered to be the weakest of the British international countries, and for this reason, particularly in the early days, the side that Scotland fielded was anything but the strongest available eleven.

1884	26 Jan	Belfast	5–0	Harrower (2) Gosland (2) Goudie	
1885	14 Mar	2nd Hampden Park	8–2	Higgins (3) Lamont Turner Calderwood Marshall Barbour	Gibb (2)
1886	20 Mar	Belfast	7–2	Heggie (4) Lambie Dunbar Gourlay	Condy Johnston
1887	19 Feb	2nd Hampden Park	4–1	Watt Jenkinson Johnstone Lowe	Browne
1888	24 Mar	Belfast	10–2	Dickson (4) Dewar Breckenridge Aitken McCallum A. Stewart Wilson o.g.	Dalton (2)
1889	9 Mar	Ibrox	7–0	Groves (3) Watt (2) Black McInnes	
1890	29 Mar	Belfast	4–1	Rankin (2) Wylie McPherson	Peden
1891	28 Mar	(Old) Celtic Park	2–1	Low Waddell	Stanfield
1892	19 Mar	Belfast	3–2	Keillor Lambie Ellis	Williamson Gaffikin

IRELAND—*contd*					
1893	25 Mar	(New) Celtic Park	6–1	Sellar (2) McMahon Kelly Hamilton S. Torrans o.g.	Gaffikin
1894	31 Mar	Belfast	2–1	Taylor Torrans o.g.	Stanfield
1895	30 Mar	Celtic Park	3–1	Walker (2) Lambie	Sherrard
1896	28 Mar	Belfast	3–3	McColl (2) Murray	Barron (2) Milne (pen)
1897	27 Mar	Ibrox	5–1	McPherson (2) Gibson McColl King	Pyper
1898	26 Mar	Belfast	3–0	Robertson McColl Stewart	
1899	25 Mar	Celtic Park	9–1	McColl (3) Hamilton (2) Campbell (2) Christie Bell	Goodall

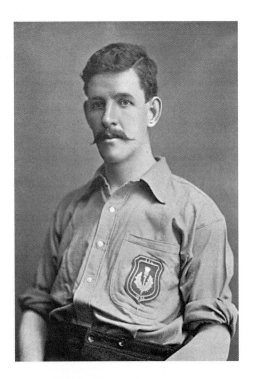

Jack Bell of Celtic was one of the scorers in the 9–1 victory over Ireland at Celtic Park in 1899. Robert McColl of Queen's Park scored a hat-trick, seven days after his hat-trick against Wales

1900	3 Mar	Belfast	3–0	Campbell (2) A. Smith	
1901	23 Feb	Celtic Park	11–0	McMahon (4) Hamilton (4) J W Campbell (2) Russell	
1902	1 Mar	Belfast	5–1	Hamilton (3) Walker Buick	Milne
1903	21 Mar	Celtic Park	0–2		Connor Kirwan
1904	26 Mar	Dublin	1–1	Hamilton	Sheridan
1905	18 Mar	Celtic Park	4–0	Thomson (2) Walker Quinn	
1906	17 Mar	Dublin	1–0	Fitchie	
1907	16 Mar	Celtic Park	3–0	O'Rourke Walker Thomson	
1908	14 Mar	Dublin	5–0	Quinn (4) Galt	
1909	15 Mar	Ibrox	5–0	McMenemy (2) MacFarlane Thomson Paul	
1910	19 Mar	Belfast	0–1		Thompson
1911	18 Mar	Celtic Park	2–0	Reid McMenemy	
1912	16 Mar	Belfast	4–1	Aitkenhead (2) Reid Walker	McKnight (pen)
1913	15 Mar	Dublin	2–1	Reid Bennett	McKnight
1914	14 Mar	Belfast	1–1	Donnachie	Young
1920	13 Mar	Celtic Park	3–0	Wilson Morton Cunningham	
1921	26 Feb	Belfast	2–0	Wilson (pen) Cassidy	
1922	4 Mar	Celtic Park	2–1	Wilson (2)	Gillespie
1923	3 Mar	Belfast	1–0	Wilson	
1924	1 Mar	Celtic Park	2–0	Cunningham Morris	

IRELAND—*contd*

1925	28 Feb	Belfast	3–0	Meiklejohn Gallacher Dunn	
1926	27 Feb	Ibrox	4–0	Gallacher (3) Cunningham	
1927	26 Feb	Belfast	2–0	Morton (2)	
1928	25 Feb	Firhill	0–1		Chambers
1929	23 Feb	Belfast	7–3	Gallacher (5) Jackson (2)	Rowley (2) Bambrick
1930	22 Feb	Celtic Park	3–1	Gallacher (2) Stevenson	McCaw
1931	21 Feb	Belfast	0–0		
1931	19 Sept	Ibrox	3–1	Stevenson McGrory McPhail	Dunne
1932	17 Sept	Belfast	4–0	McPhail (2) McGrory King	
1933	16 Sept	Celtic Park	1–2	McPhail	Martin (2)
1934	20 Oct	Belfast	1–2	Gallacher	Martin Coulter
1935	13 Nov	Tynecastle	2–1	Walker Duncan	Kelly
1936	31 Oct	Belfast	3–1	Napier Munro McCulloch	Kernaghan
1937	10 Nov	Pittodrie	1–1	Smith	Doherty
1938	8 Oct	Belfast	2–0	Delaney Walker	
1946	27 Nov	Hampden Park	0–0		
1947	4 Oct	Belfast	0–2		Smyth (2)
1948	17 Nov	Hampden Park	3–2	Houliston (2) Mason	Walsh (2)
1949	1 Oct	Belfast	8–2	Morris (3) Waddell (2) Steel Reilly Mason	Smyth (2)
1950	1 Nov	Hampden Park	6–1	Steel (4) McPhail (2)	McGarry

1951	6 Oct	Belfast	3–0	Johnstone (2) Orr	
1952	5 Nov	Hampden Park	1–1	Reilly	D'Arcy
1953	3 Oct	Belfast	3–1	Fleming (2) Henderson	Lockhart (pen)
1954	3 Nov	Hampden Park	2–2	Davidson Johnstone	Bingham McAdams
1955	8 Oct	Belfast	1–2	Reilly	J. Blanchflower Bingham
1956	7 Nov	Hampden Park	1–0	Scott	
1957	5 Oct	Belfast	1–1	Leggat	Simpson
1958	5 Nov	Hampden Park	2–2	Herd Collins	McIlroy Caldow o.g.
1959	3 Oct	Belfast	4–0	Leggat Hewie White Mulhall	
1960	9 Nov	Hampden Park	5–2	Brand (2) Law Caldow Young	D. Blanchflower (pen) McParland
1961	7 Oct	Belfast	6–1	Scott (3) Brand (2) Wilson	McLaughlin
1962	7 Nov	Hampden Park	5–1	Law (4) Henderson	Bingham
1963	12 Oct	Belfast	1–2	St John	Bingham Wilson
1964	25 Nov	Hampden Park	3–2	Wilson (2) Gilzean	Best Irvine
1965	2 Oct	Belfast	2–3	Gilzean (2)	Dougan Crossan Irvine
1966	16 Nov	Hampden Park	2–1	Murdoch Lennox	Nicholson
1967	21 Oct	Belfast	0–1		Clements
1969	6 May	Hampden Park	1–1	Stein	McMordie
1970	18 Apr	Belfast	1–0	O'Hare	
1971	18 May	Hampden Park	0–1		Greig o.g.
1972	20 May	Hampden Park	2–0	Law Lorimer	

IRELAND—*contd*						
1973	16 May	Hampden Park	1–2	Dalglish	O'Neill Anderson
1974	11 May	Hampden Park	0–1		Cassidy
1975	20 May	Hampden Park	3–0	MacDougall Dalglish Parlane	
1976	8 May	Hampden Park	3–0	Gemmill Masson Dalglish	
1977	1 June	Hampden Park	3–0	Dalglish (2) McQueen	
1978	13 May	Hampden Park	1–1	Johnstone	O'Neill
1979	22 May	Hampden Park	1–0	Graham	
1980	16 May	Belfast	0–1		Hamilton
1981	25 Mar	Hampden Park	1–1	Wark	Hamilton
1981	19 May	Hampden Park	2–0	Stewart Archibald	
1981	14 Oct	Belfast	0–0		
1982	28 Apr	Belfast	1–1	Wark	McIlroy
1983	24 May	Hampden Park	0–0		
1983	13 Dec	Belfast	0–2		Whiteside McIlroy
1992	19 Feb	Hampden Park	1–0	McCoist	
2008	20 Aug	Hampden Park	0–0		
2011	9 Feb	Dublin	3–0	Miller McArthur Commons	

IRELAND, REPUBLIC of (otherwise known as EIRE)

When Scotland lost the last match of the Nations Cup tournament in May 2011, it took the tally to won three, drawn two, and lost four.

1961	3 May	Hampden Park	4–1	Brand (2) Herd (2)	Haverty
1961	7 May	Dublin	3–0	Young (2) Brand	
1963	9 June	Dublin	0–1		Cantwell
1969	21 Sep	Dublin	1–1	Stein	

1986	15 Oct	Dublin	0–0		
1987	18 Feb	Hampden Park	0–1		Lawrenson
2000	30 May	Dublin	2–1	Hutchison Ferguson	Burley o.g.
2003	12 Feb	Hampden Park	0–2		Kilbane Morrison
2011	29 May	Dublin	0–1		Keane
2014	14 Nov	Celtic Park			
2015	13 June	Dublin			

ISRAEL

Israel qualified for the World Cup finals in 1970 and achieved a 0–0 draw with eventual finalists Italy in the group stage. Scotland has played them three times and has always beaten them, although never too convincingly.

1981	25 Feb	Tel Aviv	1–0	Dalglish	
1981	28 Apr	Hampden Park	3–1	Robertson (2) pens Provan	Sinai
1986	28 Jan	Tel Aviv	1–0	McStay	

ITALY

Scotland have only beaten Italy once, and drawn twice out of ten starts, but then again Italy are one of the best teams in the world, and were World Cup winners in 1934, 1938, 1982 and 2006. The time that Scotland beat them was a World Cup qualifier at Hampden when a late John Greig goal gave Scotland a chance of reaching the World Cup finals in England, a chance that sadly evaporated a month later when Scotland went to Naples. Sadly, Scotland have never even drawn in Italy.

1931	20 May	Rome	0–3		Constantino Meazza Orsi
1965	9 Nov	Hampden Park	1–0	Greig	
1965	7 Dec	Naples	0–3		Pascutti Facchetti Mora
1988	22 Dec	Perugia	0–2		Giannini Berti
1992	18 Nov	Ibrox	0–0		
1993	13 Oct	Rome	1–3	Gallacher	Donadoni Casiraghi Eranio

2005	26 Mar	Milan	0–2		Pirlo (2)
2005	3 Sep	Hampden Park	1–1	Miller	Grosso
2007	28 Mar	Bari	0–2		Toni (2)
2007	17 Nov	Hampden Park	1–2	Ferguson	Toni Panucci

JAPAN

Scotland did not score in their first three outings against Japan, but the game in 2009 was notable because no fewer than six Scotland players won their first cap in Yokohama (Conway, Cowie, Dorrans, Hughes, Lee Wallace and Ross Wallace).

1995	21 May	Hiroshima	0–0		
2006	13 May	Saitama	0–0		
2009	10 Oct	Yokohama	0–2		Berra o.g. Honda

LATVIA

Scotland's matches against this country on the eastern shore of the Baltic Sea have all been in the qualifying stages for the World Cup finals, and Scotland has won all four games.

1996	5 Oct	Riga	2–0	Collins Jackson	
1997	11 Oct	Celtic Park	2–0	Gallacher Durie	
2000	2 Sep	Riga	1–0	McCann	
2001	6 Oct	Hampden Park	2–1	Freedman Weir	Rubins

LITHUANIA

Scotland has played Lithuania eight times since it became an independent nation again in 1991 – winning all the home games, and winning one, drawing two and losing one in Lithuania.

1998	5 Sep	Vilnius	0–0		
1999	9 Oct	Hampden Park	3–0	Hutchison McSwegan Cameron	
2003	2 April	Kaunas	0–1		Razanauskas (pen)

2003	11 Oct	Hampden Park	1–0	Fletcher	
2006	6 Sep	Kaunas	2–1	Dailly Miller	Miceika
2007	8 Sep	Hampden Park	3–1	Boyd McManus McFadden	Danilevicius (pen)
2010	3 Sep	Kaunas	0–0		
2011	6 Sep	Hampden Park	1–0	Naismith	

LUXEMBOURG

Scotland has registered three victories over tiny Luxembourg, but in 1987 a side captained by Alex McLeish only managed a disappointing 0–0 draw. Four players won their first cap in the 2012 match (Shinnie, Kelly, Griffiths and Davidson), with Andrew Shinnie becoming the first Inverness CT player to represent Scotland at senior international level.

1947	24 May	Luxembourg-Ville	6–0	Flavell (2) Steel (2) McLaren Forbes	
1986	12 Nov	Hampden Park	3–0	Cooper (2) Johnston	
1987	2 Dec	Esch-sur-Alzette	0–0		
2012	14 Nov	Luxembourg-Ville	2–1	Rhodes (2)	Gerson

MALTA

This archipelago of islands in the Mediterranean Sea became a republic in 1974 – since when Scotland has played them five times, winning four matches and drawing one.

1988	22 Mar	Valletta	1–1	Sharp	Busuttil
1990	28 May	Valletta	2–1	McInally (2)	Degiorgio
1993	17 Feb	Ibrox	3–0	McCoist (2) Nevin	
1993	17 Nov	Valletta	2–0	McKinlay Hendry	
1997	1 June	Valletta	3–2	Jackson (2) Dailly	Suda Sultana

MOLDOVA

Scotland's game in Chisinau in the qualifying campaign for the 2006 World Cup was arguably their worst-ever performance. Scotland were lucky to get a draw and, according to one press report, 'played like a pub league team'.

| 2004 | 13 Oct | Chisinau | 1–1 | Thompson | Dadu |
| 2005 | 4 June | Hampden Park | 2–0 | Dailly McFadden | |

MOROCCO

Scotland have played Morocco only once, but it was the game which put a disorganised and outclassed Scotland out of the 1998 World Cup.

| 1998 | 23 June | St Etienne | 0–3 | | Bassir (2) Hadda |

NEW ZEALAND

Scotland have played New Zealand twice, with a win at the 1982 World Cup finals and a draw during the Berti Vogts era.

| 1982 | 15 June | Malaga | 5–2 | Wark (2) Dalglish Archibald Robertson | Sumner Wooddin |
| 2003 | 27 May | Tynecastle | 1–1 | Crawford | Nelsen |

NIGERIA

Known as 'The Super Eagles', Nigeria reached the round of sixteen at both the 1994 and 1998 World Cup finals. They played Scotland as part of their preparations for the 2014 World Cup finals and scored a last-minute equaliser against Gordon Strachan's men.

| 2002 | 17 Apr | Pittodrie | 1–2 | Dailly | Aghahowa (2) |
| 2014 | 28 May | Craven Cottage | 2–2 | Mulgrew Egwuekwe o.g. | Uchebo Nwofor |

NORTHERN IRELAND

See IRELAND. Northern Ireland's governing body is the Irish Football Association (IFA), which is not to be confused with the Republic's Football Association of Ireland (FAI). The southern part of Ireland broke away from the IFA in 1921, and Scotland's fixture in February of that year was the last occasion on which Scotland played a team that represented the whole of Ireland. From 1922 onwards, games that are listed against 'Ireland' refer to games against Northern Ireland.

Andy Cunningham of Rangers scored against the Irish when Scotland won 4–0 at Ibrox in 1926. Hughie Gallacher scored a hat-trick

Billy Steel scored four goals when Scotland won 6–1 at Hampden Park in 1950

The Scotland team that beat Ireland 3–1 at Ibrox in September 1931. Observe the players' use of their club socks!

NORWAY

Norway were Scotland's first overseas opponents in 1929 and in total there have been nine wins, six draws and three defeats. The 1998 match was one of Scotland's three games at the World Cup finals in France.

1929	28 May	Bergen	7–3	Cheyne (3) Nisbet (2) Rankin Craig	Kongsvik (2) Berg-Johannesen
1954	5 May	Hampden Park	1–0	Hamilton	
1954	19 May	Oslo	1–1	Mackenzie	Kure
1963	4 June	Bergen	3–4	Law (3)	Nilsen Johansen Pedersen Krogh
1963	7 Nov	Hampden Park	6–1	Law (4) Mackay (2)	Kristoffersen
1974	6 June	Oslo	2–1	Jordan Dalglish	Lund
1978	25 Oct	Hampden Park	3–2	Dalglish (2) Gemmill (pen)	Aas Larsen-Okland
1979	7 June	Oslo	4–0	Jordan Dalglish Robertson McQueen	
1988	14 Sep	Oslo	2–1	McStay Johnston	Fjortoft
1989	15 Nov	Hampden Park	1–1	McCoist	Johnsen
1992	3 June	Oslo	0–0		
1998	16 June	Bordeaux	1–1	Burley	Flo
2003	20 Aug	Oslo	0–0		
2004	9 Oct	Hampden Park	0–1		Iversen (pen)
2005	7 Sep	Oslo	2–1	Miller (2)	Arst
2008	11 Oct	Hampden Park	0–0		
2009	12 Aug	Oslo	0–4		J. A. Riise Pedersen (2) Huseklepp
2013	19 Nov	Molde	1–0	Brown	

PARAGUAY

This landlocked country is surrounded by Argentina, Bolivia and Brazil; Scotland have played Paraguay once, in the World Cup finals of 1958 in Sweden.

1958	11 June	Norrkoping	2–3	Mudie Collins	Aguero Re Parodi

PERU

In a game considered to be pivotal in Scottish football history, Scotland lost to Peru in the first game of the Argentina World Cup of 1978. There has also been one victory and one draw.

1972	26 Apr	Hampden Park	2–0	O'Hare Law	
1978	3 June	Cordoba	1–3	Jordan	Cubillas (2) Cueto
1979	12 Sep	Hampden Park	1–1	Hartford	Leguia

POLAND

Scotland does not enjoy a good record against Poland, with two victories and three draws in eight games, and the 2–1 defeat in 1965 was particularly disappointing. This was a key match in the qualifying campaign for the 1966 World Cup finals and Scotland were in front for most of the game – only to concede two goals in the last ten minutes.

1958	1 June	Warsaw	2–1	Collins (2)	Cieslik
1960	4 June	Hampden Park	2–3	Law St John	Baszkiewicz Brychczy Pol
1965	23 May	Chorzow	1–1	Law	Lentner
1965	13 Oct	Hampden Park	1–2	McNeill	Liberda Sadek
1980	28 May	Poznan	0–1		Boniek
1990	19 May	Hampden Park	1–1	Johnston	Gillespie o.g.
2001	25 April	Bydgoszcz	1–1	Booth (pen)	Kaluzny
2014	14 Oct	Warsaw			
2015	8 Oct	Hampden Park			

PORTUGAL

Scotland and Portugal were drawn together in the qualifying groups for the 1972 and 1980 European Championships, when Scotland won both home games and twice lost away. They were in the same World Cup qualifying group for both the 1982 and 1994 finals, but Scotland failed to win any of these four matches. Scotland's overall record against Portugal is played fourteen, won four, drawn three, and lost seven:

1950	21 May	Lisbon	2–2	Bauld Brown	Travacos Albano
1955	4 May	Hampden Park	3–0	Gemmell Liddell Reilly	
1959	3 June	Lisbon	0–1		Matateu
1966	18 June	Hampden Park	0–1		Torres
1971	21 April	Lisbon	0–2		Stanton o.g. Eusebio
1971	13 Oct	Hampden Park	2–1	O'Hare Gemmill	Rodrigues
1975	13 May	Hampden Park	1–0	Artur o.g.	
1978	29 Nov	Lisbon	0–1		Alberto
1980	26 Mar	Hampden Park	4–1	Dalglish Gray Archibald Gemmill	Gomes
1980	15 Oct	Hampden Park	0–0		
1981	18 Nov	Lisbon	1–2	Sturrock	Fernandes (2)
1992	14 Oct	Ibrox	0–0		
1993	28 April	Lisbon	0–5		Barros (2) Cadete (2) Futre
2002	20 Nov	Braga	0–2		Pauleta (2)

ROMANIA

Romania has a coastline on the Black Sea and borders Bulgaria, Hungary, Moldova, Serbia and Ukraine. Scotland's matches are all square – played six, won two, drawn two, lost two, with home advantage being significant:

1975	1 June	Bucharest	1–1	McQueen	Georgescu
1975	17 Dec	Hampden Park	1–1	Rioch	Crisan

1986	26 Mar	Hampden Park	3–0	Strachan Gough Aitken	
1990	12 Sep	Hampden Park	2–1	Robertson McCoist	Camataru
1991	16 Oct	Bucharest	0–1		Hagi (pen)
2004	31 Mar	Hampden Park	1–2	McFadden	Chivu Pancu

RUSSIA

Not to be confused with the USSR, which broke up at the end of 1991, or the CIS (Commonwealth of Independent States) that briefly followed it, the Russians have since played two draws with Scotland:

| 1994 | 16 Nov | Hampden Park | 1–1 | Booth | Radchenko |
| 1995 | 29 Mar | Moscow | 0–0 | | |

SAN MARINO

Scotland have played the tiny San Marino six times and has won them all, with San Marino yet to score a goal. Scotland will be hoping that they draw them in every competition!

1991	1 May	Serravalle	2–0	Strachan (pen) Durie	
1991	13 Nov	Hampden Park	4–0	McStay Gough Durie McCoist	
1995	26 Apr	Serravalle	2–0	Collins Calderwood	
1995	15 Nov	Hampden Park	5–0	Jess Booth McCoist Nevin Francini o.g.	
2000	7 Oct	Serravalle	2–0	Elliott Hutchison	
2001	28 Mar	Hampden Park	4–0	Hendry (2) Dodds Cameron	

SAUDI ARABIA

Saudi Arabia comprises about 80 per cent of the Arabian Peninsula, and oil extraction has brought it great wealth. When Scotland played a friendly there in 1988, Maurice Johnston (Nantes) and John Collins (Hibernian) were the scorers.

1988	17 Feb	Riyadh	2–2	Johnston Collins	Jazaa Majed

SLOVENIA

Slovenia were the side responsible for getting Scotland's World Cup bid off to a disappointing start in 2004, but Scotland (typically, perhaps) finished off in style once the damage was done, and there was no longer any possibility of qualification for the 2006 finals.

2004	8 Sep	Hampden Park	0–0		
2005	12 Oct	Celje	3–0	Fletcher McFadden Hartley	
2012	29 Feb	Kopar	1–1	Berra	Kirm

SOUTH AFRICA

Scotland have played South Africa twice since its apartheid era came to an end and the country was no longer isolated in world sport. The first occasion was at Hong Kong's Reunification Cup in 2002 and the second was a friendly international, when Barry Robson won his first senior cap.

2002	20 May	Hong Kong	0–2		Mokoena Koumantarakis
2007	22 Aug	Pittodrie	1–0	Boyd	

SOUTH KOREA

A few weeks after this friendly international, South Korea reached the semi-finals of the World Cup – beating Italy and Spain along the way. Busan was very hot and humid, and Scotland were comprehensively beaten.

2002	16 May	Busan	1–4	Dobie	Ahn (2) Lee Yoon

SPAIN

For many years the Spanish national side under-performed on the world stage, even when Spain's clubs were achieving success in European football. But they can no longer be described as under-achievers after winning the 2008 European Championship, the 2010 World Cup, and the 2012 European Championship. Scotland beat them in 1957, 1963 and 1984, but Spain has a better record overall.

1957	8 May	Hampden Park	4–2	Mudie (3) Hewie (pen)	Kubala Suarez
1957	26 May	Madrid	1–4	Smith	Basora (2) Mateos Kubala
1963	13 June	Madrid	6–2	Law Gibson McLintock Wilson Henderson St John	Adelardo Veloso

Ian Ure played in the Scotland side, captained by Denis Law, that won 6–2 in Madrid in 1963

1965	8 May	Hampden Park	0–0		
1974	20 Nov	Hampden Park	1–2	Bremner	Castro (2)
1975	5 Feb	Valencia	1–1	Jordan	Mejido
1982	24 Feb	Valencia	0–3		Munoz Castro Gallego

1984	14 Nov	Hampden Park	3–1	Johnston (2) Dalglish	Goicoechea
1985	27 Feb	Seville	0–1		Clos
1988	27 Apr	Madrid	0–0		
2004	3 Sept	Valencia	1–1	Baraja o.g.	Raul (pen)
Match abandoned after 60 minutes due to power failure					
2010	12 Oct	Hampden Park	2–3	Naismith Pique o.g.	Villa (pen) Iniesta Llorente
2011	11 Oct	Alicante	1–3	Goodwillie (pen)	Silva (2) Villa

SWEDEN

Scotland's record against Sweden is won five, drawn one, and lost six. In 1990, Andy Roxburgh's team beat the Swedes at the World Cup finals in Italy.

1952	30 May	Stockholm	1–3	Liddell	Sandberg Lofgren Bengtsson
1953	6 May	Hampden Park	1–2	Johnstone	Lofgren Eriksson
1975	16 Apr	Gothenburg	1–1	MacDougall	Sjoberg
1977	27 Apr	Hampden Park	3–1	Hellstrom o.g. Dalglish Craig	Wendt
1980	10 Sep	Stockholm	1–0	Strachan	
1981	9 Sep	Hampden Park	2–0	Jordan Robertson (pen)	
1990	16 June	Genoa	2–1	McCall Johnston (pen)	Stromberg
1995	11 Oct	Stockholm	0–2		Pettersson Schwarz
1996	10 Nov	Ibrox	1–0	McGinlay	
1997	30 Apr	Gothenburg	1–2	Gallacher	K. Andersson (2)
2004	17 Nov	Easter Road	1–4	McFadden (pen)	Allback (2) Elmander Berglund
2010	11 Aug	Stockholm	0–3		Ibrahimovic Bajrami Toivonen

SWITZERLAND

Scotland's record against the men from Europe's most mountainous country is a good one – played fifteen, won seven, drawn three, and lost five.

1931	24 May	Geneva	3–2	Easson Boyd Love	Buche Faugel
1948	17 May	Berne	1–2	Johnston	Maillard Fatton
1950	26 Apr	Hampden Park	3–1	Bauld Campbell Brown	Antenen
1957	19 May	Basle	2–1	Mudie Collins	Vonlanthen
1957	6 Nov	Hampden Park	3–2	Robertson Mudie Scott	Riva Vonlanthen
1973	22 June	Berne	0–1		Mundschin
1976	7 Apr	Hampden Park	1–0	Pettigrew	
1982	17 Nov	Berne	0–2		Sulser Egli
1983	30 Mar	Hampden Park	2–2	Wark Nicholas	Egli Hermann
1990	17 Oct	Hampden Park	2–1	Robertson (pen) McAllister	Knup (pen)
1991	11 Sep	Berne	2–2	Durie McCoist	Chapuisat Hermann
1992	9 Sep	Berne	1–3	McCoist	Knup (2) Bregy
1993	8 Sep	Pittodrie	1–1	Collins	Bregy (pen)
1996	18 June	Villa Park	1–0	McCoist	
2006	1 Mar	Hampden Park	1–3	Miller	Barnetta Gygax Cabanas

TRINIDAD AND TOBAGO

Not famous for being footballing islands, Trinidad and Tobago have nevertheless played Scotland once. Scotland's four goals came in the first thirty-five minutes.

| 2004 | 30 May | Easter Road | 4–1 | Fletcher
Holt
G. Caldwell
Quashie | John |

TURKEY

Scotland visited Turkey for a friendly international in 1960, but Andy Beattie's side, captained by Bobby Evans, lost. In 2002 the Turks finished in third place at the World Cup finals.

1960	8 June	Ankara	2–4	Caldow (pen) Young	Lefter (2) Metin Senol

UKRAINE

A former republic of the Soviet Union, Ukraine has a coastline on the northern shore of the Black Sea and shares a land border with seven other countries. It gained its independence in 1991 and Scotland played twice against this country in the qualification section for Euro 2008.

2006	11 Oct	Kiev	0–2		Kucher Shevchenko (pen)
2007	13 Oct	Hampden Park	3–1	Miller McCulloch McFadden	Shevchenko

URUGUAY

Uruguay delivered one of the biggest shocks of all time to the Scottish system with their 7–0 victory in the 1954 World Cup in Switzerland. In a subsequent World Cup (1986) they produced a shock of a different kind with their cynical approach to the game. Played four, won one, drawn one and lost two.

1954	19 June	Basle	0–7		Borges (3) Miguez (2) Abbadie (2)
1962	2 May	Hampden Park	2–3	Baxter Brand	Cubilla (2) Sacia
1983	21 Sep	Hampden Park	2–0	Robertson (pen) Dodds	
1986	13 June	Nezahualcoyotl	0–0		

USA

Comparative newcomers to the football scene (although they famously beat England in the World Cup of 1950), the USA are now respected opponents. Played seven, won two, drawn three, and lost two. Matt Phillips of Blackpool made his international debut in the 2012 friendly, whilst Gordon Greer and Gary Mackay-Steven were awarded a first cap in the following year's friendly international.

Gordon Smith of Hibernian was in the Scotland side that beat the USA 6–0 at Hampden Park in 1952. His team-mate Lawrie Reilly scored a hat-trick

1952	30 Apr	Hampden Park	6–0	Reilly (3) McMillan (2) O'Connell o.g.	
1992	17 May	Denver	1–0	Nevin	
1996	26 May	New Britain	1–2	Durie	Wynalda (pen) Jones
1998	30 May	Washington	0–0		
2005	11 Nov	Hampden Park	1–1	Webster	Wolff (pen)
2012	26 May	Jacksonville	1–5	Cameron o.g.	Donovan (3) Bradley Jones
2013	15 Nov	Hampden Park	0–0		

USSR

Scotland never beat the USSR in the four times that they met, and now they will never have an opportunity to do so, as the USSR is no more. The best result was a draw in Malaga, which effectively put Scotland out of the 1982 World Cup in Spain. Scotland did beat a team called the

Commonwealth of Independent States in the European Championships in Sweden in 1992. This team was effectively the USSR, but for political reasons could no longer be so called. Played four, drawn one, and lost three.

1967	10 May	Hampden Park	0–2		Gemmell o.g. Medved
1971	14 June	Moscow	0–1		Yevryuzhikhin
1982	22 June	Malaga	2–2	Jordan Souness	Chivadze Shengalia
1991	6 Feb	Ibrox	0–1		Kuznetsov

WALES

Scotland played Wales annually in the Home International Championship from 1876 until 1985. Sometimes Scotland fielded teams which they would not necessarily have fielded against England, but this practice stopped once Wales began to improve as a team in the Edwardian era. The defeat by Wales at Tynecastle in 1906 in particular was a major shock to the Scottish national psyche, and marked the end of Scotland fielding a 'reserve team' against Wales. Some of the fixtures were World Cup or European Championship qualifying games, including the famous game in 1977 when Scotland qualified for Argentina at Anfield, and the time in 1985 when they earned a play-off for Mexico. Tragically this was the night that Jock Stein collapsed and died. After Scotland's Nations Cup victory against Wales in May 2011, the record book showed Scotland sixty-one victories, Wales twenty-three, and twenty-three draws.

1876	25 Mar	Hamilton Crescent	4–0	Ferguson Lang MacKinnon H. McNeil	
1877	5 Mar	Wrexham	2–0	Campbell Evans o.g.	
1878	23 Mar	1st Hampden Park	9–0	Campbell (2) Weir (2) Ferguson (2) Baird Watson Lang	
1879	7 April	Wrexham	3–0	Smith (2) Campbell	
1880	27 Mar	1st Hampden Park	5–1	Davidson Beveridge Lindsay McAdam Campbell	W. Roberts

1881	14 Mar	Wrexham	5–1	Ker (2) McNeil Bell o.g. Morgan o.g.	Crosse
1882	25 Mar	1st Hampden Park	5–0	Fraser (2) Kay Ker McAulay	
1883	12 Mar	Wrexham	3–0	Smith Fraser Anderson	
1884	29 Mar	Cathkin Park	4–1	Lindsay Shaw Kay Ker	R. Roberts
1885	23 Mar	Wrexham	8–1	Lindsay (3) Calderwood (2) Anderson (2) Allan	R. Jones
1886	10 April	2nd Hampden Park	4–1	McCormack McCall Allan Harrower	Vaughan
1887	21 Mar	Wrexham	2–0	Robertson Allan	
1888	10 Mar	Easter Road	5–1	Latta (2) Paul Munro Groves	J. Doughty
1889	15 April	Wrexham	0–0		
1890	22 Mar	Underwood, Paisley	5–0	Paul (4) Wilson	
1891	21 Mar	Wrexham	4–3	Boyd (2) Logan Buchanan	Bowdler (2) Owen
1892	26 Mar	Tynecastle	6–1	Hamilton (2) McPherson (2) Thomson Baird	B. Lewis
1893	18 Mar	Wrexham	8–0	Madden (4) Barker (3) Lambie	
1894	24 Mar	Rugby Park	5–2	Berry Barker Chambers Alexander Johnstone	Morris (2)

WALES—*contd*					
1895	23 Mar	Wrexham	2–2	Madden Divers	W. Lewis Chapman
1896	21 Mar	Carolina Port, Dundee	4–0	Neil (2) Keillor Paton	
1897	20 Mar	Wrexham	2–2	Ritchie (pen) Walker	Morgan-Owen Pugh
1898	19 Mar	Fir Park	5–2	Gillespie (3) McKie (2)	Thomas Morgan-Owen
1899	18 Mar	Wrexham	6–0	McColl (3) Campbell (2) Marshall	
1900	3 Feb	Pittodrie	5–2	Wilson (2) Bell Hamilton A. Smith	Parry Butler
1901	2 Mar	Wrexham	1–1	Robertson	T. Parry
1902	15 Mar	Cappielow	5–1	Smith (3) Buick Drummond	Morgan-Owen
1903	9 Mar	Cardiff	1–0	Speedie	
1904	12 Mar	Dens Park	1–1	R. Walker	Atherton
1905	6 Mar	Wrexham	1–3	Robertson	Watkins A. Morris Meredith

*Neil Gibson of Rangers played in the Scotland
team that won 6–0 at Wrexham in 1899. Robert
McColl scored a hat-trick in this match*

1906	3 Mar	Tynecastle	0–2		W. Jones J. Jones
1907	4 Mar	Wrexham	0–1		A. Morris
1908	7 Mar	Dens Park	2–1	Bennett Lennie	Jones
1909	1 Mar	Wrexham	2–3	Walker Paul	Davies (2) Jones
1910	5 Mar	Rugby Park	1–0	Devine	
1911	6 Mar	Cardiff	2–2	Hamilton (2)	A. Morris (2)
1912	2 Mar	Tynecastle	1–0	Quinn	
1913	3 Mar	Wrexham	0–0		
1914	28 Feb	Celtic Park	0–0		
1920	26 Feb	Cardiff	1–1	Cairns	Evans
1921	12 Feb	Pittodrie	2–1	Wilson (2)	Collier
1922	4 Feb	Wrexham	1–2	Archibald	L. Davies S. Davies
1923	17 Mar	Love Street	2–0	Wilson (2)	
1924	16 Feb	Cardiff	0–2		W. Davies L. Davies
1925	14 Feb	Tynecastle	3–1	Gallacher (2) Meiklejohn	Williams
1925	31 Oct	Cardiff	3–0	Duncan McLean Clunas	
1926	30 Oct	Ibrox	3–0	Jackson (2) Gallacher	
1927	29 Oct	Wrexham	2–2	Gallacher Hutton	Curtis Gibson o.g.
1928	27 Oct	Ibrox	4–2	Gallacher (3) Dunn	W. Davies (2)
1929	26 Oct	Cardiff	4–2	Gallacher (2) James Gibson	O'Callaghan L. Davies
1930	25 Oct	Ibrox	1–1	Battles	Bamford
1931	31 Oct	Wrexham	3–2	Stevenson Thomson McGrory	Curtis O'Callaghan
1932	26 Oct	Tynecastle	2–5	Dewar Duncan	O'Callaghan (2) Griffiths Astley J. Thomson o.g.

WALES—*contd*					
1933	4 Oct	Cardiff	2–3	McFadyen Duncan	Evans Robbins Astley
1934	21 Nov	Pittodrie	3–2	Napier (2) Duncan	Phillips Astley
1935	5 Oct	Cardiff	1–1	Duncan	Phillips
1936	2 Dec	Dens Park	1–2	Walker	Glover (2)
1937	30 Oct	Cardiff	1–2	Massie	B. Jones Morris
1938	9 Nov	Tynecastle	3–2	Walker (2) Gillick	Astley L. Jones
1946	19 Oct	Wrexham	1–3	Waddell (pen)	B. Jones Ford Stephen o.g.
1947	12 Nov	Hampden Park	1–2	McLaren	Ford Lowrie
1948	23 Oct	Cardiff	3–1	Waddell (2) Howie	B. Jones
1949	9 Nov	Hampden Park	2–0	McPhail Linwood	
1950	21 Oct	Cardiff	3–1	Reilly (2) Waddell	A. Powell
1951	14 Nov	Hampden Park	0–1		Allchurch
1952	18 Oct	Cardiff	2–1	Brown Liddell	Ford
1953	4 Nov	Hampden Park	3–3	Brown Johnstone Reilly	Charles (2) Allchurch
1954	16 Oct	Cardiff	1–0	Buckley	
1955	9 Nov	Hampden Park	2–0	Johnstone (2)	
1956	20 Oct	Cardiff	2–2	Fernie Reilly	Ford Medwin
1957	13 Nov	Hampden Park	1–1	Collins	Medwin
1958	18 Oct	Cardiff	3–0	Leggat Law Collins	
1959	4 Nov	Hampden Park	1–1	Leggat	Charles
1960	22 Oct	Cardiff	0–2		Jones Vernon
1961	8 Nov	Hampden Park	2–0	St John (2)	

Action from Scotland v Wales at Hampden Park in 1959. Scotland's Graham Leggat, in the centre of the photograph, scored Scotland's goal in a 1–1 draw

1962	20 Oct	Cardiff	3–2	Caldow Law Henderson	Allchurch Charles
1963	20 Nov	Hampden Park	2–1	White Law	B. Jones
1964	3 Oct	Cardiff	2–3	Chalmers Gibson	Leek (2) Davies
1965	24 Nov	Hampden Park	4–1	Murdoch (2) Henderson Greig	Allchurch
1966	22 Oct	Cardiff	1–1	Law	R. Davies
1967	22 Nov	Hampden Park	3–2	Gilzean (2) McKinnon	R. Davies Durban
1969	3 May	Wrexham	5–3	McNeill Stein Gilzean Bremner McLean	R. Davies (2) Toshack
1970	22 April	Hampden Park	0–0		
1971	15 May	Cardiff	0–0		
1972	24 May	Hampden Park	1–0	Lorimer	
1973	12 May	Wrexham	2–0	Graham (2)	
1974	14 May	Hampden Park	2–0	Dalglish Jardine (pen)	

WALES—*contd*

1975	17 May	Cardiff	2–2	Jackson Rioch	Toshack Flynn
1976	6 May	Hampden Park	3–1	Pettigrew Rioch Gray	Griffiths (pen)
1976	17 Nov	Hampden Park	1–0	Evans o.g.	
1977	28 May	Wrexham	0–0		
1977	12 Oct	Anfield, Liverpool	2–0	Masson (pen) Dalglish	
1978	17 May	Hampden Park	1–1	Johnstone	Donachie o.g.
1979	19 May	Cardiff	0–3		Toshack (3)
1980	21 May	Hampden Park	1–0	Miller	
1981	16 May	Swansea	0–2		Walsh (2)
1982	24 May	Hampden Park	1–0	Hartford	
1983	28 May	Cardiff	2–0	A. Gray Brazil	
1984	28 Feb	Hampden Park	2–1	Cooper (pen) Johnston	James
1985	27 Mar	Hampden Park	0–1		Rush
1985	10 Sept	Cardiff	1–1	Cooper (pen)	Hughes
1997	27 May	Rugby Park	0–1		Hartson
2004	18 Feb	Cardiff	0–4		Earnshaw (3) Taylor
2009	14 Nov	Cardiff	0–3		Edwards Church Ramsey
2011	25 May	Dublin	3–1	Morrison Miller Berra	Earnshaw
2012	12 Oct	Cardiff	1–2	Morrison	Bale (2) (1 pen)
2013	22 Mar	Hampden Park	1–2	Hanley	Ramsey (pen) Robson-Kanu

Standing room only for the vast Hampden Park crowd, with over 110,000
attending this fixture against England in the 1920s

YUGOSLAVIA

Scotland played the former Socialist Federal Republic of Yugoslavia eight times before the country began to break up in the early 1990s. They won two, drew five and lost only once.

1955	15 May	Belgrade	2–2	Reilly Smith	Veselinovic Vukas
1956	21 Nov	Hampden Park	2–0	Mudie Baird	
1958	8 June	Vasteras	1–1	Murray	Petakovic
1972	29 June	Belo Horizonte (Brazil)	2–2	Macari (2)	Bajevic Jerkovic
1974	22 June	Frankfurt	1–1	Jordan	Karasi
1984	12 Sep	Hampden Park	6–1	Cooper Souness Dalglish Sturrock Johnston Nicholas	Vokri
1988	19 Oct	Hampden Park	1–1	Johnston	Katanec
1989	6 Sep	Zagreb	1–3	Durie	Katanec Nicol o.g. Gillespie o.g.

ZAIRE

When Scotland played Zaire at the World Cup finals of 1974, beating them 2–0, it was Scotland's first-ever win at a World Cup finals tournament. The country is now known as the Democratic Republic of the Congo.

1974	14 June	Dortmund	2–0	Lorimer Jordan	

Danny McGrain and Kenny Dalglish celebrate with the Home International Championship trophy in 1976

THE MEN WHO HAVE PLAYED FOR SCOTLAND

A - International Appearances for Scotland
B - Goals Scored for Scotland

Last Match Included	
Nigeria v Scotland	28 May 2014

			A	B	
ADAM	Charlie	Rangers Blackpool Liverpool Stoke City	25	0	2007–2014
ADAMS	James	Hearts	3	0	1889–1893
AGNEW	William	Kilmarnock	3	0	1907–1908
AIRD	John	Burnley	4	0	1954
AITKEN	Andrew	Newcastle Utd. Middlesbrough Leicester Fosse	14	0	1901–1911
AITKEN	George	East Fife Sunderland	8	0	1949–1954
AITKEN	Ralph	Dumbarton	2	1	1886–1888
AITKEN	Roy	Celtic Newcastle Utd. St Mirren	57	1	1980–1992
AITKENHEAD	Walter	Blackburn Rovers	1	2	1912
ALBISTON	Arthur	Man. Utd.	14	0	1982–1986
ALEXANDER	David	East Stirlingshire	2	0	1894
ALEXANDER	Graham	Preston N E Burnley	40	0	2002–2009
ALEXANDER	Neil	Cardiff City	3	0	2006
ALLAN	David	Queen's Park	3	1	1885–1886
ALLAN	George	Liverpool	1	0	1897
ALLAN	Henry	Hearts	1	0	1902
ALLAN	John	Queen's Park	2	1	1887
ALLAN	Thomson	Dundee	2	0	1974
ANCELL	Bobby	Newcastle Utd.	2	0	1937
ANDERSON	Andrew	Hearts	23	0	1933–1939
ANDERSON	Fred	Clydesdale	1	1	1874

ANDERSON	George	Kilmarnock	1	0	1901
ANDERSON	Harry	Raith Rovers	1	0	1914
ANDERSON	John	Leicester City	1	0	1954
ANDERSON	Kenny	Queen's Park	3	0	1896–1898
ANDERSON	Russell	Aberdeen Plymouth Argyle	11	0	2003–2008
ANDERSON	William	Queen's Park	6	2	1882–1885
ANDREWS	Peter	Eastern	1	1	1875
ANYA	Ikechi	Watford	6	1	2013–2014
ARCHIBALD	Sandy	Rangers	8	1	1921–1932
ARCHIBALD	Steve	Aberdeen Tottenham H. Barcelona	27	4	1980–1986
ARMSTRONG	Matt	Aberdeen	3	0	1936–1937
ARNOT	Wattie	Queen's Park	14	0	1883–1893
AULD	Bertie	Celtic	3	0	1959–1960
AULD	John	Third Lanark	3	0	1887–1889

BAIRD	Andrew	Queen's Park	2	0	1892–1894
BAIRD*	Archie	Aberdeen			
BAIRD	David	Hearts	3	1	1890–1892
BAIRD	Hugh	Airdrie	1	0	1956
BAIRD	John	Vale of Leven	3	2	1876–1880
BAIRD	Sammy	Rangers	7	2	1957–1958
BAIRD	William	St Bernard's	1	0	1897
BANNAN	Barry	Aston Villa Crystal Palace	17	0	2010–2014
BANNON	Eamonn	Dundee Utd.	11	1	1980–1986
BARBOUR	Alexander	Renton	1	1	1885
BARDSLEY	Phil	Sunderland	13	0	2010–2014
BARKER	John	Rangers	2	4	1893–1894
BARR	Darren	Falkirk	1	0	2008
BARRETT	Francis	Dundee	2	0	1894–1895
BATTLES	Barney sr.	Celtic	3	0	1901
BATTLES	Barney jr.	Hearts	1	1	1931
BAULD	Willie	Hearts	3	2	1950

BAXTER	Jim	Rangers Sunderland	34	3	1961–1968
BAXTER	Robert	Middlesbrough	3	0	1939
BEATTIE	Andy	Preston N E	7	0	1937–1939
BEATTIE	Craig	Celtic W B A	7	1	2005–2007
BEATTIE	Robert	Preston N E	1	0	1939
BEGBIE	Isaac	Hearts	4	0	1890–1894
BELL	Alec	Man. Utd.	1	0	1912
BELL	Cammy	Kilmarnock	1	0	2010
BELL	Jack	Dumbarton Everton Celtic	10	5	1890–1900
BELL	Mark	Hearts	1	0	1901
BELL	William	Leeds United	2	0	1966
BENNETT	Alec	Celtic Rangers	11	2	1904–1913
BENNIE	Bob	Airdrieonians	3	0	1925–1926
BERNARD	Paul	Oldham Ath.	2	0	1995
BERRA	Christophe	Hearts Wolves	28	2	2008–2013
BERRY	Davidson	Queen's Park	3	1	1894–1899
BERRY	William	Queen's Park	4	0	1888–1891
BETT	Jim	Rangers Lokeren Aberdeen	25	1	1982–1990
BEVERIDGE	William	Glasgow Univ.	3	1	1879–1880
BLACK	Andrew	Hearts	3	3	1938–1939
BLACK	David	Hurlford	1	0	1889
BLACK	Eric	Metz	2	0	1988
BLACK	Ian	Southampton	1	0	1948
BLACK	Ian	Rangers	1	0	2012
BLACKBURN	John	Royal Engineers	1	0	1873
BLACKLAW	Adam	Burnley	3	0	1963–1965
BLACKLEY	John	Hibernian	7	0	1974–1977
BLAIR	Danny	Clyde Aston Villa	8	0	1929–1933

BLAIR	Jimmy	Sheffield Wed. Cardiff City	8	0	1920–1924
BLAIR	Jimmy	Blackpool	1	0	1947
BLAIR	John	Motherwell	1	0	1934
BLAIR	William	Third Lanark	1	0	1896
BLESSINGTON	Jimmy	Celtic	4	0	1894–1896
BLYTH	Jim	Coventry City	2	0	1978
BONE	Jimmy	Norwich City	2	1	1972
BOOTH	Scott	Aberdeen B. Dortmund Twente	21	6	1993–2001
BOWIE	James	Rangers	2	0	1920
BOWIE	William	Linthouse	1	0	1891
BOWMAN	Dave	Dundee United	6	0	1992–1994
BOWMAN	George	Montrose	1	0	1892
BOYD	George	Hull City	2	0	2013–2014
BOYD	James	Newcastle Utd.	1	0	1934
BOYD	Kris	Rangers Middlesbrough	18	7	2006–2010
BOYD	Robert	Mossend Swifts	2	2	1889–1891
BOYD	Tom	Motherwell Chelsea Celtic	72	1	1991–2001
BOYD	William	Clyde	2	1	1931
BRADSHAW	Tom	Bury	1	0	1928
BRAND	Ralph	Rangers	8	8	1961–1962
BRANDON	Thomas	Blackburn Rovers	1	0	1896
BRAZIL	Alan	Ipswich Town Tottenham H.	13	1	1980–1983
BRECKENRIDGE	Thomas	Hearts	1	1	1888
BREMNER	Billy	Leeds United	54	3	1965–1975
BREMNER	Des	Hibernian	1	0	1976
BRENNAN**	Frank	Newcastle Utd.	7	0	1947–1954
BRESLIN	Bernard	Hibernian	1	0	1897
BREWSTER	George	Everton	1	0	1921
BRIDCUTT	Liam	Brighton	1	0	2013
BROADFOOT	Kirk	Rangers	4	1	2008–2010

BROGAN	Jim	Celtic	4	0	1971
BROWN	Alex	Middlesbrough	1	0	1904
BROWN	Allan	East Fife Blackpool	14	6	1950–1954
BROWN	Andrew	St Mirren	2	0	1890–1891
BROWN	Bill	Dundee Tottenham H.	28	0	1958–1965
BROWN***	Bobby	Rangers	3	0	1946–1952
BROWN	George	Rangers	19	0	1931–1938
BROWN	Hugh	Partick Thistle	3	0	1946–1947
BROWN	James	Cambuslang	1	0	1890
BROWN	James	Sheffield United	1	0	1975
BROWN	John	Clyde	1	0	1938
BROWN	Robert	Dumbarton	2	0	1884
BROWN	Robert	Dumbarton	1	0	1885
BROWN	Scott	Hibernian Celtic	38	4	2005–2014
BROWNING	Johnny	Celtic	1	0	1914
BROWNLIE	Jimmy	Third Lanark	16	0	1909–1914
BROWNLIE	John	Hibernian	7	0	1971–1975
BRUCE	Daniel	Vale of Leven	1	0	1890
BRUCE	Robert	Middlesbrough	1	0	1934
BRYSON	Craig	Kilmarnock Derby County	2	0	2010–2013
BUCHAN	Martin	Aberdeen Man. Utd.	34	0	1971–1978
BUCHANAN	Jock	Rangers	2	0	1929–1930
BUCHANAN	John	Cambuslang	1	0	1889
BUCHANAN	Peter	Chelsea	1	1	1937
BUCHANAN	Robert	Abercorn	1	1	1891
BUCKLEY	Paddy	Aberdeen	3	1	1954
BUICK	Albert	Hearts	2	2	1902
BURCHILL	Mark	Celtic	6	0	1999–2000
BURKE	Chris	Rangers Birmingham City	7	2	2006–2014

BURLEY	Craig	Chelsea Celtic Derby County	46	3	1995–2002
BURLEY	George	Ipswich Town	11	0	1979–1982
BURNS	Frank	Man. Utd	1	0	1969
BURNS	Kenny	Birmingham C. Nottingham F.	20	1	1974–1981
BURNS	Tommy	Celtic	8	0	1981–1988
BUSBY	Matt	Manchester C.	1	0	1933

CAIRNS	Tommy	Rangers	8	1	1920–1925
CALDERHEAD	David	Q. Of South Wanderers	1	0	1889
CALDERWOOD	Colin	Tottenham H. Aston Villa	36	1	1995–1999
CALDERWOOD	Robert	Cartvale	3	3	1885
CALDOW	Eric	Rangers	40	4	1957–1963
CALDWELL	Gary	Newcastle Utd. Hibernian Celtic Wigan Athletic	55	2	2002–2013
CALDWELL	Steven	Newcastle Utd. Sunderland Burnley Wigan Athletic	12	0	2001–2011
CALLAGHAN	Pat	Hibernian	1	0	1900
CALLAGHAN	Willie	Dunfermline Ath.	2	0	1969–70
CAMERON	Colin	Hearts Wolves	28	2	1999–2004
CAMERON	John	Rangers	1	0	1886
CAMERON	John	Queen's Park	1	0	1896
CAMERON	John	St Mirren Chelsea	2	0	1904–1909
CAMPBELL	Charles	Queen's Park	13	1	1874–1886
CAMPBELL	Henry	Renton	1	0	1889
CAMPBELL	James	Kilmarnock	2	0	1891–1892
CAMPBELL	James	Sheffield Wed.	1	0	1913
CAMPBELL*	James	Clyde			
CAMPBELL	John	South Western	1	1	1880
CAMPBELL	John	Celtic	12	5	1893–1903

CAMPBELL	John	Rangers	4	4	1899–1901
CAMPBELL	Kenneth	Liverpool Partick Thistle	8	0	1920–1922
CAMPBELL	Peter	Rangers	2	3	1878–1879
CAMPBELL	Peter	Morton	1	0	1898
CAMPBELL	Robert	Falkirk Chelsea	5	1	1947–1950
CAMPBELL**	William	Morton	4	0	1946–1948
CANERO	Peter	Leicester City	1	0	2004
CARABINE	Jimmy	Third Lanark	3	0	1938–1939
CARR	Willie	Coventry	6	0	1970–1972
CASSIDY	Joe	Celtic	4	1	1921–1924
CHALMERS	Steve	Celtic	5	3	1964–1966
CHALMERS	William	Rangers	1	0	1885
CHALMERS	William	Queen's Park	1	0	1929
CHAMBERS	Thomas	Hearts	1	1	1894
CHAPLIN	George	Dundee	1	0	1908
CHEYNE	Alec	Aberdeen	5	4	1929–1930
CHRISTIE	Alec	Queen's Park	3	1	1898–1899
CHRISTIE	Robert	Queen's Park	1	0	1884
CLARK	Bobby	Aberdeen	17	0	1967–1973
CLARK	John	Celtic	4	0	1966–1967
CLARKE	Steve	Chelsea	6	0	1987–1994
CLARKSON	David	Motherwell	2	1	2008
CLELAND	James	Royal Albert	1	0	1891
CLEMENTS	Robert	Leith Athletic	1	0	1891
CLUNAS	William	Sunderland	2	1	1924–1926
COLLIER	Will	Raith Rovers	1	0	1922
COLLINS	Bobby	Celtic Everton Leeds United	31	10	1950–1965
COLLINS	John	Hibernian Celtic Monaco Everton	58	12	1988–1999
COLLINS	Thomas	Hearts	1	0	1909

COLMAN	Donald	Aberdeen	4	0	1911–1913
COLQUHOUN	Eddie	Sheffield Utd.	9	0	1971–1973
COLQUHOUN	John	Hearts	2	0	1988
COMBE	James	Hibernian	3	1	1948
COMMONS	Kris	Derby County Celtic	12	2	2008–2013
CONN	Alfie jr.	Tottenham H.	2	0	1975
CONN	Alfie sr.	Hearts	1	1	1956
CONNACHAN	Eddie	Dunfermline Ath.	2	0	1961–1962
CONNELLY	George	Celtic	2	0	1973
CONNOLLY	John	Everton	1	0	1973
CONNOR	James	Airdrieonians	1	0	1886
CONNOR	James	Sunderland	4	0	1930–1934
CONNOR	Robert	Dundee Aberdeen	4	0	1986–1990
CONWAY	Craig	Dundee United Cardiff City Brighton	7	0	2009–2013
COOK	Willie	Everton	3	0	1934
COOKE	Charlie	Dundee Chelsea	16	0	1965–1975
COOPER	Davie	Rangers Motherwell	22	6	1979–1990
CORMACK	Peter	Hibernian Nottingham F.	9	0	1966–1971
COWAN	James	Aston Villa	3	0	1896–1898
COWAN	James	Morton	25	0	1948–1952
COWAN	William	Newcastle Utd.	1	1	1924
COWIE	Don	Watford Cardiff City	10	0	2009–2012
COWIE	Doug	Dundee	20	0	1953–1958
COX	Sammy	Rangers	24	0	1948–1954
CRAIG	Allan	Motherwell	3	0	1929–1932
CRAIG	Jim	Celtic	1	0	1967
CRAIG	Joe	Celtic	1	1	1977
CRAIG	Tom	Rangers	8	1	1927–1930
CRAIG	Tommy	Newcastle Utd.	1	0	1976

CRAINEY	Stephen	Celtic Southampton Blackpool	12	0	2002–2011
CRAPNELL	James	Airdrieonians	9	0	1929–1932
CRAWFORD	David	St Mirren Rangers	3	0	1894–1900
CRAWFORD	James	Queen's Park	5	0	1931–1933
CRAWFORD	Steve	Raith Rovers Dunfermline Plymouth Arg.	25	4	1995–2004
CRERAND	Pat	Celtic Man. Utd.	16	0	1961–1965
CRINGAN	Willie	Celtic	5	0	1920–1923
CROAL	James	Falkirk	3	0	1913–1914
CROPLEY	Alex	Hibernian	2	0	1971
CROSBIE	James	Ayr United Birmingham	2	0	1920–1922
CROSS	John	Third Lanark	1	0	1903
CRUICKSHANK	Jim	Hearts	6	0	1964–1975
CRUM	Johnny	Celtic	2	0	1936–1938
CULLEN	Michael	Luton Town	1	0	1956
CUMMING	David	Middlesbrough	1	0	1938
CUMMING	John	Hearts	9	0	1954–1960
CUMMINGS	George	Partick Thistle Aston Villa	9	0	1935–1939
CUMMINGS	Warren	Chelsea	1	0	2002
CUNNINGHAM	Andy	Rangers	12	5	1920–1927
CUNNINGHAM	Willie	Preston N E	8	0	1954–1955
CURRAN	Hugh	Wolves	5	1	1969–1971

DAILLY	Christian	Derby County Blackburn R. West Ham Utd. Rangers	67	6	1997–2008
DALGLISH	Kenny	Celtic Liverpool	102	30	1971–1986
DAVIDSON	Callum	Blackburn R. Leicester City Burnley	19	0	1998–2009
DAVIDSON	David	Queen's Park	5	1	1878–1881

DAVIDSON	Jimmy	Partick Thistle	8	1	1954–1955
DAVIDSON	Murray	St Johnstone	1	0	2012
DAVIDSON	Stewart	Middlesbrough	1	0	1921
DAWSON	Ally	Rangers	5	0	1980–1983
DAWSON	Jerry	Rangers	14	0	1934–1939
DEAKIN*	John	St Mirren			
DEANS	Dixie	Celtic	2	0	1974
DELANEY***	Jimmy	Celtic Man. Utd.	13	3	1935–1948
DEVINE	Andrew	Falkirk	1	1	1910
DEVLIN	Paul	Birmingham C.	10	0	2002–2003
DEWAR	George	Dumbarton	2	1	1888–1889
DEWAR	Neil	Third Lanark	3	4	1932
DICK	John	West Ham U.	1	0	1959
DICKIE	Matthew	Rangers	3	0	1897–1900
DICKOV	Paul	Manchester C. Leicester City Blackburn R.	10	1	2000–2004
DICKSON	William	Dundee Strathmore	1	4	1888
DICKSON	Willie	Kilmarnock	5	0	1970–1971
DIVERS	John	Celtic	1	1	1895
DIVERS	John	Celtic	1	0	1938
DIXON	Paul	Huddersfield T.	3	0	2012
DOBIE	Scott	W B A	6	1	2002
DOCHERTY	Tommy	Preston N E Arsenal	25	1	1951–1959
DODDS	Billy	Aberdeen Dundee Utd. Rangers	26	7	1996–2001
DODDS	Davie	Dundee Utd.	2	1	1983
DODDS	Joe	Celtic	3	0	1914
DOIG	Ned	Arbroath Sunderland	5	0	1887–1903
DONACHIE	Willie	Manchester C.	35	0	1972–1978
DONALDSON	Alex	Bolton Wandrs.	6	1	1914–1922
DONNACHIE	Joe	Oldham Ath.	3	1	1913–1914
DONNELLY	Simon	Celtic	10	0	1997–1998

DORRANS	Graham	W B A	10	0	2009–2013
DOUGALL	Cornelius	Birmingham C.	1	0	1946
DOUGALL	Jimmy	Preston N E	1	1	1939
DOUGAN	Bobby	Hearts	1	0	1950
DOUGLAS	Angus	Chelsea	1	0	1911
DOUGLAS	James	Renfrew	1	0	1880
DOUGLAS	Rab	Celtic	19	0	2002–2005
DOWDS	Peter	Celtic	1	0	1892
DOWNIE	Robert	Third Lanark	1	0	1892
DOYLE	Dan	Celtic	8	0	1892–1898
DOYLE	Johnny	Ayr United	1	0	1975
DRUMMOND	John	Falkirk Rangers	14	1	1892–1903
DUNBAR	Mick	Cartvale	1	1	1886
DUNCAN	Arthur	Hibernian	6	0	1975
DUNCAN	David	East Fife	3	1	1948
DUNCAN	Dally	Derby County	14	7	1932–1937
DUNCAN	James	Alexandra A.	2	0	1878–1882
DUNCAN	John	Leicester City	1	1	1925
DUNCANSON	Jimmy	Rangers	1	0	1946
DUNLOP	Jimmy	St Mirren	1	0	1890
DUNLOP	Willie	Liverpool	1	0	1906
DUNN	Jimmy	Hibernian Everton	6	2	1925–1928
DURIE	Gordon	Chelsea Tottenham H. Rangers	43	7	1987–1998
DURRANT	Ian	Rangers Kilmarnock	20	0	1987–2000
DYKES	James	Hearts	2	0	1938

EASSON	James	Portsmouth	3	1	1931–1933
ELLIOTT	Matt	Leicester City	18	1	1997–2001
ELLIS	James	Mossend Swifts	1	1	1892
EVANS	Allan	Aston Villa	4	0	1982
EVANS	Bobby	Celtic Chelsea	48	0	1948–1960

EWART	Jock	Bradford City	1	0	1921
EWING	Tommy	Partick Thistle	2	0	1957–1958

FARM	George	Blackpool	10	0	1952–1959
FERGUSON	Barry	Rangers Blackburn R. Rangers	45	3	1998–2009
FERGUSON	Bobby	Kilmarnock	7	0	1965–1966
FERGUSON	Derek	Rangers	2	0	1988
FERGUSON	Duncan	Dundee Utd. Everton	7	0	1992–1997
FERGUSON	Ian	Rangers	9	0	1988–1997
FERGUSON	John	Vale of Leven	6	5	1874–1878
FERNIE	Willie	Celtic	12	1	1954–1958
FINDLAY	Robert	Kilmarnock	1	0	1898
FITCHIE	Tommy	Arsenal Queen's Park	4	1	1905–1907
FLAVELL	Robert	Airdrieonians	2	2	1947
FLECK	Robert	Norwich City	4	0	1990–1991
FLEMING	Charlie	East Fife	1	2	1953
FLEMING	James	Rangers	3	3	1929–1930
FLEMING	Robert	Morton	1	0	1886
FLETCHER	Darren	Man. Utd.	62	5	2003–2014
FLETCHER	Steven	Hibernian Burnley Wolves Sunderland	14	1	2008–2014
FORBES	Alex	Sheffield Utd Arsenal	14	1	1947–1952
FORBES	John	Vale of Leven	5	0	1884–1887
FORD	Donald	Hearts	3	0	1973–1974
FORREST	James	Celtic	9	0	2011–2013
FORREST	James	Motherwell	1	0	1958
FORREST	Jim	Rangers Aberdeen	5	0	1965–1971
FORSYTH	Alex	Partick Thistle Man. Utd.	10	0	1972–1975
FORSYTH	Campbell	Kilmarnock	4	0	1964
FORSYTH	Craig	Derby County	1	0	2014

FORSYTH	Tom	Motherwell Rangers	22	0	1971–1978
FOX	Danny	Celtic Southampton	4	0	2009–2012
FOYERS	Robert	St Bernard's	2	0	1893–1894
FRASER	Douglas	W B A	2	0	1968
FRASER	J ?	Moffat	1	0	1891
FRASER	John	Dundee	1	0	1907
FRASER	Malcolm	Queen's Park	5	0	1880–1883
FRASER	William	Sunderland	2	0	1954
FREEDMAN	Dougie	Crystal Palace	2	1	2001–2002
FULTON	William	Abercorn	1	0	1884
FYFE	John	Third Lanark	1	0	1895

GABRIEL	Jimmy	Everton	2	0	1960–1963
GALLACHER	Hughie	Airdrieonians Newcastle Utd. Chelsea Derby County	20	24	1924–1935
GALLACHER	Kevin	Dundee Utd. Coventry City Blackburn R. Newcastle Utd.	53	9	1988–2001
GALLACHER	Patrick	Sunderland	1	1	1934
GALLACHER	Paul	Dundee Utd.	8	0	2002–2004
GALLAGHER	Paul	Blackburn R.	1	0	2004
GALLOWAY	Mike	Celtic	1	0	1991
GALT	Jimmy	Rangers	2	1	1908
GARDINER	James	Motherwell	1	0	1957
GARDNER	David	Third Lanark	1	0	1897
GARDNER	Robert	Queen's Park Clydesdale	5	0	1872–1878
GEMMELL	Tommy	St Mirren	2	1	1955
GEMMELL	Tommy	Celtic	18	1	1966–1971
GEMMILL	Archie	Derby County Nottingham F. Birmingham C.	43	8	1971–1981
GEMMILL	Scot	Nottingham F. Everton	26	1	1995–2003

GIBB	William	Clydesdale	1	1	1873
GIBSON	David	Leicester City	7	3	1963–1964
GIBSON	James	Partick Thistle Aston Villa	8	1	1926–1930
GIBSON	Neil	Rangers Partick Thistle	14	1	1895–1905
GILCHRIST	Johnny	Celtic	1	0	1922
GILHOOLEY	Michael	Hull City	1	0	1922
GILKS	Matt	Blackpool	3	0	2012–2013
GILLESPIE	Gary	Liverpool	13	0	1987–1990
GILLESPIE	George	Rangers Queen's Park	7	0	1880–1891
GILLESPIE	James	Third Lanark	1	3	1898
GILLESPIE	John	Queen's Park	1	0	1896
GILLESPIE	Robert	Queen's Park	4	0	1926–1933
GILLICK	Torry	Everton	5	3	1937–1938
GILMOUR	John	Dundee	1	0	1930
GILZEAN	Alan	Dundee Tottenham H.	22	12	1963–1971
GLASS	Stephen	Newcastle U.	1	0	1998
GLAVIN	Ronnie	Celtic	1	0	1977
GLEN	Archie	Aberdeen	2	0	1955–1956
GLEN	Robert	Renton Hibernian	3	0	1895–1900
GOODWILLIE	David	Dundee United Blackburn R.	3	1	2010–2011
GORAM	Andy	Oldham Ath. Hibernian Rangers	43	0	1985–1998
GORDON	Craig	Hearts Sunderland	40	0	2004–2010
GORDON	Jimmy	Rangers	10	0	1912–1920
GOSSLAND	James	Rangers	1	2	1884
GOUDIE	John	Abercorn	1	1	1884
GOUGH	Richard	Dundee Utd. Tottenham H. Rangers	61	6	1983–1993
GOULD	Jonathan	Celtic	2	0	1999–2000

GOURLAY	Jimmy	Cambuslang	2	1	1886–1888
GOVAN	John	Hibernian	6	0	1947–1948
GOW	Donald	Rangers	1	0	1888
GOW	John J	Queen's Park	1	0	1885
GOW	John R	Rangers	1	0	1888
GRAHAM	Arthur	Leeds United	11	2	1977–1981
GRAHAM	George	Arsenal Man. Utd.	12	3	1971–1973
GRAHAM	John	Annbank	1	0	1884
GRAHAM	John	Arsenal	1	0	1921
GRANT	John	Hibernian	2	0	1958
GRANT	Peter	Celtic	2	0	1989
GRAY	Andy	Aston Villa Wolves Everton	20	7	1975–1985
GRAY	Andy	Bradford City	2	0	2003
GRAY	Archie	Hibernian	1	0	1903
GRAY	Duggie	Rangers	10	0	1928–1932
GRAY	Eddie	Leeds United	12	3	1969–1976
GRAY	Frank	Leeds United Nottingham F.	32	1	1976–1983
GRAY	Woodville	Pollokshields	1	0	1886
GREEN	Tony	Blackpool Newcastle U.	6	0	1971–1972
GREER	Gordon	Brighton	4	0	2013–2014
GREIG	John	Rangers	44	3	1964–1975
GRIFFITHS	Leigh	Hibernian Wolverhampton	4	0	2012–2013
GROVES	Willie	Hibernian Celtic	3	4	1888–1890
GULLILAND	William	Queen's Park	4	0	1891–1895
GUNN	Bryan	Norwich City	6	0	1990–1994

HADDOCK	Harry	Clyde	6	0	1954–1958
HADDOW	David	Rangers	1	0	1894
HAFFEY	Frank	Celtic	2	0	1960–1961
HAMILTON	Alex	Queen's Park	4	0	1885–1888

HAMILTON	Alex	Dundee	24	0	1961–1965
HAMILTON	Bob	Rangers Dundee	11	15	1899–1911
HAMILTON	George	Aberdeen	5	4	1946–1954
HAMILTON	Gladstone	Port Glasgow A.	1	0	1906
HAMILTON	James	Queen's Park	3	3	1892–1893
HAMILTON	James	St Mirren	1	0	1924
HAMILTON	T ?	Hurlford	1	0	1891
HAMILTON	Tom	Rangers	1	0	1932
HAMILTON	Willie	Hibernian	1	0	1965
HAMMELL	Steve	Motherwell	1	0	2004
HANLEY	Grant	Blackburn R.	13	1	2011–2014
HANNAH	Andrew	Renton	1	0	1888
HANNAH	James	Third Lanark	1	0	1889
HANSEN	Alan	Liverpool	26	0	1979–1987
HANSEN	John	Partick Thistle	2	0	1971–1972
HARKNESS	Jack	Queen's Park Hearts	12	0	1927–1933
HARPER	Joe	Aberdeen Hibernian	4	2	1972–1978
HARPER	Willie	Hibernian Arsenal	11	0	1923–1926
HARRIS	Joe	Partick Thistle	2	0	1921
HARRIS	Neil	Newcastle Utd.	1	0	1924
HARROWER	Willie	Queen's Park	3	4	1882–1886
HARTFORD	Asa	W B A Manchester City Everton	50	4	1972–1982
HARTLEY	Paul	Hearts Celtic Bristol City	25	1	2005–2010
HARVEY	David	Leeds United	16	0	1972–1976
HASTINGS	Alex	Sunderland	2	0	1935–1937
HAUGHNEY	Mike	Celtic	1	0	1954
HAY	Davie	Celtic	27	0	1970–1974
HAY	James	Celtic Newcastle Utd.	11	0	1905–1914
HEGARTY	Paul	Dundee Utd.	8	0	1979–1983

HEGGIE	Charles	Rangers	1	4	1886
HENDERSON	George	Rangers	1	0	1904
HENDERSON	Jack	Portsmouth	7	1	1953–1958
HENDERSON	Willie	Rangers	29	5	1962–1971
HENDRY	Colin	Blackburn R. Rangers Coventry City Bolton Wandrs	51	3	1993–2001
HEPBURN	James	Alloa	1	0	1891
HEPBURN	Bob	Ayr United	1	0	1931
HERD	Andrew	Hearts	1	0	1934
HERD	David	Arsenal	5	3	1958–1961
HERD	George	Clyde	5	1	1958–1960
HERRIOT	Jim	Birmingham C.	8	0	1968–1969
HEWIE	John	Charlton Athletic	19	2	1956–1960
HIGGINS	Alex	Kilmarnock	1	3	1885
HIGGINS	Sandy	Newcastle Utd.	4	1	1910–1911
HIGHET	Thomas	Queen's Park	4	1	1875–1878
HILL	David	Rangers	3	1	1881–1882
HILL	David	Third Lanark	1	0	1906
HILL	Frank	Aberdeen	3	0	1930–1931
HILL	John	Hearts	2	0	1891–1892
HOGG	Bobby	Celtic	1	0	1937
HOGG	George	Hearts	2	0	1896
HOGG	James	Ayr United	1	0	1922
HOLM	Andrew	Queen's Park	3	0	1882–1883
HOLT	Davie	Hearts	5	0	1963–1964
HOLT	Gary	Kilmarnock Norwich City	10	1	2000–2004
HOLTON	Jim	Man. Utd.	15	2	1973–1974
HOPE	Bobby	W B A	2	0	1968
HOPKIN	David	Crystal Palace Leeds United	7	2	1997–1999
HOULISTON	Billy	Queen of the S.	3	2	1948–1949
HOUSTON	Stewart	Man. Utd.	1	0	1975
HOWDEN	William	Partick Thistle	1	0	1905

HOWE	Robert	Hamilton Ac.	2	0	1929
HOWIE	Hugh	Hibernian	1	1	1948
HOWIE	James	Newcastle Utd.	3	2	1905–1908
HOWIESON	Jimmy	St Mirren	1	0	1927
HUGHES	Billy	Sunderland	1	0	1975
HUGHES	John	Celtic	8	1	1965–1969
HUGHES	Richard	Portsmouth	5	0	2004–2005
HUGHES	Stephen	Norwich City	1	0	2009
HUMPHRIES	Wilson	Motherwell	1	0	1952
HUNTER	Ally	Kilmarnock Celtic	4	0	1972–1973
HUNTER	John	Eastern Third Lanark	4	0	1874–1877
HUNTER	John	Dundee	1	0	1909
HUNTER	R?	St Mirren	1	0	1890
HUNTER	Willie	Motherwell	3	1	1960
HUSBAND**	Jackie	Partick Thistle	1	0	1946
HUTCHISON	Don	Everton Sunderland West Ham Utd.	26	6	1999–2003
HUTCHISON	Tom	Coventry City	17	1	1973–1975
HUTTON	Alan	Rangers Tottenham H. Aston Villa RCD Mallorca Aston Villa Bolton Wanderers Aston Villa	40	0	2007–2014
HUTTON	J?	St Bernard's	1	0	1887
HUTTON	Jock	Aberdeen Blackburn R.	10	1	1923–1928
HYSLOP	Tommy	Stoke City Rangers	2	1	1896–1897

IMLACH	Stewart	Nottingham F.	4	0	1958
IMRIE	Willie	St Johnstone	2	1	1929
INGLIS	John	Rangers	2	0	1883
INGLIS	John	Kilmarnock Ath.	1	0	1884
IRONS	James	Queen's Park	1	0	1900
IRVINE	Brian	Aberdeen	9	0	1990–1994
IWELUMO	Chris	Wolves Burnley	4	0	2008–2010

JACKSON	Alex	Aberdeen Huddersfield T.	17	8	1925–1930
JACKSON	Andrew	Cambuslang	2	0	1886–1888
JACKSON	Colin	Rangers	8	1	1975–1976
JACKSON	Darren	Hibernian Celtic	28	4	1995–1998
JACKSON	John	Partick Thistle Chelsea	8	0	1931–1935
JACKSON	Thomas	St Mirren	6	0	1904–1907
JAMES	Alex	Preston N E Arsenal	8	3	1925–1932
JARDINE	Sandy	Rangers	38	1	1970–1979
JARVIE	Drew	Airdrieonians	3	0	1971
JENKINSON	Tommy	Hearts	1	1	1887
JESS	Eoin	Aberdeen Coventry City	18	2	1992–1999
JOHNSTON	Allan	Sunderland Rangers Middlesbrough	18	2	1998–2002
JOHNSTON	Leslie	Clyde	2	1	1948
JOHNSTON	Mo	Watford Celtic Nantes Rangers	38	14	1984–1991
JOHNSTON	Robert	Sunderland	1	0	1937
JOHNSTON	Willie	Rangers W B A	22	2	1965–1978
JOHNSTONE	Bobby	Hibernian Manchester C.	17	10	1951–1956
JOHNSTONE	Derek	Rangers	14	2	1973–1979
JOHNSTONE	James	Abercorn	1	0	1888
JOHNSTONE	Jimmy	Celtic	23	2	1964–1974
JOHNSTONE	John	Hearts	3	0	1929–1932
JOHNSTONE	John	Kilmarnock	1	1	1894
JOHNSTONE	William	Third Lanark	3	1	1887–1890
JORDAN	Joe	Leeds United Man. Utd. AC Milan	52	11	1973–1982

KAY	John	Queen's Park	6	5	1880–1884
KEILLOR	Alex	Montrose Dundee	6	2	1891–1897

KEIR	Leitch	Renton Dumbarton	5	1	1885–1888
KELLY	Hugh	Blackpool	1	0	1952
KELLY	James	Renton Celtic	8	1	1888–1896
KELLY	John	Barnsley	2	0	1948
KELLY	Liam	Kilmarnock	1	0	2012
KELSO	Robert	Renton Dundee	7	0	1885–1898
KELSO	Thomas	Dundee	1	0	1914
KENNAWAY	Joe	Celtic	1	0	1934
KENNEDY	Alex	Eastern Third Lanark	6	0	1875–1884
KENNEDY	John	Hibernian	1	0	1897
KENNEDY	John	Celtic	1	0	2004
KENNEDY	Jim	Celtic	6	0	1963–1964
KENNEDY	Sam	Partick Thistle	1	0	1905
KENNEDY	Stewart	Rangers	5	0	1975
KENNEDY	Stuart	Aberdeen	8	0	1978–1981
KENNETH	Garry	Dundee United	2	0	2010
KER	Geordie	Queen's Park	5	10	1880–1882
KER	William	Queen's Park	2	0	1872–1873
KERR	Andy	Partick Thistle	2	0	1955
KERR	Brian	Newcastle Utd.	3	0	2003–2004
KERR	Peter	Hibernian	1	0	1924
KEY	George	Hearts	1	0	1902
KEY	William	Queen's Park	1	0	1907
KING	Alex	Hearts Celtic	6	1	1896–1899
KING	James	Hamilton Ac.	2	1	1932–1933
KING	William	Queen's Park	1	0	1929
KINLOCH	James	Partick Thistle	1	0	1922
KINNAIRD	Arthur	Wanderers	1	0	1873
KINNEAR	Davie	Rangers	1	1	1937
KYLE	Kevin	Sunderland Kilmarnock	10	1	2002–2009

LAMBERT	Paul	Motherwell Borussia Dort. Celtic	40	1	1995–2003
LAMBIE	John	Queen's Park	3	1	1886–1888
LAMBIE	William	Queen's Park	9	5	1892–1897
LAMONT	W?	Pilgrims	1	1	1885
LANG	Archie	Dumbarton	1	0	1880
LANG	James	Clydesdale Third Lanark	2	2	1876–1878
LATTA	Alex	Dumbarton Ath.	2	2	1888–1889
LAW	Denis	Huddersfield T. Manchester C. Torino Man. Utd	55	30	1958–1974
LAW	George	Rangers	3	0	1910
LAW	Tommy	Chelsea	2	0	1928–1930
LAWRENCE	James	Newcastle Utd.	1	0	1911
LAWRENCE	Tommy	Liverpool	3	0	1963–1969
LAWSON	Denis	St Mirren	1	0	1923
LECKIE	Robert	Queen's Park	1	0	1872
LEGGAT	Graham	Aberdeen Fulham	18	8	1956–1960
LEIGHTON	Jim	Aberdeen Man. Utd Hibernian	91	0	1982–1998
LENNIE	Willie	Aberdeen	2	1	1908
LENNOX	Bobby	Celtic	10	3	1966–1970
LESLIE	Lawrie	Airdrieonians	5	0	1960–1961
LEVEIN	Craig	Hearts	16	0	1990–1994
LIDDELL**	Billy	Liverpool	28	6	1946–1955
LIDDLE	Danny	East Fife	3	0	1931
LINDSAY	David	St Mirren	1	0	1903
LINDSAY	John	Renton	3	0	1888–1893
LINDSAY	Joseph	Dumbarton	8	6	1880–1886
LINWOOD	Alex	Clyde	1	1	1949
LITTLE	John	Rangers	1	0	1953
LIVINGSTONE	George	Manchester C. Rangers	2	0	1906–07

LOCHHEAD	Alex	Third Lanark	1	0	1889
LOGAN	James	Ayr United	1	1	1891
LOGAN	Thomas	Falkirk	1	0	1913
LOGIE	Jimmy	Arsenal	1	0	1952
LONEY	Willie	Celtic	2	0	1910
LONG	Hugh	Clyde	1	0	1946
LONGAIR	William	Dundee	1	0	1894
LORIMER	Peter	Leeds United	21	4	1969–1975
LOVE	Andrew	Aberdeen	3	1	1931
LOW	Alex	Falkirk	1	0	1933
LOW	James	Cambuslang	1	1	1891
LOW	Thomas	Rangers	1	0	1897
LOW	Wilfred	Newcastle Utd.	5	0	1911–1920
LOWE	James	St Bernard's	1	1	1887
LUNDIE	James	Hibernian	1	0	1886
LYALL	John	Sheffield Wed.	1	0	1905

McADAM	J?	Third Lanark	1	1	1880
McALLISTER	Brian	Wimbledon	3	0	1997
McALLISTER	Gary	Leicester City Leeds United Coventry City	57	5	1990–1999
McALLISTER	Jamie	Livingston	1	0	2004
MACARI	Lou	Celtic Man. Utd.	24	5	1972–1978
McARTHUR	Dan	Celtic	3	0	1895–1899
McARTHUR	James	Wigan Athletic	15	1	2010–2013
McATEE	Andy	Celtic	1	0	1913
MACAULAY	Archie	Brentford Arsenal	7	0	1947–1948
McAULAY	J?	Arthurlie	1	0	1884
McAULAY	James	Dumbarton	9	1	1882–1887
McAULAY	Robert	Rangers	2	0	1931
McAVENNIE	Frank	West Ham Utd. Celtic	5	1	1985–1988
McBAIN	Edward	St Mirren	1	0	1894

McBAIN	Neil	Man. Utd Everton	3	0	1922–1924
McBRIDE	Joe	Celtic	2	0	1966
McBRIDE	Peter	Preston N E	6	0	1904–1909
McCALL	Archie	Renton	1	0	1888
McCALL	James	Renton	5	2	1886–1890
McCALL	Stuart	Everton Rangers	40	1	1990–1998
McCALLIOG	Jim	Sheffield Wed. Wolves	5	1	1967–1971
McCALLUM	Neil	Renton	1	1	1888
McCANN	Bert	Motherwell	5	0	1959–1961
McCANN	Neil	Hearts Rangers Southampton	26	1	1998–2005
McCARTNEY	Willie	Hibernian	1	0	1902
McCLAIR	Brian	Celtic Man. Utd	30	2	1986–1993
McCLORY	Allan	Motherwell	3	0	1926–1934
McCLOY	Peter	Rangers	4	0	1973
McCLOY	Philip	Ayr United	4	0	1924–1925
McCOIST	Ally	Rangers Kilmarnock	61	19	1986–1998
McCOLL	Ian	Rangers	14	0	1950–1958
McCOLL	Robert	Queen's Park Newcastle Utd.	13	13	1896–1908
McCOLL	William	Renton	1	0	1895
McCOMBIE	Andrew	Sunderland Newcastle Utd.	4	0	1903–1905
McCORKINDALE	J?	Partick Thistle	1	0	1891
McCORMACK	Ross	Motherwell Cardiff City Leeds Utd.	11	2	2008–2014
McCORMICK	Robert	Abercorn	1	1	1886
McCRAE	David	St Mirren	2	0	1929
McCREADIE	Andrew	Rangers	2	0	1893–1894
McCREADIE	Eddie	Chelsea	23	0	1965–1969
McCULLOCH	David	Hearts Brentford Derby County	7	3	1934–1938

McCULLOCH	Lee	Wigan Rangers	18	1	2004–2010
MacDONALD	Alec	Rangers	1	0	1976
McDONALD	Joe	Sunderland	2	0	1955
McDONALD	John	Edinburgh Univ.	1	0	1886
MacDOUGALL	Eddie	Norwich City	7	3	1975
McDOUGALL	James	Liverpool	2	0	1931
McDOUGALL	John	Airdrie	1	0	1926
McDOUGALL	John	Vale of Leven	5	4	1877–1879
McEVELEY	James	Derby County	3	0	2007–2008
McFADDEN	James	Motherwell Everton Birmingham C.	48	15	2002–2010
McFADYEN	Willie	Motherwell	2	2	1933
MacFARLANE	Sandy	Dundee	5	1	1904–1911
MacFARLANE	Willie	Hearts	1	0	1947
McFARLANE	Robert	Morton	1	0	1896
McGARR	Ernie	Aberdeen	2	0	1969
McGARVEY	Frank	Liverpool Celtic	7	0	1979–1984
McGEOCH	Alex	Dumbreck	4	0	1876–1877
McGHEE	Jimmy	Hibs	1	0	1886
McGHEE	Mark	Aberdeen	4	2	1983–1984
McGINLAY	John	Bolton Wandrs.	13	4	1994–1997
McGONAGLE	Peter	Celtic	6	0	1933–1934
McGOWAN*	James	Partick Thistle			
McGRAIN	Danny	Celtic	62	0	1973–1982
McGREGOR	Allan	Rangers Besiktas Hull City	32	0	2007–2014
McGREGOR	John	Vale of Leven	4	1	1877–1880
McGRORY	John	Kilmarnock	3	0	1964–1965
McGRORY	Jimmy	Celtic	7	6	1928–1933
McGUIRE	William	Beith	2	0	1881
McGURK	Frank	Birmingham	1	0	1933
McHARDY	Hugh	Rangers	1	0	1885
McINALLY	Alan	Aston Villa Bayern Munich	8	3	1989–1990

McINALLY	Jim	Dundee United	10	0	1987–1993
McINALLY	Tommy	Celtic	2	0	1926
McINNES	Derek	W B A	2	0	2002
McINNES	Thomas	Cowlairs	1	1	1889
McINTOSH	William	Third Lanark	1	0	1905
McINTYRE	Andrew	Vale of Leven	2	0	1878–1882
McINTYRE	Hugh	Rangers	1	0	1880
McINTYRE	James	Rangers	1	0	1884
MACKAIL-SMITH	Craig	Peterborough U. Brighton	7	1	2011–2012
MACKAY	Dave	Hearts Tottenham H.	22	4	1957–1965
MacKAY	Dunky	Celtic	14	0	1959–1962
MACKAY	Gary	Hearts	4	1	1987–1988
MACKAY	Malky	Norwich City	5	0	2004
McKAY	Bob	Newcastle Utd	1	0	1927
McKAY	John	Blackburn R.	1	0	1924
MACKAY-STEVEN	Gary	Dundee United	1	0	2013
McKEAN	Bobby	Rangers	1	0	1976
MacKENZIE	John	Partick Thistle	9	1	1953–1956
McKENZIE	Duncan	Brentford	1	0	1937
McKEOWN	Michael	Celtic	2	0	1889–1890
McKIE	James	E. Stirlingshire	1	2	1898
MACKIE	Jamie	Q P R	9	2	2010–2012
McKILLOP	Tommy	Rangers	1	0	1938
McKIMMIE	Stewart	Aberdeen	40	1	1989–1996
McKINLAY	Billy	Dundee United Blackburn R.	29	4	1993–1998
McKINLAY	Donald	Liverpool	2	0	1922
McKINLAY	Tosh	Celtic	22	0	1995–1998
MacKINNON	William	Dumbarton	4	0	1883–1884
MacKINNON	William	Queen's Park	9	5	1872–1879
McKINNON	Angus	Queen's Park	1	1	1874
McKINNON	Rob	Motherwell	3	0	1993–1995
McKINNON	Ron	Rangers	28	1	1965–1971

McLAREN	Alan	Hearts Rangers	24	0	1992–1995
McLAREN	Alex	St Johnstone	5	0	1929–1932
McLAREN	Andy	Preston N E	4	3	1947
McLAREN	Andy	Kilmarnock	1	0	2001
McLAREN	James	Hibernian Celtic	3	1	1888–1890
McLEAN	Adam	Celtic	4	1	1925–1927
McLEAN	Davie	Sheffield Wed.	1	0	1912
McLEAN	Duncan	St Bernard's	2	0	1896–1897
McLEAN	George	Dundee	1	0	1968
McLEAN	Tommy	Kilmarnock	6	1	1968–1971
McLEISH	Alex	Aberdeen	77	0	1980–1993
MacLEOD	John	Hibernian	4	0	1961
MacLEOD	Murdo	Celtic Borussia Dort. Hibernian	20	1	1985–1991
McLEOD	Donny	Celtic	4	0	1905–1906
McLEOD	John	Dumbarton	5	0	1888–1893
McLEOD	William	Cowlairs	1	0	1886
McLINTOCK	Alexander	Vale of Leven	3	0	1875–1880
McLINTOCK	Frank	Leicester City Arsenal	9	1	1963–1971
McLUCKIE	James	Manchester C.	1	0	1933
McMAHON	Sandy	Celtic	6	6	1892–1902
McMANUS	Stephen	Celtic Middlesbrough	26	2	2006–2010
McMENEMY	Jimmy	Celtic	12	5	1905–1920
McMENEMY	John	Motherwell	1	0	1933
McMILLAN	Ian	Airdrieonians Rangers	6	2	1952–1961
McMILLAN	J?	St Bernard's	1	0	1897
McMILLAN	Thomas	Dumbarton	1	0	1887
McMULLAN	Jimmy	Partick Thistle Manchester C.	16	0	1920–1929
McNAB	Alex	Morton	2	0	1921
McNAB	Alex	Sunderland W B A	2	0	1937–1939

McNAB	Colin	Dundee	6	0	1930–1932
McNAB	John	Liverpool	1	0	1923
McNAIR	Alec	Celtic	15	0	1906–1920
McNAMARA	Jackie	Celtic Wolves	33	0	1996–2005
McNAMEE	David	Livingston	4	0	2004–2006
McNAUGHT	Willie	Raith Rovers	5	0	1950–1954
McNAUGHTON	Kevin	Aberdeen Cardiff City	4	0	2002–2008
McNEILL	Billy	Celtic	29	3	1961–1972
McNIEL	Henry	Queen's Park	10	6	1874–1881
McNIEL	Moses	Rangers	2	0	1876–1880
McPHAIL	Bob	Airdrieonians Rangers	17	7	1927–1937
McPHAIL	John	Celtic	5	3	1949–1953
McPHERSON	Dave	Hearts Rangers	27	0	1989–1993
McPHERSON	David	Kilmarnock	1	0	1892
McPHERSON	John	Clydesdale	1	0	1875
McPHERSON	John	Hearts	1	0	1891
McPHERSON	John	Kilmarnock Cowlairs Rangers	9	7	1888–1897
McPHERSON	John	Vale of Leven	8	0	1879–1885
McPHERSON	Robert	Arthurlie	1	1	1882
McQUEEN	Gordon	Leeds United Man. Utd	30	5	1974–1981
McQUEEN	Matthew	Leith Athletic	2	0	1890–1891
McRORIE	Danny	Morton	1	0	1930
McSPADYEN	Alex	Partick Thistle	2	0	1938–1939
McSTAY	Paul	Celtic	76	9	1983–1997
McSTAY	Willie	Celtic	13	0	1921–1928
McSWEGAN	Gary	Hearts	2	1	1999
McTAVISH	John	Falkirk	1	0	1910
McWATTIE	George	Queen's Park	2	0	1901
McWILLIAM	Peter	Newcastle Utd.	8	0	1905–1911
MADDEN	Johnnie	Celtic	2	5	1893–1895

MAGUIRE	Chris	Aberdeen	2	0	2011
MAIN	James	Hibernian	1	0	1909
MAIN	Robert	Rangers	1	0	1937
MALEY	Willie	Celtic	2	0	1893
MALONEY	Shaun	Celtic Aston Villa Celtic Wigan Athletic	32	2	2005–2014
MALPAS	Maurice	Dundee United	55	0	1984–1992
MARSHALL	David	Celtic Cardiff City	11	0	2004–2014
MARSHALL	Gordon	Celtic	1	0	1992
MARSHALL	Harry	Celtic	2	1	1899–1900
MARSHALL	James	Rangers	3	0	1932–1934
MARSHALL	John	Middlesbrough Llanelli	7	0	1921–1924
MARSHALL	John	Third Lanark	4	1	1885–1887
MARSHALL	Robert	Rangers	2	0	1892–1894
MARTIN	Brian	Motherwell	2	0	1995
MARTIN	Chris	Derby County	1	0	2014
MARTIN	Fred	Aberdeen	6	0	1954–1955
MARTIN	Neil	Hibernian Sunderland	3	0	1965
MARTIN	Russell	Norwich City	11	0	2011–2014
MARTIS	John	Motherwell	1	0	1960
MASON	Jimmy	Third Lanark	7	4	1948–1951
MASSIE	Alec	Hearts Aston Villa	18	1	1931–1937
MASSON	Don	Q P R Derby County	17	5	1976–1978
MATHERS	David	Partick Thistle	1	0	1954
MATTEO	Dominic	Leeds United	6	0	2000–2002
MAXWELL	William	Stoke City	1	0	1898
MAY	John	Rangers	5	0	1906–1909
MEECHAN	Peter	Celtic	1	0	1896
MEIKLEJOHN	Davie	Rangers	15	3	1922–1933
MENZIES	Alec	Hearts	1	0	1906
MERCER	Bob	Hearts	2	0	1912–1913
MIDDLETON	Bob	Cowdenbeath	1	0	1930

MILLAR	James	Rangers	3	2	1897–1898
MILLAR	Jimmy	Rangers	2	0	1963
MILLER	Archie	Hearts	1	0	1938
MILLER	Charlie	Dundee United	1	0	2001
MILLER	John	St Mirren	5	0	1931–1934
MILLER	Kenny	Rangers Wolves Celtic Derby County Rangers Bursaspor Cardiff City Vancouver W.	69	18	2001–2013
MILLER	Lee	Dundee United Aberdeen	3	0	2006–2009
MILLER	Peter	Dumbarton	3	0	1882–1883
MILLER	Tommy	Liverpool Man. Utd	3	2	1920–1921
MILLER	William	Third Lanark	1	0	1876
MILLER	Willie	Aberdeen	65	1	1975–1989
MILLER	Willie	Celtic	6	0	1946–1947
MILLS	Willie	Aberdeen	3	0	1935–1936
MILNE	Jackie	Middlesbrough	2	0	1938–1939
MITCHELL	Bobby	Newcastle Utd.	2	1	1951
MITCHELL	David	Rangers	5	0	1890–1894
MITCHELL	James	Kilmarnock	3	0	1908–1910
MOCHAN	Neil	Celtic	3	0	1954
MOIR	Willie	Bolton Wandrs.	1	0	1950
MONCUR	Bobby	Newcastle Utd.	16	0	1968–1972
MORGAN	Hugh	St Mirren Liverpool	2	0	1898–1899
MORGAN	Willie	Burnley Man. Utd	21	1	1967–1974
MORRIS	David	Raith Rovers	6	1	1923–1925
MORRIS	Henry	East Fife	1	3	1949
MORRISON	James	W B A	31	3	2008–2014
MORRISON	Tommy	St Mirren	1	0	1927
MORTON	Alan	Queen's Park Rangers	31	5	1920–1932
MORTON	Hugh	Kilmarnock	2	0	1929

MUDIE	Jackie	Blackpool	17	9	1956–1958
MUIR	William	Dundee	1	0	1907
MUIRHEAD	Tommy	Rangers	8	0	1922–1929
MULGREW	Charlie	Celtic	13	2	2012–2014
MULHALL	George	Aberdeen Sunderland	3	1	1959–1963
MUNRO	Alex	Hearts Blackpool	3	1	1936–1938
MUNRO	Frank	Wolves	9	0	1971–1975
MUNRO	Iain	St Mirren	7	0	1979–1980
MUNRO	Neil	Abercorn	2	2	1888–1889
MURDOCH	Bobby	Celtic	12	5	1965–1969
MURDOCH	John	Motherwell	1	0	1931
MURPHY	Frank	Celtic	1	1	1938
MURRAY	Ian	Hibernian Rangers	6	0	2002–2006
MURRAY	Jimmy	Hearts	5	1	1958
MURRAY	John	Vale of Leven	1	0	1890
MURRAY	John	Renton	1	0	1895
MURRAY	Patrick	Hibernian	2	1	1896–1897
MURRAY	Stevie	Aberdeen	1	0	1971
MURTY	Graeme	Reading	4	0	2004–2007
MUTCH	George	Preston N E	1	0	1938
NAISMITH	Steven	Kilmarnock Rangers Everton	29	3	2007–2014
NAPIER	Charlie	Celtic Derby County	5	3	1932–1937
NAREY	Dave	Dundee United	35	1	1977–1989
NAYSMITH	Gary	Hearts Everton Sheffield United	46	1	2000–2009
NEIL	Robert	Hibernian Rangers	2	2	1896–1900
NEILL	Robert	Queen's Park	5	0	1876–1880
NEILSON	Robbie	Hearts	1	0	2006
NELLIES	Peter	Hearts	2	0	1913–1914
NELSON	James	Cardiff City	4	0	1925–1930

NEVIN	Pat	Chelsea Everton Tranmere Rov.	28	5	1986–1996
NIBLO	Thomas	Aston Villa	1	0	1904
NIBLOE	Joe	Kilmarnock	11	0	1929–1932
NICHOLAS	Charlie	Celtic Arsenal Aberdeen	20	5	1983–1989
NICHOLSON	Barry	Dunfermline A.	3	0	2001–2004
NICOL	Steve	Liverpool	27	0	1984–1991
NISBET	James	Ayr United	3	2	1929
NIVEN	James	Moffat	1	0	1885

O'CONNOR	Garry	Hibernian Lok. Moscow Birmingham C.	16	4	2002–2009
O'DONNELL	Frank	Preston N E Blackpool	6	2	1937–1938
O'DONNELL	Phil	Motherwell	1	0	1993
OGILVIE	Duncan	Motherwell	1	0	1933
O'HARE	John	Derby County	13	5	1970–1972
O'NEIL	Brian	Celtic Wolfsburg Derby County Preston N E	7	0	1996–2005
O'NEIL	John	Hibernian	1	0	2001
ORMOND	Willie	Hibernian	6	2	1954–1959
O'ROURKE	Frank	Airdrieonians	1	1	1907
ORR	James	Kilmarnock	1	0	1892
ORR	Ronald	Newcastle Utd.	2	1	1902–1904
ORR	Tommy	Morton	2	1	1951
ORR	Willie	Celtic	3	0	1900–1904
ORROCK	Robert	Falkirk	1	0	1913
OSWALD	James	Third Lanark St Bernard's Rangers	3	1	1889–1897

PARKER	Alex	Falkirk Everton	15	0	1955–1958
PARLANE	Derek	Rangers	12	1	1973–1977
PARLANE	Robert	Vale of Leven	3	0	1878–1879

PATERSON*	George	Celtic	1	0	1938
PATERSON	James	Cowdenbeath	3	0	1931
PATERSON	John	Leicester City	1	0	1920
PATON*	Andy	Motherwell	2	0	1952
PATON	Daniel	St Bernard's	1	1	1896
PATON	Michael	Dumbarton	5	0	1883–1886
PATON	Robert	Vale of Leven	2	0	1879
PATRICK	John	St Mirren	2	0	1897
PAUL	Harold	Queen's Park	3	2	1909
PAUL	William	Dykebar	1	0	1891
PAUL	William	Partick Thistle	3	5	1888–1890
PEARSON	Stephen	Celtic Derby County	10	0	2003–2007
PEARSON	Tommy	Newcastle Utd.	2	0	1947
PENMAN	Andy	Dundee	1	0	1966
PETTIGREW	Willie	Motherwell	5	2	1976–1977
PHILLIPS	James	Queen's Park	3	0	1877–1878
PHILLIPS	Matt	Blackpool	2	0	2012
PLENDERLEITH	John	Manchester C.	1	0	1961
PORTEOUS	William	Hearts	1	0	1903
PRESSLEY	Steven	Hearts	32	0	2000–2006
PRINGLE	Charles	St Mirren	1	0	1921
PROVAN	Davie	Rangers	5	0	1963–1966
PROVAN	Davie	Celtic	10	1	1979–1982
PURSELL	Peter	Queen's Park	1	0	1914

QUASHIE	Nigel	Portsmouth Southampton W B A	14	1	2004–2006
QUINN	Jimmy	Celtic	11	7	1905–1912
QUINN	Pat	Motherwell	4	1	1961–1962

RAE	Gavin	Dundee Rangers Cardiff City	14	0	2001–2009
RAE	James	Third Lanark	2	0	1889–1890
RAESIDE	James	Third Lanark	1	0	1906

RAISBECK	Alex	Liverpool	8	0	1900–1907
RANKIN	Gilbert	Vale of Leven	2	2	1890–1891
RANKIN	Robert	St Mirren	3	2	1929
REDPATH	Willie	Motherwell	9	0	1948–1952
REID	James	Airdrie	3	0	1914–1924
REID	Robert	Brentford	2	0	1937–1938
REID	Willie	Rangers	9	4	1911–1914
REILLY	Lawrie	Hibernian	38	22	1948–1957
RENNIE	Harry	Hearts Hibernian	13	0	1900–1908
RENNY-TAILYOUR	Henry	R. Engineers	1	1	1873
RHIND	Alex	Queen's Park	1	0	1872
RHODES	Jordan	Huddersfield T. Blackburn Rvrs.	11	3	2011–2013
RICHMOND	Andrew	Queen's Park	1	0	1906
RICHMOND	James	Clydesdale Queen's Park	3	1	1877–1882
RING	Tommy	Clyde	12	2	1953–1957
RIOCH	Bruce	Derby County Everton	24	6	1975–1978
RIORDAN	Derek	Hibs	3	0	2005–2009
RITCHIE	Archibald	E. Stirlingshire	1	0	1891
RITCHIE	Billy	Rangers	1	0	1962
RITCHIE	Henry	Hibernian	2	0	1923–1928
RITCHIE	John	Queen's Park	1	1	1897
RITCHIE	Paul	Hearts Bolton W. Walsall	7	1	1999–2004
ROBB	Davie	Aberdeen	5	0	1971
ROBB	Willie	Hibernian Rangers	2	0	1925–1927
ROBERTSON	Andrew	Dundee Utd	2	0	2014
ROBERTSON	Archie	Clyde	5	2	1955–1958
ROBERTSON	David	Rangers	3	0	1992–1994
ROBERTSON	George	Motherwell Sheffield Wed.	4	0	1910–1913
ROBERTSON	George	Kilmarnock	1	0	1937
ROBERTSON	Hugh	Dundee	1	0	1961
ROBERTSON	James	Dundee	2	0	1931

ROBERTSON	James	Tottenham H.	1	0	1964
ROBERTSON	John	Hearts	16	3	1990–1995
ROBERTSON	John	Nottingham F. Derby County	28	8	1978–1983
ROBERTSON	John	Everton Southampton Rangers	16	2	1898–1905
ROBERTSON	Peter	Dundee	1	0	1903
ROBERTSON	Scott	Dundee United	2	0	2008–2010
ROBERTSON	Tom	Queen's Park	4	0	1889–1892
ROBERTSON	Tom	Hearts	1	1	1898
ROBERTSON	William	Dumbarton	2	1	1887
ROBINSON	Robert	Dundee	4	0	1974–1975
ROBSON	Barry	Dundee Utd. Celtic Middlesbrough	17	0	2007–2012
ROSS	Maurice	Rangers	13	0	2002–2003
ROUGH	Alan	Partick Thistle	53	0	1976–1986
ROUGVIE	Doug	Aberdeen	1	0	1983
ROWAN	Archibald	Caledonian Queen's Park	2	0	1880–1882
RUSSELL	David	Hearts Celtic	6	1	1895–1901
RUSSELL	J?	Cambuslang	1	0	1890
RUSSELL	Willie	Airdrieonians	2	0	1924–1925
RUTHERFORD	Eddie	Rangers	1	0	1948
ST JOHN	Ian	Motherwell Liverpool	21	9	1959–1965
SAUNDERS	Steven	Motherwell	1	0	2010
SAWERS	William	Dundee	1	0	1895
SCARFF	Peter	Celtic	1	0	1931
SCHAEDLER	Erich	Hibernian	1	0	1974
SCOTT	Alec	Rangers Everton	16	5	1956–1966
SCOTT	Jim	Hibernian	1	0	1966
SCOTT	Jocky	Dundee	2	0	1971
SCOTT	Matthew	Airdrieonians	1	0	1898

SCOTT	Robert	Airdrieonians	1	0	1894
SCOULAR	Jimmy	Portsmouth	9	0	1951–1952
SELLAR	William	Battlefield Queen's Park	9	4	1885–1893
SEMPLE	William	Cambuslang	1	0	1886
SEVERIN	Scott	Hearts Aberdeen	15	0	2001–2006
SHANKLY	Bill	Preston N E	5	0	1938–1939
SHARP	Graeme	Everton	12	1	1985–1988
SHARP	James	Dundee Arsenal Fulham	5	0	1904–1909
SHAW**	Davie	Hibernian	8	0	1946–1948
SHAW	Frank	Pollokshields A.	2	1	1884
SHAW***	Jock	Rangers	4	0	1947
SHEARER	Bobby	Rangers	4	0	1961
SHEARER	Duncan	Aberdeen	7	2	1994–1995
SHINNIE	Andrew	Inverness CT	1	0	2012
SILLARS	Donald	Queen's Park	5	0	1891–1895
SIMPSON	James	Third Lanark	3	0	1895
SIMPSON	Jimmy	Rangers	14	1	1934–1937
SIMPSON	Neil	Aberdeen	5	0	1983–1988
SIMPSON	Ronnie	Celtic	5	0	1967–1968
SINCLAIR	George	Hearts	3	0	1910–1912
SINCLAIR	John	Leicester City	1	0	1966
SKENE	Leslie	Queen's Park	1	0	1904
SLOAN	Thomas	Third Lanark	1	0	1904
SMELLIE	Robert	Queen's Park	6	0	1887–1893
SMITH	Alex	Rangers	20	5	1898–1911
SMITH	Dave	Aberdeen Rangers	2	0	1966–1968
SMITH	Eric	Celtic	2	0	1959
SMITH*	Gordon	Hibernian	18	4	1946–1957
SMITH	Henry	Hearts	3	0	1988–1992
SMITH	James	Queen's Park	1	0	1872
SMITH	Jamie	Celtic	2	0	2003

SMITH	John	Ayr United	1	0	1924
SMITH	John	Mauchline Edinburgh Univ. Queen's Park	10	10	1877–1884
SMITH	Jimmy	Rangers	2	1	1934–1937
SMITH	Jimmy	Aberdeen Newcastle Utd.	4	0	1968–1974
SMITH	Nick	Rangers	12	0	1897–1902
SMITH	Robert	Queen's Park	2	0	1872–1873
SMITH	Tommy	Kilmarnock Preston N E	2	0	1934–1938
SNODGRASS	Robert	Leeds United Norwich City	15	3	2011–2013
SOMERS	Peter	Celtic	4	0	1905–1909
SOMERS	William	Third Lanark Queen's Park	3	0	1879–1880
SOMERVILLE	George	Queen's Park	1	0	1886
SOUNESS	Graeme	Middlesbrough Liverpool Sampdoria	54	4	1974–1986
SPEEDIE	David	Chelsea Coventry City	10	0	1985–1989
SPEEDIE	Finlay	Rangers	3	2	1903
SPEIRS	James	Rangers	1	0	1908
SPENCER	John	Chelsea QPR	14	0	1994–1997
STANTON	Pat	Hibernian	16	0	1966–1974
STARK	James	Rangers	2	0	1909
STEEL	Billy	Morton Derby County Dundee	30	12	1947–1953
STEELE	David	Huddersfield T.	3	0	1923
STEIN	Colin	Rangers Coventry City	21	10	1968–1973
STEPHEN	James	Bradford PA	2	0	1946–1947
STEVENSON	George	Motherwell	12	4	1927–1934
STEWART	Allan	Queen's Park	2	1	1888–1889
STEWART	Andrew	Third Lanark	1	0	1894
STEWART	David	Queen's Park	3	0	1893–1897
STEWART	David	Leeds United	1	0	1977

STEWART	Duncan	Dumbarton	1	0	1888
STEWART	George	Hibernian Manchester C.	4	0	1906–1907
STEWART	James	Kilmarnock Middlesbrough	2	0	1977–1978
STEWART	Michael	Man. Utd. Hearts	4	0	2002–2008
STEWART	Ray	West Ham Utd.	10	1	1981–1987
STEWART	William	Queen's Park	2	1	1898–1900
STOCKDALE	Robbie	Middlesbrough	5	0	2002
STORRIER	Davie	Celtic	3	0	1899
STRACHAN	Gordon	Aberdeen Man. Utd. Leeds United	50	5	1980–1992
STURROCK	Paul	Dundee United	20	3	1981–1987
SULLIVAN	Neil	Wimbledon Tottenham H.	28	0	1997–2003
SUMMERS	William	St Mirren	1	0	1926
SYMON	Scott	Rangers	1	0	1938

TAIT	Thomas	Sunderland	1	0	1911
TAYLOR	John	Dumbarton St Mirren	4	1	1892–1895
TAYLOR	Joseph	Queen's Park	6	0	1872–1876
TAYLOR	William	Hearts	1	0	1892
TEALE	Gary	Wigan Athletic Derby County	13	0	2006–2009
TELFER	Paul	Coventry City	1	0	2000
TELFER	Willie	Motherwell	2	0	1932
TELFER	Willie	St Mirren	1	0	1953
TEMPLETON	Bobby	Aston Villa Newcastle Utd. Arsenal Celtic Kilmarnock	11	1	1902–1913
THOMPSON	Steve	Dundee United Rangers	16	3	2002–2004
THOMSON	Alec	Airdrieonians	1	1	1909
THOMSON	Alec	Celtic	3	0	1926–1932
THOMSON	Andrew	Arthurlie	1	0	1886

THOMSON	Andrew	Third Lanark	1	0	1889
THOMSON	Bertie	Celtic	1	1	1931
THOMSON	Billy	St Mirren	7	0	1980–1983
THOMSON	Charlie	Hearts Sunderland	21	4	1904–1914
THOMSON	Charlie	Sunderland	1	0	1937
THOMSON	David	Dundee	1	0	1920
THOMSON	James	Queen's Park	3	0	1872–1874
THOMSON	John	Celtic	5	0	1930–1931
THOMSON	John	Everton	1	0	1932
THOMSON	Kevin	Rangers Middlesbrough	3	0	2008–2010
THOMSON	Robert	Falkirk	1	0	1927
THOMSON	Samuel	Lugar Boswell	2	0	1884
THOMSON	William	Dumbarton	4	1	1892–1898
THOMSON	William	Dundee	1	0	1896
THORNTON**	Willie	Rangers	7	1	1946–1952
TONER	Willie	Kilmarnock	2	0	1958
TOWNSLEY	Tom	Falkirk	1	0	1925
TROUP	Alec	Dundee Everton	5	0	1920–1926
TURNBULL	Eddie	Hibernian	9	0	1948–1958
TURNER	Thomas	Arthurlie	1	0	1884
TURNER	William	Pollokshields A.	2	1	1885–1886

URE	Ian	Dundee Arsenal	11	0	1961–1967
URQUHART	Duncan	Hibernian	1	0	1933

VALLANCE	Thomas	Rangers	7	0	1877–1881
VENTERS	Alex	Cowdenbeath Rangers	3	0	1933–1939

WADDELL	Thomas	Queen's Park	6	1	1891–1895
WADDELL**	Willie	Rangers	17	6	1946–1954
WALES	Hugh	Motherwell	1	0	1932
WALKER	Andy	Celtic	3	0	1988–1994

WALKER	Bobby	Hearts	29	7	1900–1913
WALKER	Frank	Third Lanark	1	0	1922
WALKER	George	St Mirren	4	0	1930–1931
WALKER*	Jimmy	Hearts			
WALKER	John	Hearts Rangers	5	3	1895–1904
WALKER	John	Swindon Town	9	0	1911–1913
WALKER	Nicky	Hearts Partick Thistle	2	0	1993–1996
WALKER**	Tommy	Hearts	20	9	1934–1939
WALKER	William	Clyde	2	0	1909–1910
WALLACE	Ian	Coventry City	3	1	1978–1979
WALLACE	Lee	Hearts Rangers	8	0	2009–2013
WALLACE	Ross	Preston N E	1	0	2009
WALLACE	Willie	Hearts Celtic	7	0	1964–1969
WARDHAUGH	Jimmy	Hearts	2	0	1954–1956
WARK	John	Ipswich Town Liverpool	29	7	1979–1984
WATSON	Andrew	Queen's Park	3	0	1881
WATSON	Bobby	Motherwell	1	0	1971
WATSON	James	Motherwell Huddersfield T.	2	0	1947–1953
WATSON	James	Sunderland Middlesbrough	6	0	1903–1909
WATSON	James	Rangers	1	1	1878
WATSON	Philip	Blackpool	1	0	1933
WATSON	W?	Falkirk	1	0	1898
WATT	Frank	Balbirnie	4	3	1889–1891
WATT	William	Queen's Park	1	1	1887
WAUGH	William	Hearts	1	0	1937
WEBSTER	Andy	Hearts Dundee United Hearts	28	1	2003–2013
WEIR	Andy	Motherwell	6	1	1959–1960
WEIR	David	Hearts Everton Rangers	69	1	1997–2010

WEIR	James	Queen's Park	4	2	1872–1878
WEIR	John	Third Lanark	1	0	1887
WEIR	Peter	St Mirren Aberdeen	6	0	1980–1983
WHITE	John	Albion Rovers Hearts	2	0	1922–1923
WHITE	John	Falkirk Tottenham H.	22	3	1959–1964
WHITE	Walter	Bolton W.	2	0	1907–1908
WHITELAW	Andrew	Vale of Leven	2	0	1887–1890
WHITTAKER	Steven	Rangers Norwich City	24	0	2009–2014
WHYTE	Derek	Celtic Middlesbrough Aberdeen	12	0	1987–1999
WILKIE	Lee	Dundee	11	1	2002–2004
WILLIAMS	Gareth	Nottingham F.	5	0	2002
WILSON	Andrew	Sheffield Wed.	6	2	1907–1914
WILSON	Andrew Nesbit	Dunfermline A. Middlesbrough	12	13	1920–1923
WILSON	Alex	Portsmouth	1	0	1954
WILSON	Bob	Arsenal	2	0	1971
WILSON	Danny	Liverpool	5	1	2010–2011
WILSON	David	Queen's Park	1	2	1900
WILSON	David	Oldham Ath.	1	0	1913
WILSON	Davie	Rangers	22	9	1960–1965
WILSON	George	Hearts Everton Newcastle Utd.	6	0	1904–1909
WILSON	Hugh	Newmilns Sunderland Third Lanark	4	1	1890–1904
WILSON	Ian	Leicester City Everton	5	0	1987
WILSON	James	Vale of Leven	4	0	1888–1891
WILSON	Mark	Celtic	1	0	2011
WILSON	Paul	Celtic	1	0	1975
WILSON	Peter	Celtic	4	0	1926–1933
WINTERS	Robbie	Aberdeen	1	0	1999

WISEMAN	William	Queen's Park	2	0	1926–1930
WOOD	George	Everton Arsenal	4	0	1979–1982
WOODBURN	Willie	Rangers	24	0	1947–1952
WOTHERSPOON	David	Queen's Park	2	0	1872–1873
WRIGHT	Keith	Hibernian	1	0	1992
WRIGHT	Stephen	Aberdeen	2	0	1993
WRIGHT	Tommy	Sunderland	3	0	1952–1953
WYLIE	Tom	Rangers	1	1	1890

YEATS	Ron	Liverpool	2	0	1964–1965
YORSTON	Benny	Aberdeen	1	0	1931
YORSTON	Harry	Aberdeen	1	0	1954
YOUNG	Alec	Everton	2	0	1905–1907
YOUNG	Alec	Hearts Everton	8	5	1960–1966
YOUNG	George	Rangers	53	0	1946–1957
YOUNG	Jim	Celtic	1	0	1906
YOUNGER	Tommy	Hibernian Liverpool	24	0	1955–1958

Names marked with one or more asterisks are players who took part in the 2–2 draw against Belgium on 23 January 1946 and/or the 3–1 victory over Switzerland on 15 May 1946, which are sometimes regarded as unofficial internationals. Jimmy Delaney (2) scored against Belgium; Billy Liddell (2) and Jimmy Delaney scored against Switzerland.

Players are identified as follows: * played against Belgium, ** played against Switzerland, *** played against both Belgium and Switzerland. Appearances in these two matches are not included in the figures shown for total international appearances.

SCOTLAND MANAGERS

- Andy Beattie: 1954 (WC)
- Matt Busby: 1958
- Andy Beattie (again): 1959–60
- Ian McColl: 1960–65
- Jock Stein: 1965
- John Prentice: 1966
- Malky MacDonald: 1966
- Bobby Brown: 1967–71
- Tommy Docherty: 1971–72
- Willie Ormond: 1973–77 (WC)
- Ally MacLeod: 1977–78 (WC)
- Jock Stein (again): 1978–85 (WC)
- Alex Ferguson: 1985–86 (WC)
- Andy Roxburgh: 1986–93 (WC) (EC)
- Craig Brown: 1993–2001 (WC) (EC)
- Berti Vogts: 2001–04
- Tommy Burns: 2004
- Walter Smith: 2005–07
- Alex McLeish: 2007
- George Burley: 2008–09
- Craig Levein: 2009–12
- Billy Stark: 2012
- Gordon Strachan: 2013 onwards

Andy Beattie: 1954 and 1959–60

(WC) Manager at the World Cup finals; (EC) Manager at the European Championship finals

Of these men, the following managed the national side for fewer than five matches:

Craig Brown: 1993–2001

- Matt Busby (2): Wales v Scotland (18 Oct 1958) and Scotland v N. Ireland (5 Nov 1958). He was still recovering from injuries sustained in the Munich air crash at the time of the 1958 World Cup finals
- John Prentice (4): Scotland v England (2 April 1966), Scotland v Holland (11 May 1966), Scotland v Portugal (18 Jun 1966) and Scotland v Brazil (25 Jun 1966)
- Malky MacDonald (2): Wales v Scotland (22 Oct 1966) and Scotland v N. Ireland (16 Nov 1966)
- Tommy Burns (1): Scotland v Sweden (17 Nov 2004)
- Billy Stark (1): Luxembourg v Scotland (14 Nov 2012)

Jock Stein: 1965 and 1978–85

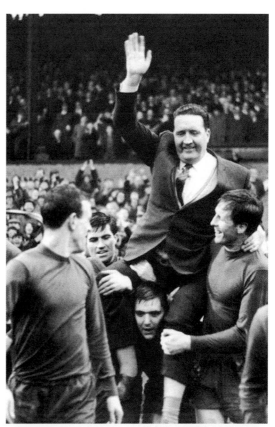

Alex McLeish: 2007

INTERNATIONAL TOURNAMENTS

EUROPEAN FOOTBALL CHAMPIONSHIP

- First match at the European Championship finals: Scotland's first match was a 1–0 defeat to Holland on 12 June 1992 in Gothenburg. They qualified for the 1992 finals in Sweden by coming top of their qualifying group.

- First goal at the European Championship finals: Paul McStay of Celtic scored the first goal in Scotland's 3–0 victory over the Commonwealth of Independent States (formerly the Soviet Union) at Norrkoping on 18 June 1992.

- 1996 finals in England: Scotland had to finish in the top two of a group that also contained England, Holland and Switzerland in order to progress. England topped the group, whilst Scotland and Holland were behind them with equal points and equal goal difference. Holland took second place as they had scored more goals, but they would have had a worse goal difference than Scotland if Patrick Kluivert had not scored a late goal in their 4–1 defeat by England.

- 2000 qualifying campaign: After finishing second in their group, behind the Czech Republic, Scotland had to take part in a two-legged play-off against England. They lost the first leg 0–2 at Hampden Park on 13 November 1999, but four days later they won 1–0 at Wembley, thanks to a Don Hutchison header from a Neil McCann cross.

- 2008 qualifying campaign: Scotland finished third in their group, behind Italy and France, but nevertheless achieved a memorable double over the French. They beat them 1–0 at Hampden Park on 7 October 2006, with a goal from Gary Caldwell, and then won 1–0 in Paris on 12 September 2007 when James McFadden scored with a spectacular long-range shot. These were the only two matches that France lost whilst qualifying.

Known as the European Nations' Cup until 1968, this tournament for national teams is held every four years, at two-year intervals from the World Cup. The winners are presented with the 'Henri Delaunay Cup', which is named after the first General Secretary of UEFA. Henri Delaunay (1883–1955) campaigned for the introduction of such a championship, but died before his vision became reality.

Scotland showed no interest in the first two tournaments of 1960 or 1964 (even though the Scottish team was a strong one around 1964), but have entered every competition since. The British international championships of 1966/67 and 1967/68 were used as a qualifying section. Since then there has been a draw for the qualifying sections. However, Scotland's record is poor; for only in 1992 and 1996 have they qualified.

1968   Qualifying Section

22 Oct 1966	Wales	Cardiff	1–1
16 Nov 1966	Northern Ireland	Hampden Park	2–1
15 Apr 1967	England	Wembley	3–2
21 Oct 1967	Northern Ireland	Belfast	0–1
22 Nov 1967	Wales	Hampden Park	3–2
24 Feb 1968	England	Hampden Park	1–1
Scotland failed to qualify for Italy			

1972   Qualifying Section

11 Nov 1970	Denmark	Hampden Park	1–0
3 Feb 1971	Belgium	Liege	0–3
21 Apr 1971	Portugal	Lisbon	0–2
9 June 1971	Denmark	Copenhagen	0–1
13 Oct 1971	Portugal	Hampden Park	2–1
10 Nov 1971	Belgium	Pittodrie	1–0
Scotland failed to qualify for Belgium			

1976   Qualifying Section

20 Nov 1974	Spain	Hampden Park	1–2
5 Feb 1975	Spain	Valencia	1–1
1 June 1975	Romania	Bucharest	1–1
3 Sep 1975	Denmark	Copenhagen	1–0
29 Oct 1975	Denmark	Hampden Park	3–1
17 Dec 1975	Romania	Hampden Park	1–1
Scotland failed to qualify for Yugoslavia			

1980   Qualifying Section

20 Sep 1978	Austria	Vienna	2–3
25 Oct 1978	Norway	Hampden Park	3–2
29 Nov 1978	Portugal	Lisbon	0–1
7 June 1979	Norway	Oslo	4–0
17 Oct 1979	Austria	Hampden Park	1–1
21 Nov 1979	Belgium	Brussels	0–2
19 Dec 1979	Belgium	Hampden Park	1–3
26 Mar 1980	Portugal	Hampden Park	4–1
Scotland failed to qualify for Italy			

1984   Qualifying Section

13 Oct 1982	East Germany	Hampden Park	2–0
17 Nov 1982	Switzerland	Berne	0–2
15 Dec 1982	Belgium	Brussels	2–3
30 Mar 1983	Switzerland	Hampden Park	2–2
12 Oct 1983	Belgium	Hampden Park	1–1
16 Nov 1983	East Germany	Halle	1–2
Scotland failed to qualify for France			

Archie Gemmill nets from the penalty spot as Scotland defeat Norway 3–2 in a European Championship qualifier at Hampden Park in October 1978

1988 Qualifying Section

10 Sep 1986	Bulgaria	Hampden Park	0–0
15 Oct 1986	Republic of Ireland	Dublin	0–0
12 Nov 1986	Luxembourg	Hampden Park	3–0
18 Feb 1987	Republic of Ireland	Hampden Park	0–1
1 Apr 1987	Belgium	Brussels	1–4
14 Oct 1987	Belgium	Hampden Park	2–0
11 Nov 1987	Bulgaria	Sofia	1–0
2 Dec 1987	Luxembourg	Esch	0–0
Scotland failed to qualify for Germany			

1992 Qualifying Section

12 Sep 1990	Romania	Hampden Park	2–1
17 Oct 1990	Switzerland	Hampden Park	2–1
14 Nov 1990	Bulgaria	Sofia	1–1
27 Mar 1991	Bulgaria	Hampden Park	1–1
1 May 1991	San Marino	Serravalle	2–0
11 Sep 1991	Switzerland	Berne	2–2
16 Oct 1991	Romania	Bucharest	0–1
13 Nov 1991	San Marino	Hampden Park	4–0

Finals in Sweden

12 June 1992	Holland	Gothenburg	0–1
15 June 1992	Germany	Norrkoping	0–2
18 June 1992	CIS	Norrkoping	3–0

It was felt by many observers that Andy Roxburgh's side did not enjoy the best of fortunes in the 1992 championships. The first game saw Scotland against the strong Dutch side, and after Scotland had weathered an early storm, they held their own until a late Dennis Bergkamp goal. Against Germany, Scotland lost a goal in the first half, then early in the second half a wicked deflection from Stefan Effenberg deceived Andy Goram and put Germany two up. Hard though Scotland tried, they could not get back into the game. In the final game, with only pride at stake, Scotland turned on some of the best football seen by any team at the tournament, against the Commonwealth of Independent States, who had previously been known as the USSR. Paul McStay was outstanding in midfield, and he scored one of the goals, the other two coming from Brian McClair and Gary McAllister.

1996 Qualifying Section

7 Sep 1994	Finland	Helsinki	2–0
12 Oct 1994	Faeroe Islands	Hampden Park	5–1

16 Nov 1994	Russia	Hampden Park	1–1
18 Dec 1994	Greece	Athens	0–1
29 Mar 1995	Russia	Moscow	0–0
26 Apr 1995	San Marino	Serravalle	2–0
7 June 1995	Faeroe Islands	Toftir	2–0
16 Aug 1995	Greece	Hampden Park	1–0
6 Sep 1995	Finland	Hampden Park	1–0
15 Nov 1995	San Marino	Hampden Park	5–0

Finals in England

10 June 1996	Holland	Villa Park	0–0
15 June 1996	England	Wembley	0–2
18 June 1996	Switzerland	Villa Park	1–0

Scotland, under Craig Brown, were very unfortunate not to qualify from this section. The first game was a creditable 0–0 draw with Holland at Villa Park, and then it was on to Wembley for the key match against England. Scotland held their own until Alan Shearer scored early in the second half, then Gary McAllister missed the penalty that has haunted him ever since before Paul Gascoigne, minutes later, scored a wonder goal to defeat Scotland 2–0. Even then Scotland might just have qualified if they had scored one more goal against Switzerland, or Holland one goal fewer against England. Although Ally McCoist scored for Scotland, the game finished 1–0, and Holland's late consolation goal against England was enough to put them into the next round.

2000   Qualifying Section

5 Sep 1998	Lithuania	Vilnius	0–0
10 Oct 1998	Estonia	Tynecastle	3–2
14 Oct 1998	Faeroe Islands	Pittodrie	2–1
31 Mar 1999	Czech Republic	Celtic Park	1–2
5 June 1999	Faeroe Islands	Toftir	1–1
9 June 1999	Czech Republic	Prague	2–3
4 Sep 1999	Bosnia	Sarajevo	2–1
8 Sep 1999	Estonia	Tallinn	0–0
5 Oct 1999	Bosnia	Ibrox	1–0
9 Oct 1999	Lithuania	Hampden Park	3–0

Play-Offs

13 Nov 1999	England	Hampden Park	0–2
17 Nov 1999	England	Wembley	1–0
Scotland failed to qualify for Holland / Belgium			

2004 Qualifying Section

7 Sep 2002	Faeroe Islands	Toftir	2–2
12 Oct 2002	Iceland	Reykjavik	2–0
29 Mar 2003	Iceland	Hampden Park	2–1
2 Apr 2003	Lithuania	Kaunas	0–1
7 June 2003	Germany	Hampden Park	1–1
6 Sep 2003	Faeroe Islands	Hampden Park	3–1
10 Sep 2003	Germany	Dortmund	1–2
11 Oct 2003	Lithuania	Hampden Park	1–0

Play-Offs

15 Nov 2003	Holland	Hampden Park	1–0
19 Nov 2003	Holland	Amsterdam	0–6
Scotland failed to qualify for Portugal			

2008 Qualifying Section

2 Sep 2006	Faeroe Islands	Celtic Park	6–0
6 Sep 2006	Lithuania	Kaunas	2–1
7 Oct 2006	France	Hampden Park	1–0
11 Oct 2006	Ukraine	Kiev	0–2
24 Mar 2007	Georgia	Hampden Park	2–1
28 Mar 2007	Italy	Bari	0–2
6 June 2007	Faeroe Islands	Toftir	2–0
8 Sep 2007	Lithuania	Hampden Park	3–1
12 Sep 2007	France	Paris	1–0
13 Oct 2007	Ukraine	Hampden Park	3–1
17 Oct 2007	Georgia	Tbilisi	0–2
17 Nov 2007	Italy	Hampden Park	1–2
Scotland failed to qualify for Austria / Switzerland			

2012 Qualifying Section

3 Sep 2010	Lithuania	Kaunas	0–0
7 Sep 2010	Liechtenstein	Hampden Park	2–1
8 Oct 2010	Czech Republic	Prague	0–1
12 Oct 2010	Spain	Hampden Park	2–3
3 Sep 2011	Czech Republic	Hampden Park	2–2
6 Sep 2011	Lithuania	Hampden Park	1–0
8 Oct 2011	Liechtenstein	Vaduz	1–0
11 Oct 2011	Spain	Alicante	1–3
Scotland failed to qualify for Poland / Ukraine			

2016   Qualifying Section

7 Sep 2014	Germany	Dortmund	
11 Oct 2014	Georgia	Hampden Park	
14 Oct 2014	Poland	Warsaw	
14 Nov 2014	Rep. Of Ireland	Hampden Park	
29 Mar 2015	Gibraltar	Hampden Park	
13 Jun 2015	Rep. Of Ireland	Dublin	
4 Sep 2015	Georgia	Tblisi	
7 Sep 2015	Germany	Hampden Park	
8 Oct 2015	Poland	Hampden Park	
11 Oct 2015	Gibraltar	Faro	

WORLD CUP

- First match at the World Cup finals: Scotland's first match was a 1–0 defeat by Austria on 16 June 1954 in Zurich. They qualified for the 1954 finals in Switzerland by coming second in the Home International Championship of 1953/54.

- First goal at the World Cup finals: Jimmy Murray of Hearts scored in the 1–1 draw against Yugoslavia at Vasteras on 8 June 1958, when the 1958 finals were held in Sweden.

- 1974 finals in West Germany: Scotland returned without losing a match and only failed to progress from their group on goal difference. They beat Zaire 2–0 (Scorers: Peter Lorimer and Joe Jordan), drew 0–0 with Brazil and drew 1–1 with Yugoslavia (Scorer: Joe Jordan).

- 1978 finals in Argentina: Archie Gemmill scored one of the most memorable goals in the history of the competition when Scotland defeated eventual finalists Holland 3–2 at Mendoza on 11 June 1978. The Scottish Football Museum at Hampden Park set up a continuous loop so that it could be watched over and over again.

- 1982 finals in Spain: Joe Jordan became the only Scotsman to have scored in the final stages of three World Cup tournaments when he (and Graeme Souness) scored in the 2–2 draw against the USSR.

Scotland have entered every World Cup tournament since 1950, and have qualified for the final stages in 1954, 1958, 1974, 1978, 1982, 1986, 1990 and 1998. In common with other British nations, they showed no interest in the first three World Cup competitions of 1930, 1934 and 1938, and even in 1950, when they were invited to enter, they refused to do so unless they were British Champions! England beat them in the crucial game, and thus Scotland was deprived of a trip to Brazil. Since then qualification for the World Cup has become an important part of the Scottish psyche. Whilst Jimmy Murray of Hearts was the first player to score for Scotland in the World Cup finals, the first Scotsman to score was Jimmy Brown, an Ayrshire man who scored for the USA versus Argentina in the semi-final of the 1930 World Cup.

1950   Qualifying Stages

1 Oct 1949	Northern Ireland	Belfast	8–2
9 Nov 1949	Wales	Hampden Park	2–0
15 Apr 1950	England	Hampden Park	0–1
Scotland refused to go to Brazil			

1954   Qualifying Stages

3 Oct 1953	Northern Ireland	Belfast	3–1
4 Nov 1953	Wales	Hampden Park	3–3
3 Apr 1954	England	Hampden Park	2–4

Finals in Switzerland

16 June 1954	Austria	Zurich	0–1
19 June 1954	Uruguay	Basle	0–7

Scotland's half-hearted and amateurish approach to this tournament got what it deserved in terms of results. Only thirteen men were in the squad (although twenty-two would have been allowed) and no training kit was supplied. Only one goalkeeper, Fred Martin of Aberdeen, was chosen. The strips supplied were the thick ones that one would have expected for a cold day in February, not for the sweltering heat of Switzerland in midsummer. Scotland played only two games, for they were to play the other team in the group, Czechoslovakia, only if there was a tie. In spite of this, Scotland played respectably in their first game against Austria and were unlucky to see a late Neil Mochan shot saved by the goalkeeper. Then before the next game against Uruguay, Andy Beattie the manager announced his resignation, although he would stay with the squad for the duration of the World Cup. For inept timing, this was breathtaking, and Scotland, suffering from a lack of leadership, the heat and a total lack of preparation for their South American opponents, went down 0–7 before a 43,000 crowd and a live TV audience.

1958   Qualifying Stages

8 May 1957	Spain	Hampden Park	4–2
19 May 1957	Switzerland	Basle	2–1
26 May 1957	Spain	Madrid	1–4
6 Nov 1957	Switzerland	Hampden Park	3–2

Finals in Sweden

8 June 1958	Yugoslavia	Vasteras	1–1
11 June 1958	Paraguay	Norrkoping	2–3
15 June 1958	France	Orebro	1–2

Incredibly, Scotland approached a World Cup finals tournament without a manager, Matt Busby having not yet fully recovered from the injuries sustained in the Munich air crash in February. The job was not offered to any other accredited manager and the organisation of the team was in the hands of the selectors. Team talks were given by trainer Dawson Walker and a few more experienced players. In each of the three games played, Scotland lost an early goal. The first game against Yugoslavia was a respectable draw, and indeed Scotland might have won if the referee had not disallowed a late goal. It was against Paraguay that Scotland came a real cropper, losing 2–3 in a game that was

George Young was captain of the Scottish side that defeated Switzerland 2–1 in a World Cup qualifier in May 1957

characterised by heavy tackling and a weak referee, as well as Scottish naivety. The final game against France saw Scotland 0–2 down, then fight back and they were unlucky not to get an equaliser after Jimmy Murray had pulled one back. It is hard to resist the feeling that a little organisation and leadership would not have gone amiss.

1962   Qualifying Stages

3 May 1961	Eire	Hampden Park	4–1
7 May 1961	Eire	Dublin	3–0
14 May 1961	Czechoslovakia	Bratislava	0–4
26 Sep 1961	Czechoslovakia	Hampden Park	3–2
29 Nov 1961	Czechoslovakia	Brussels	2–4
(After extra time in a play-off on a neutral ground)			
Scotland failed to qualify for Chile			

Matt Busby with Ian St John, who scored Scotland's two goals in the World Cup play-off against Czechoslovakia in 1961

1966   Qualifying Stages

21 Oct 1964	Finland	Hampden Park	3–1
23 May 1965	Poland	Chorzow	1–1
27 May 1965	Finland	Helsinki	2–1
13 Oct 1965	Poland	Hampden Park	1–2
9 Nov 1965	Italy	Hampden Park	1–0
7 Dec 1965	Italy	Naples	0–3
Scotland failed to qualify for England			

1970   Qualifying Stages

6 Nov 1968	Austria	Hampden Park	2–1
11 Dec 1968	Cyprus	Nicosia	5–0
16 Apr 1969	West Germany	Hampden Park	1–1
17 May 1969	Cyprus	Hampden Park	8–0
22 Oct 1969	West Germany	Hamburg	2–3
5 Nov 1969	Austria	Vienna	0–2
Scotland failed to qualify for Mexico			

1974   Qualifying Stages

18 Oct 1972	Denmark	Copenhagen	4–1
15 Nov 1972	Denmark	Hampden Park	2–0
26 Sep 1973	Czechoslovakia	Hampden Park	2–1
17 Oct 1973	Czechoslovakia	Bratislava	0–1

Finals in West Germany

14 June 1974	Zaire	Dortmund	2–0
18 June 1974	Brazil	Frankfurt	0–0
22 June 1974	Yugoslavia	Frankfurt	1–1

This was arguably Scotland's best-ever performance in the World Cup finals, but Willie Ormond's side, although undefeated, did not get past the group stage, largely as a result of not having scored enough goals in the first game against Zaire. The goals by Lorimer and Jordan were satisfactory but both Yugoslavia and Brazil beat Zaire by more goals. In the second game against Brazil, Scotland were distinctly unlucky. Billy Bremner missed one good chance and several others might have been put away as well, and a 0–0 draw was all that Scotland could claim. It was, however, a good result against Brazil, although it meant that Scotland now had to beat Yugoslavia to qualify. Once again a draw was all that could be achieved, both goals coming late. Yugoslavia scored with eight minutes to go, then Jordan equalised at the death. Some thought

Billy Bremner nearly scores against Brazil in the 1974 World Cup game that ended 0–0

Kenny Dalglish in the game against Yugoslavia at the 1974 World Cup finals which ended in a 1–1 draw

that Scotland had qualified because Zaire were holding Brazil to two goals in the other game, but a comical error by the Zaire goalkeeper allowed Brazil to score again and qualify. In spite of the disappointment, Scotland deserved the acclaim that they received when they came back to Scotland.

1978   Qualifying Stages

13 Oct 1976	Czechoslovakia	Prague	0–2
17 Nov 1976	Wales	Hampden Park	1–0
21 Sep 1977	Czechoslovakia	Hampden Park	3–1
12 Oct 1977	Wales	Anfield	2–0

Finals in Argentina

3 June 1978	Peru	Cordoba	1–3
7 June 1978	Iran	Cordoba	1–1
11 June 1978	Holland	Mendoza	3–2

Archie Gemmill's goal against Holland at the 1978 World Cup is arguably the most famous Scottish goal of all time

The events in Argentina were a major disaster for Scotland that affected the credibility of Scottish football for a time, and rocked the whole nation in a way that is hard to parallel elsewhere. Following the winter of 1977/78, in which unrestrained optimism and euphoria was the order of the day, manager Ally MacLeod failed to read the danger signals highlighted by some dreadful performances in the British International Championship, particularly a poor performance against England. The draw was looked upon as comparatively easy, but no research had been done on Peru or Iran, whom the management took far too lightly. Scotland went ahead in the first game against Peru through Jordan, then at a crucial stage missed a penalty and subsequently collapsed. Following the sending home of Willie Johnston for using an illegal substance, Scotland then proceeded to draw with Iran, needing an own goal to do so. Then, ironically, once the damage had been done, Scotland beat Holland on the night of Archie Gemmill's famous goal (Dalglish scored the first goal, then Gemmill scored a penalty for the second) but the 3–2 scoreline was not enough.

10 Sep 1980	Sweden	Stockholm	1–0
15 Oct 1980	Portugal	Hampden Park	0–0
25 Feb 1981	Israel	Tel Aviv	1–0
25 Mar 1981	Northern Ireland	Hampden Park	1–1
28 Apr 1981	Israel	Hampden Park	3–0
9 Sep 1981	Sweden	Hampden Park	2–0
14 Oct 1981	Northern Ireland	Belfast	0–0
18 Nov 1981	Portugal	Lisbon	1–2

Finals in Spain

15 June 1982	New Zealand	Malaga	5–2
18 June 1982	Brazil	Seville	1–4
22 June 1982	USSR	Malaga	2–2

Jock Stein's men did creditably in Spain, but once again disappointment was the order of the day. The game against New Zealand brought five good goals (Dalglish, Wark 2, Robertson and Archibald), but two were conceded through defensive errors, and at one point New Zealand brought it back to 3–2. The game against Brazil was the game of Dave Narey's famous goal as Scotland went ahead. Unfortunately it was too good to last, and Scotland then conceded four. Thus Scotland had to beat the USSR in the final game. For a while it looked possible as Jordan opened the scoring, but then after the USSR had equalised, with time running out, Miller and Hansen made the classic mistake of going for the same ball and collided with one another, allowing the USSR the chance to go ahead. Although Graeme Souness scored near the end, the 2–2 draw was not enough, and for the third successive time, Scotland went out of the tournament on goal difference.

Gordon Strachan played in the World Cup finals of 1982 and 1986

1986   Qualifying Stages

17 Oct 1984	Iceland	Hampden Park	3–0
14 Nov 1984	Spain	Hampden Park	3–1
27 Feb 1985	Spain	Seville	0–1

27 Mar 1985	Wales	Hampden Park	0–1
28 May 1985	Iceland	Reykjavik	1–0
10 Sep 1985	Wales	Cardiff	1–1

Play-Offs

| 20 Nov 1985 | Australia | Hampden Park | 2–0 |
| 4 Dec 1985 | Australia | Melbourne | 0–0 |

Finals in Mexico

4 June 1986	Denmark	Nezahualcoyotl	0–1
8 June 1986	West Germany	Queretaro	1–2
13 June 1986	Uruguay	Nezahualcoyotl	0–0

Scotland, under the temporary charge of Alex Ferguson, was placed into what was called the 'group of death' by the draw, and it was generally acknowledged to be the most difficult of all. The first game against Denmark saw a good performance from Scotland, but it was Denmark who got the only goal of the game. The game against the Germans produced a great goal by Gordon Strachan to put Scotland ahead, but then Germany scored twice in a game played in searing heat. Scotland might yet have qualified as one of the best-placed third countries if they beat Uruguay, but in spite of the Uruguayans losing a man, Batista sent off in the first minute for a bad tackle on Strachan, Scotland could not score against a defensive-minded Uruguayan side.

1990   Qualifying Stages

14 Sep 1988	Norway	Oslo	2–1
19 Oct 1988	Yugoslavia	Hampden Park	1–1
8 Feb 1989	Cyprus	Limassol	3–2
8 Mar 1989	France	Hampden Park	2–0
26 Apr 1989	Cyprus	Hampden Park	2–1
6 Sep 1989	Yugoslavia	Zagreb	1–3
11 Oct 1989	France	Paris	0–3
15 Nov 1989	Norway	Hampden Park	1–1

Finals in Italy

11 June 1990	Costa Rica	Genoa	0–1
16 June 1990	Sweden	Genoa	2–1
20 June 1990	Brazil	Turin	0–1

Scotland shot themselves in the foot in this tournament with a disgraceful first game against Costa Rica which the third-world unknowns won 1–0. This result was greeted with incredulity throughout the world, but then Scotland bounced back with a fine win over Sweden five days later. Stuart McCall and Mo Johnston (with a penalty) scored for Scotland, and although Sweden pulled a goal back in the last few minutes, Scotland held out for a deserved victory. It now all depended on the game against Brazil, who had already qualified, and it looked as if a draw might be sufficient. Everything went well until a ball bounced off Jim Leighton's chest and Muller tapped the ball in to win the game for Brazil and to put Andy Roxburgh's side out.

1994   Qualifying Stages

9 Sep 1992	Switzerland	Berne	1–3
14 Oct 1992	Portugal	Ibrox	0–0
18 Nov 1992	Italy	Ibrox	0–0
17 Feb 1993	Malta	Ibrox	3–0
28 Apr 1993	Portugal	Lisbon	0–5
19 May 1993	Estonia	Tallinn	3–0
2 June 1993	Estonia	Pittodrie	3–1
8 Sep 1993	Switzerland	Pittodrie	1–1
13 Oct 1993	Italy	Rome	1–3
17 Nov 1993	Malta	Valletta	2–0
Scotland failed to qualify for the USA			

1998   Qualifying Stages

31 Aug 1996	Austria	Vienna	0–0
5 Oct 1996	Latvia	Riga	2–0
10 Nov 1996	Sweden	Ibrox	1–0
11 Feb 1997	Estonia	Monaco	0–0
29 Mar 1997	Estonia	Rugby Park	2–0
2 Apr 1997	Austria	Celtic Park	2–0
30 Apr 1997	Sweden	Gothenburg	1–2
8 June 1997	Belarus	Minsk	1–0
7 Sep 1997	Belarus	Pittodrie	4–1
11 Oct 1997	Latvia	Celtic Park	2–0

Finals in France

10 June 1998	Brazil	Paris	1–2
16 June 1998	Norway	Bordeaux	1–1
23 June 1998	Morocco	St Etienne	0–3

Craig Brown's team found themselves opening the tournament by playing against Brazil (yet again) and once again not getting the breaks from Lady Luck. Brazil scored early, but then Scotland equalised through a penalty from John Collins, and looked for a long time as if they might get a draw, until a freakish own goal, when the ball bounced off Tom Boyd to give the Brazilians the lead. A creditable draw against Norway followed, with Craig Burley equalising for Scotland and a little luck might well have brought a winner. Scotland had to beat Morocco in their final game, but collapsed and went down 0–3 before a large and disappointed Scottish support.

2002   Qualifying Stages

2 Sep 2000	Latvia	Riga	1–0
7 Oct 2000	San Marino	Serravalle	2–0
11 Oct 2000	Croatia	Zagreb	1–1
24 Mar 2001	Belgium	Hampden Park	2–2
28 Mar 2001	San Marino	Hampden Park	4–0
1 Sep 2001	Croatia	Hampden Park	0–0
5 Sep 2001	Belgium	Brussels	0–2
6 Oct 2001	Latvia	Hampden Park	2–1
Scotland failed to qualify for Korea / Japan			

2006   Qualifying Stages

8 Sep 2004	Slovenia	Hampden Park	0–0
9 Oct 2004	Norway	Hampden Park	0–1
13 Oct 2004	Moldova	Chisinau	1–1
26 Mar 2005	Italy	Milan	0–2
4 June 2005	Moldova	Hampden Park	2–0
8 June 2005	Belarus	Minsk	0–0
3 Sep 2005	Italy	Hampden Park	1–1
7 Sep 2005	Norway	Oslo	2–1
8 Oct 2005	Belarus	Hampden Park	0–1
12 Oct 2005	Slovenia	Celje	3–0
Scotland failed to qualify for Germany			

2010   Qualifying Stages

6 Sep 2008	Macedonia	Skopje	0–1
10 Sep 2008	Iceland	Reykjavik	2–1
11 Oct 2008	Norway	Hampden Park	0–0
28 Mar 2009	Holland	Amsterdam	0–3
1 Apr 2009	Iceland	Hampden Park	2–1
12 Aug 2009	Norway	Oslo	0–4

5 Sep 2009	Macedonia	Hampden Park	2–0
9 Sep 2009	Holland	Hampden Park	0–1
Scotland failed to qualify for South Africa			

2014   Qualifying Stages

8 Sep 2012	Serbia	Hampden Park	0–0
11 Sep 2012	Macedonia	Hampden Park	1–1
12 Oct 2012	Wales	Cardiff	1–2
16 Oct 2012	Belgium	Brussels	0–2
22 Mar 2013	Wales	Hampden Park	1–2
26 Mar 2013	Serbia	Novi Sad	0–2
7 Jun 2013	Croatia	Zagreb	1–0
6 Sep 2013	Belgium	Hampden Park	0–2
10 Sep 2013	Macedonia	Skopje	2–1
15 Oct 2013	Croatia	Hampden Park	2–0
Scotland failed to qualify for Brazil			

Craig Levein was Scotland manager for the first four fixtures of the campaign, whilst his replacement Gordon Strachan was in charge for the final six matches.

April 1944, and Field Marshal Montgomery is introduced to Scotland's team by captain Matt Busby before a wartime international at Hampden Park against England